Big Dweeb Energy

A FoxTrot Collection by Bill Amend

Andrews McMeel
PUBLISHING®

Other FoxTrot Books by Bill Amend

Anthologies

Thinking Ahead

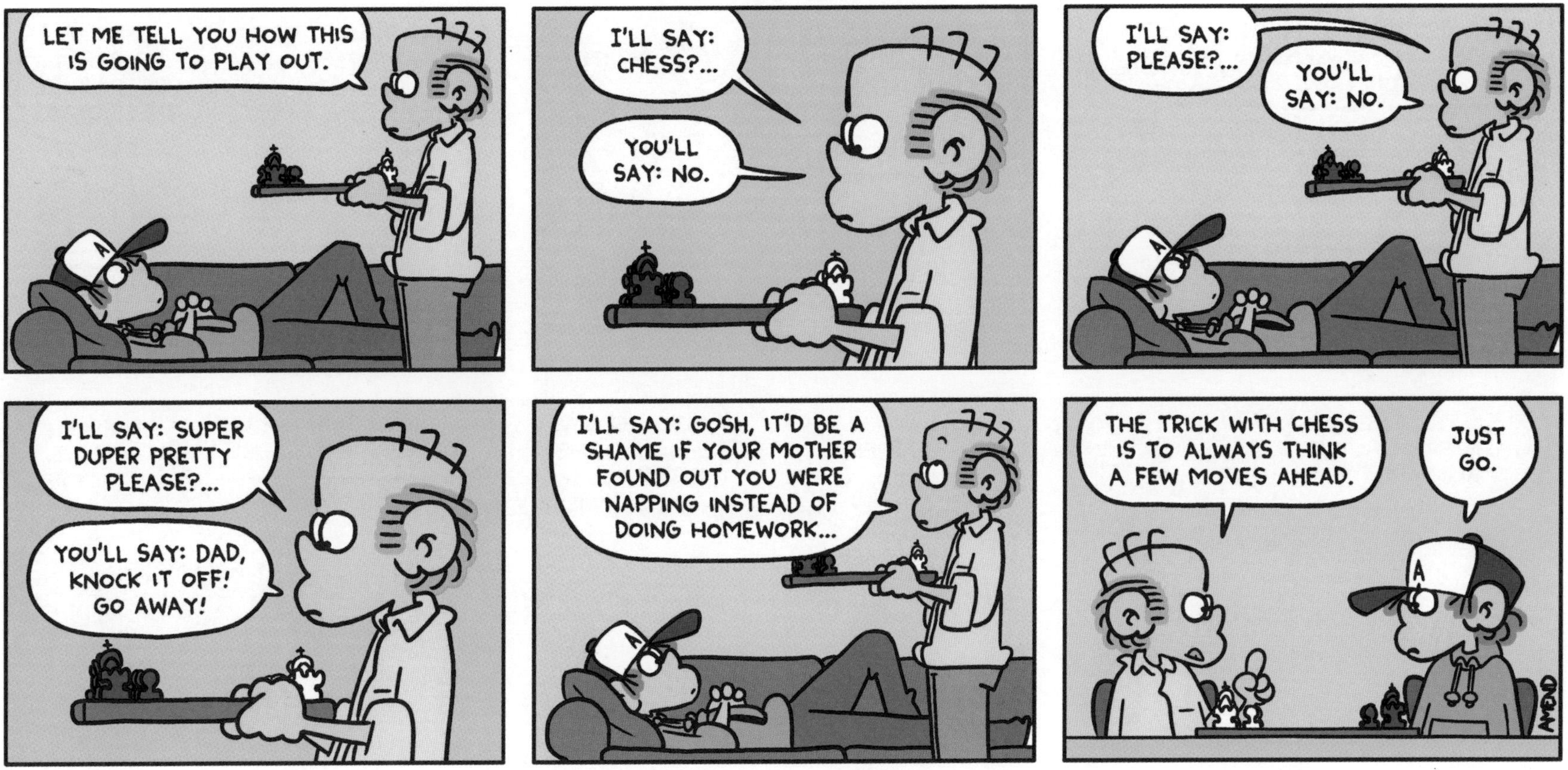

LET ME TELL YOU HOW THIS IS GOING TO PLAY OUT.
I'LL SAY: CHESS?...
YOU'LL SAY: NO.
I'LL SAY: PLEASE?...
YOU'LL SAY: NO.
I'LL SAY: SUPER DUPER PRETTY PLEASE?...
YOU'LL SAY: DAD, KNOCK IT OFF! GO AWAY!
I'LL SAY: GOSH, IT'D BE A SHAME IF YOUR MOTHER FOUND OUT YOU WERE NAPPING INSTEAD OF DOING HOMEWORK...
THE TRICK WITH CHESS IS TO ALWAYS THINK A FEW MOVES AHEAD.
JUST GO.
AMEND

Homesick

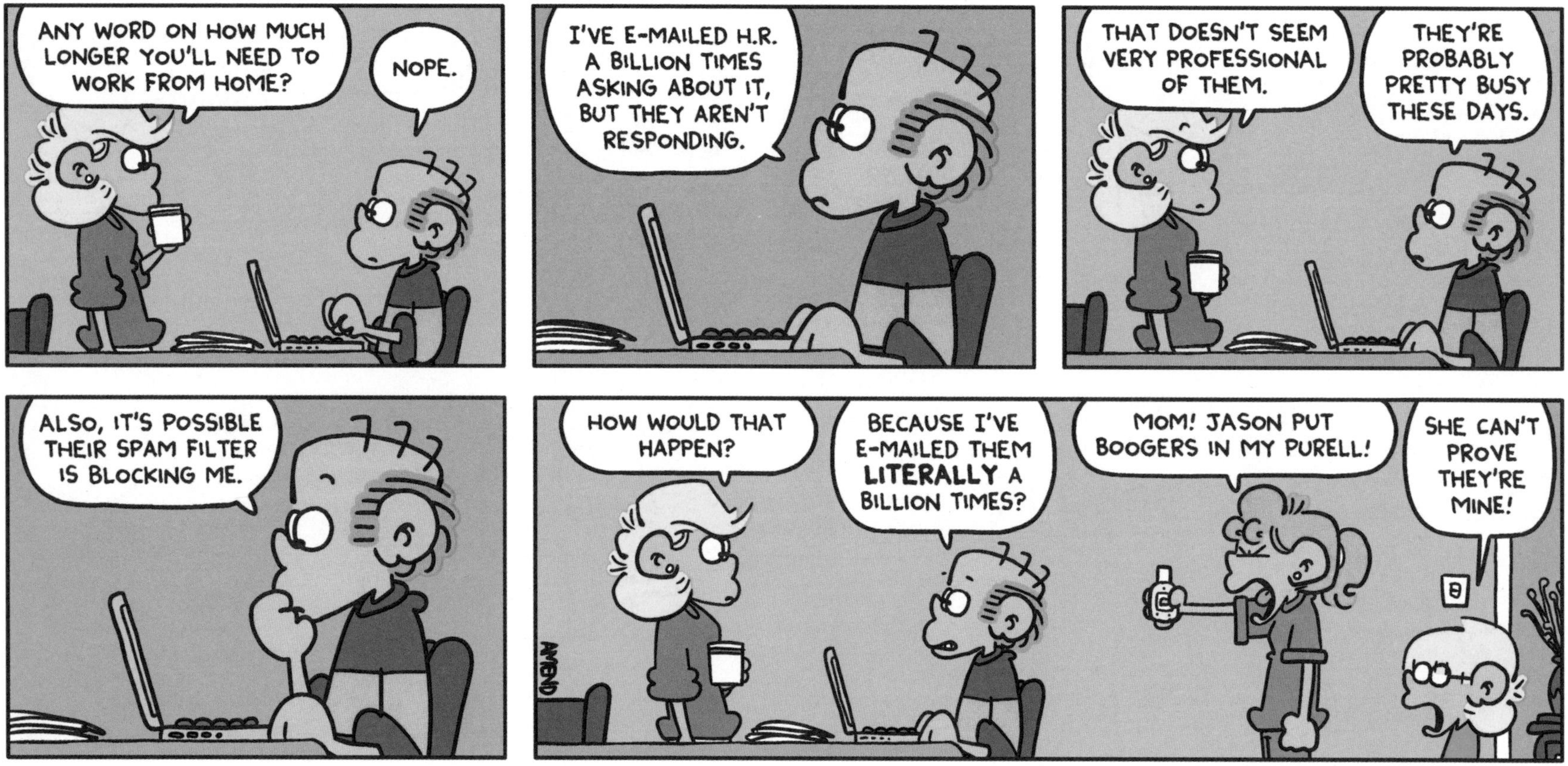
ANY WORD ON HOW MUCH LONGER YOU'LL NEED TO WORK FROM HOME?
NOPE.
I'VE E-MAILED H.R. A BILLION TIMES ASKING ABOUT IT, BUT THEY AREN'T RESPONDING.
THAT DOESN'T SEEM VERY PROFESSIONAL OF THEM.
THEY'RE PROBABLY PRETTY BUSY THESE DAYS.
ALSO, IT'S POSSIBLE THEIR SPAM FILTER IS BLOCKING ME.
HOW WOULD THAT HAPPEN?
BECAUSE I'VE E-MAILED THEM **LITERALLY** A BILLION TIMES?
MOM! JASON PUT BOOGERS IN MY PURELL!
SHE CAN'T PROVE THEY'RE MINE!
AMEND

So Bored

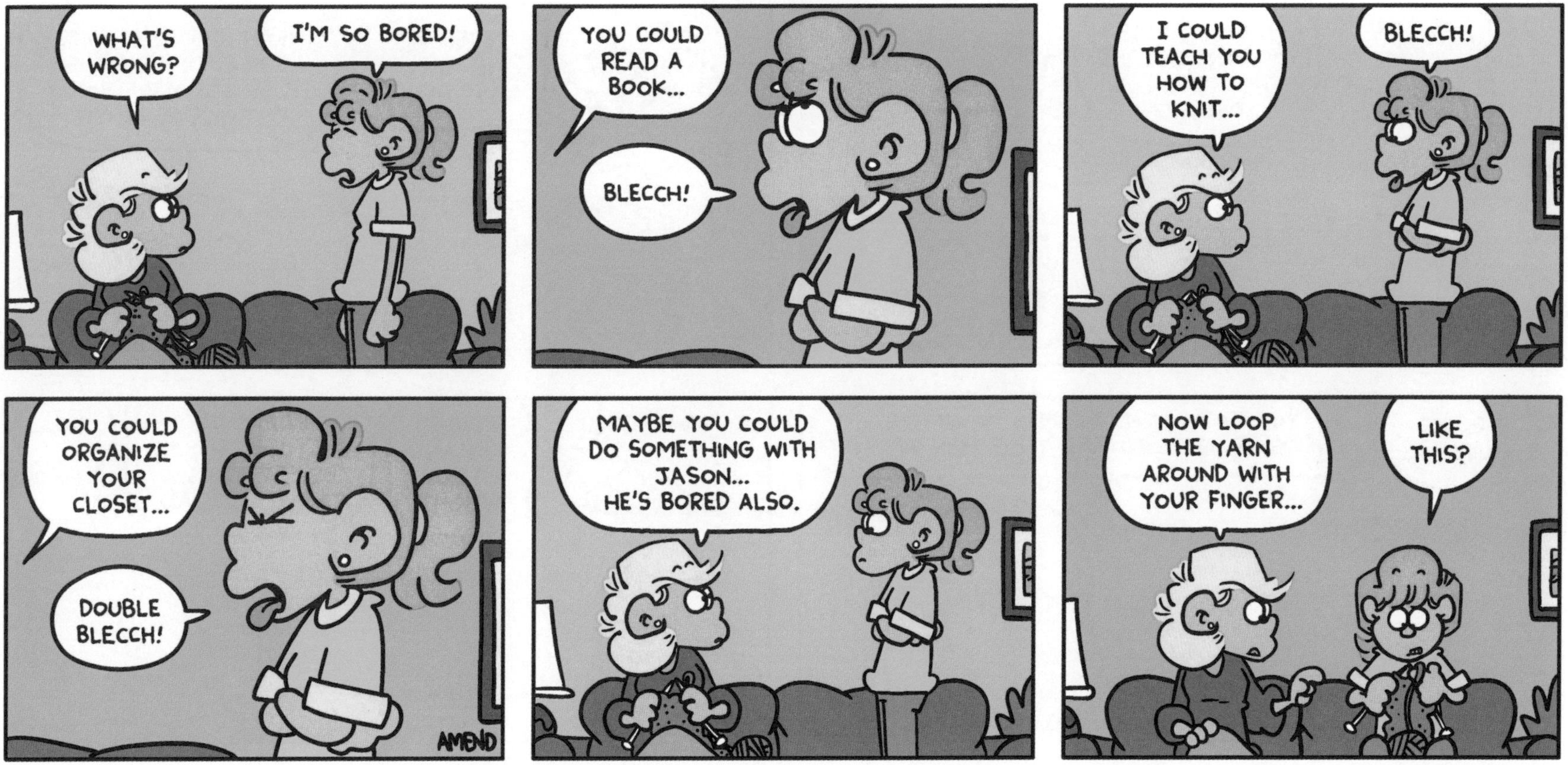
WHAT'S WRONG?
I'M SO BORED!
YOU COULD READ A BOOK...
BLECCH!
I COULD TEACH YOU HOW TO KNIT...
BLECCH!
YOU COULD ORGANIZE YOUR CLOSET...
DOUBLE BLECCH!
AMEND
MAYBE YOU COULD DO SOMETHING WITH JASON... HE'S BORED ALSO.
NOW LOOP THE YARN AROUND WITH YOUR FINGER...
LIKE THIS?

Weighty Matters

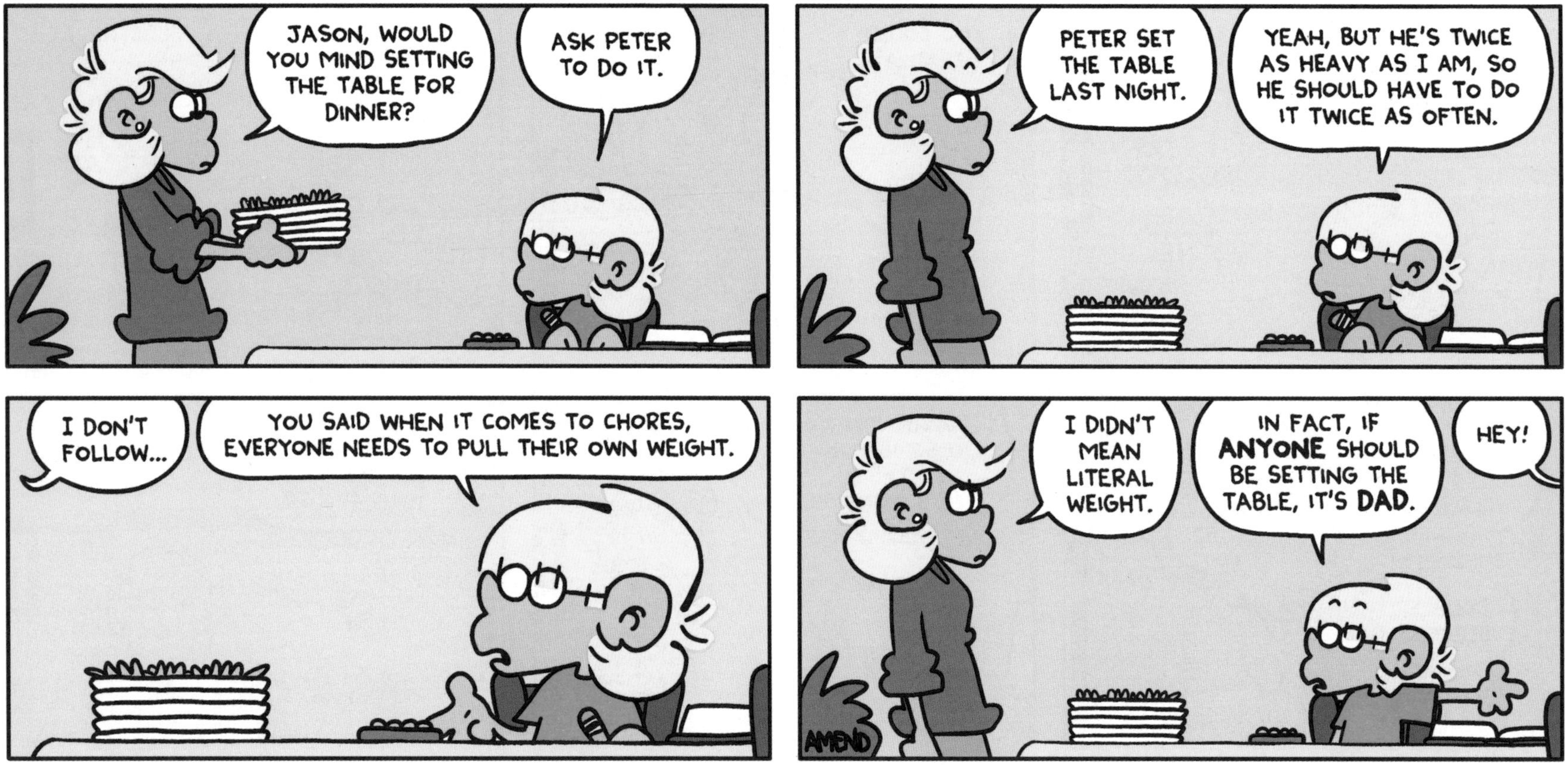
JASON, WOULD YOU MIND SETTING THE TABLE FOR DINNER?
ASK PETER TO DO IT.
PETER SET THE TABLE LAST NIGHT.
YEAH, BUT HE'S TWICE AS HEAVY AS I AM, SO HE SHOULD HAVE TO DO IT TWICE AS OFTEN.
I DON'T FOLLOW...
YOU SAID WHEN IT COMES TO CHORES, EVERYONE NEEDS TO PULL THEIR OWN WEIGHT.
AMEND
I DIDN'T MEAN LITERAL WEIGHT.
IN FACT, IF **ANYONE** SHOULD BE SETTING THE TABLE, IT'S **DAD**.
HEY!

Business Casual

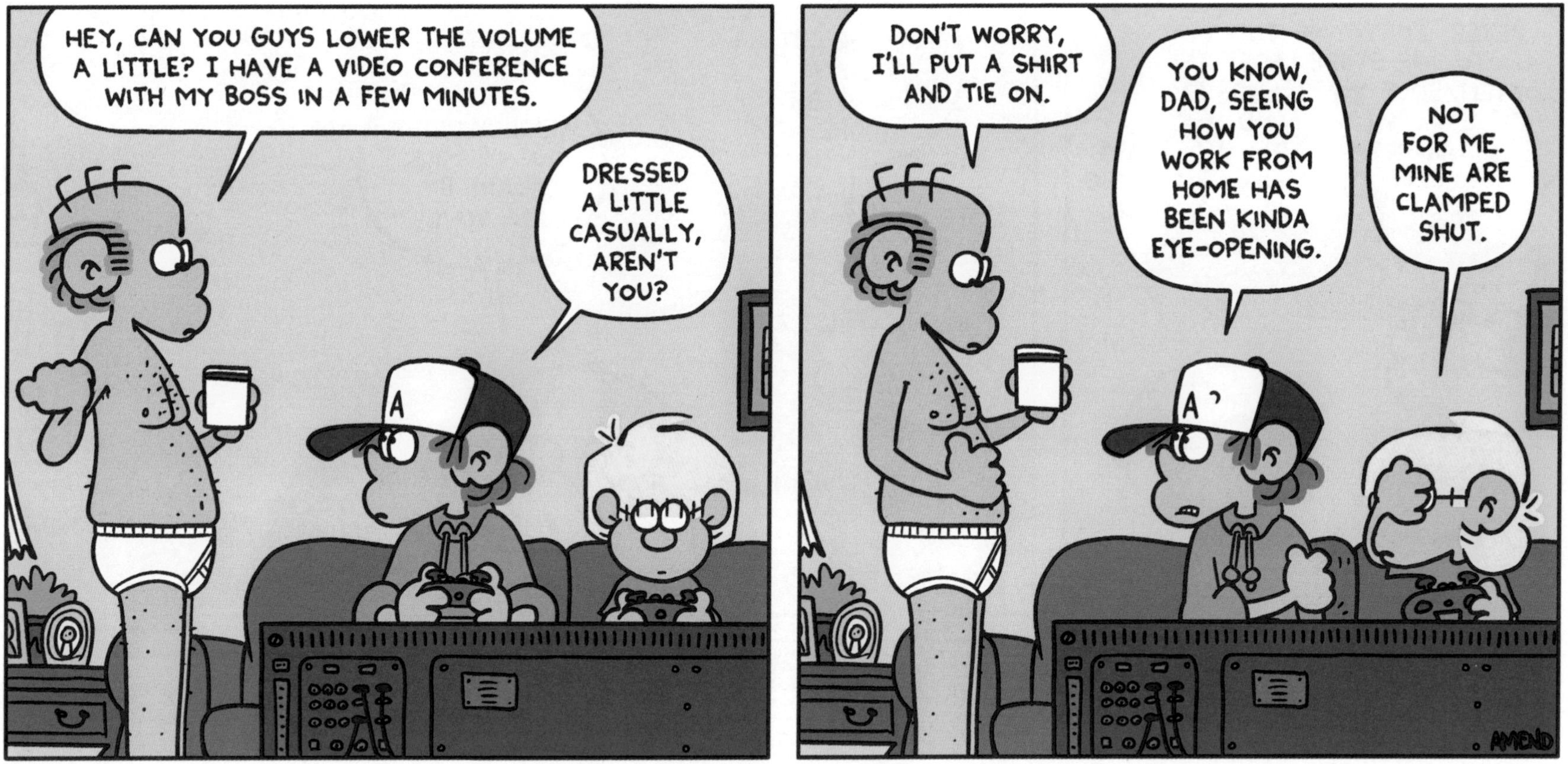
HEY, CAN YOU GUYS LOWER THE VOLUME A LITTLE? I HAVE A VIDEO CONFERENCE WITH MY BOSS IN A FEW MINUTES.
DRESSED A LITTLE CASUALLY, AREN'T YOU?
DON'T WORRY, I'LL PUT A SHIRT AND TIE ON.
YOU KNOW, DAD, SEEING HOW YOU WORK FROM HOME HAS BEEN KINDA EYE-OPENING.
NOT FOR ME. MINE ARE CLAMPED SHUT.
AMEND

Cereal Killer

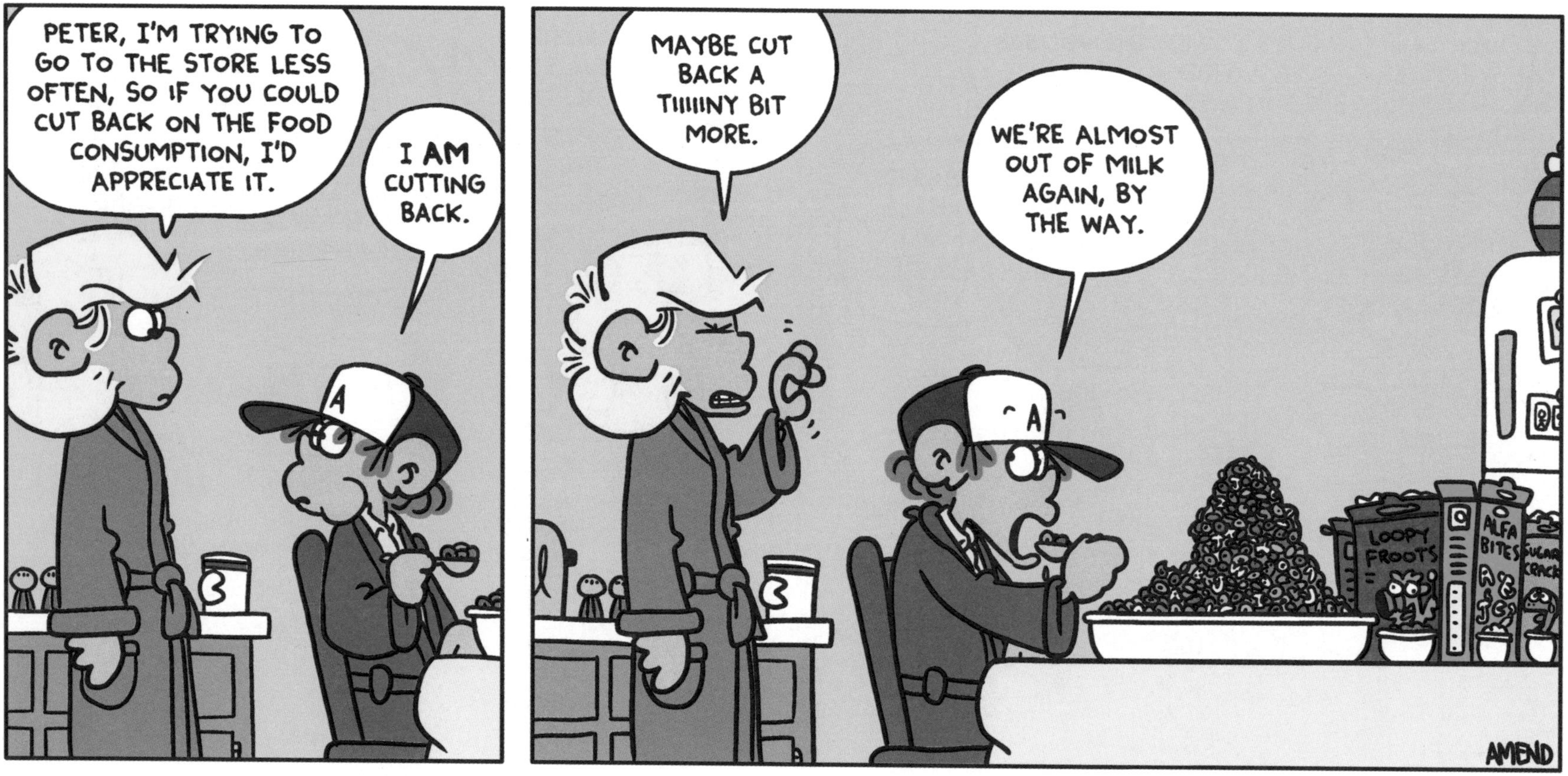

PETER, I'M TRYING TO GO TO THE STORE LESS OFTEN, SO IF YOU COULD CUT BACK ON THE FOOD CONSUMPTION, I'D APPRECIATE IT.
I AM CUTTING BACK.
MAYBE CUT BACK A TIIIIINY BIT MORE.
WE'RE ALMOST OUT OF MILK AGAIN, BY THE WAY.
LOOPY FROOTS
ALFA BITES
AMEND

House of Cards

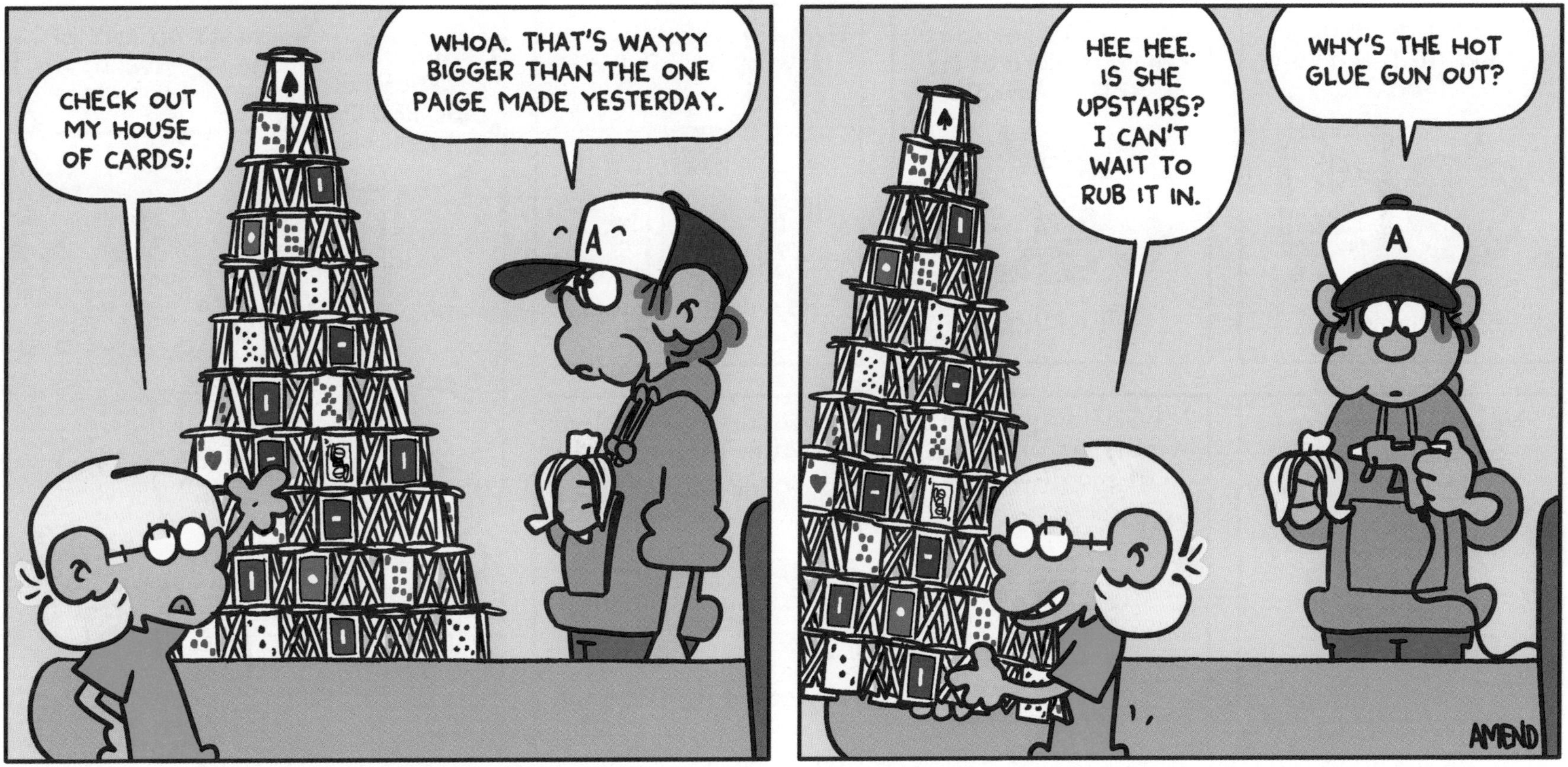

CHECK OUT MY HOUSE OF CARDS!
WHOA. THAT'S WAYYY BIGGER THAN THE ONE PAIGE MADE YESTERDAY.
HEE HEE. IS SHE UPSTAIRS? I CAN'T WAIT TO RUB IT IN.
WHY'S THE HOT GLUE GUN OUT?
AMEND

Laughable

What is an apple's favorite thing to teach?

S.T.E.M. classes!

What 1994 movie received a score of N95 on Rotten Tomatoes?

"The Mask"!

Why did the software developer visit the cutlery shop?

He wanted to fork his project!

How do you make cattle turn left and right?

With a steer-ing wheel!

What do you call really small bottles of mouthwash?

Micro Scopes!

How can you tell the age of anthropomorphic shopping carts?

By counting the bags under their eyes!

THEY SAY LAUGHTER IS THE BEST MEDICINE.

WHAT DO ANY OF THESE HAVE TO DO WITH LAUGHTER?

AMEND

Tough Cookie

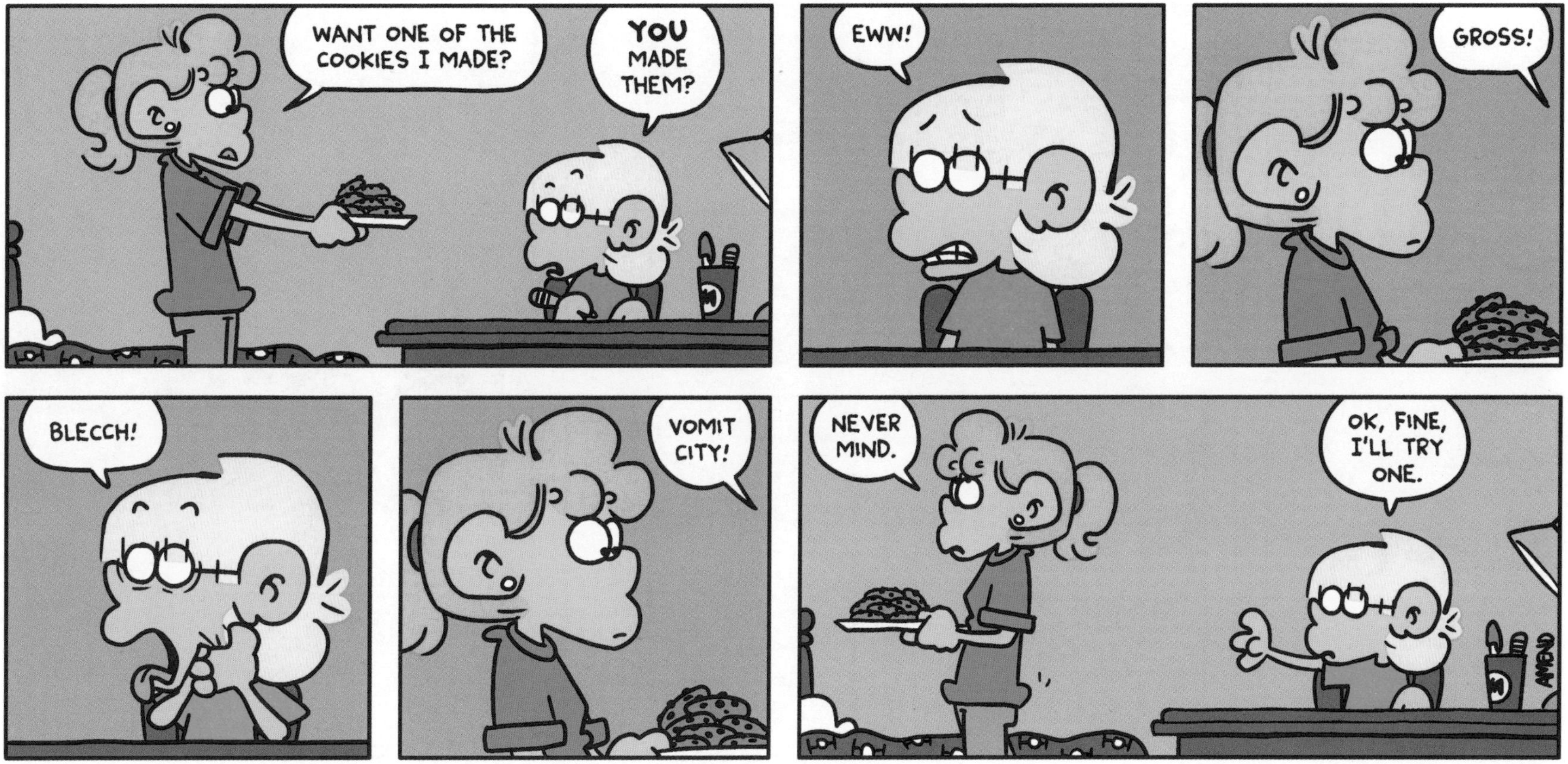
WANT ONE OF THE COOKIES I MADE?
YOU MADE THEM?
EWW!
GROSS!
BLECCH!
VOMIT CITY!
NEVER MIND.
OK, FINE, I'LL TRY ONE.
AMEND

Bangin'

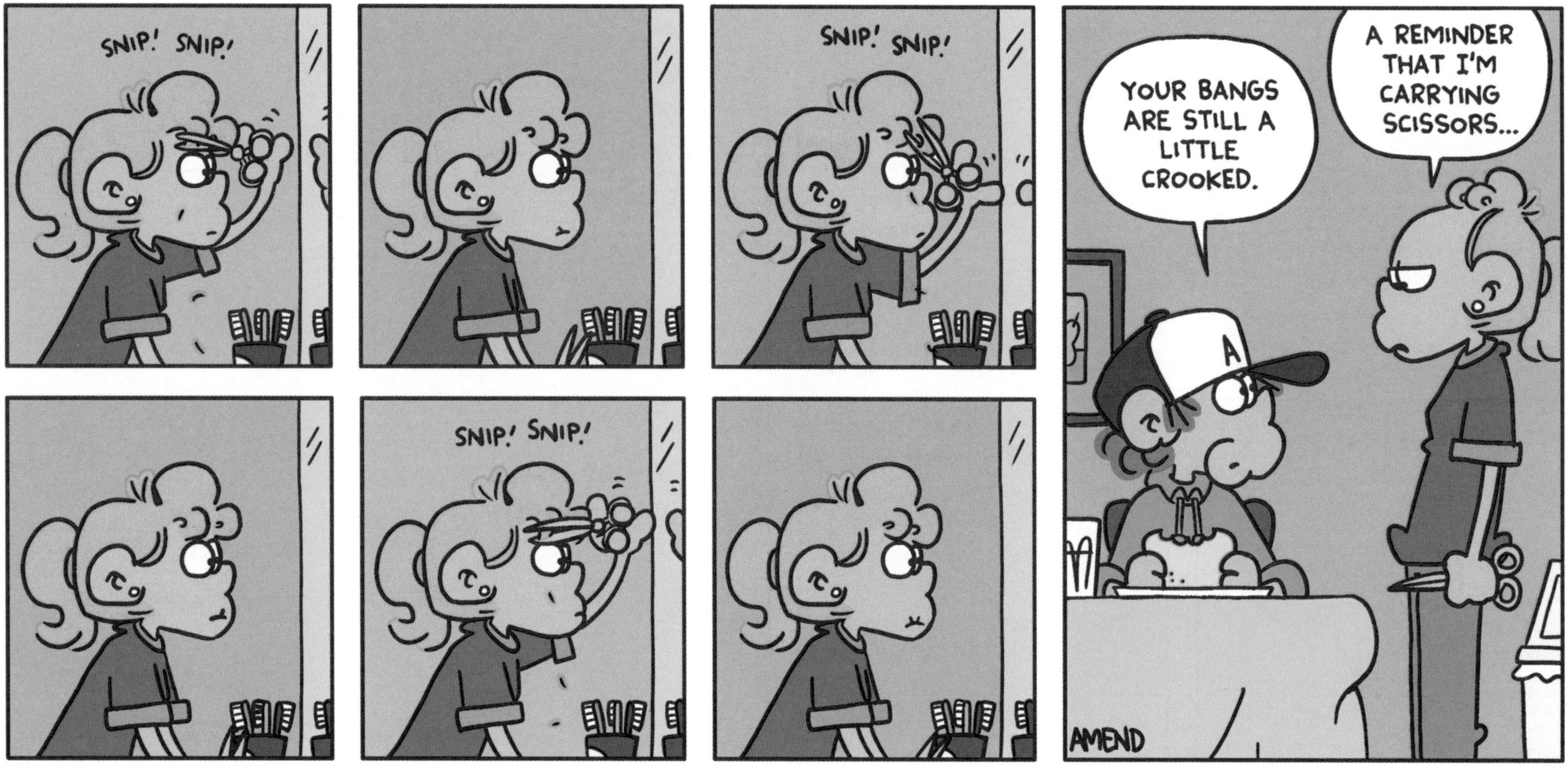
SNIP! SNIP!
SNIP! SNIP!
SNIP! SNIP!
YOUR BANGS ARE STILL A LITTLE CROOKED.
A REMINDER THAT I'M CARRYING SCISSORS...
AMEND

Fertile Mind

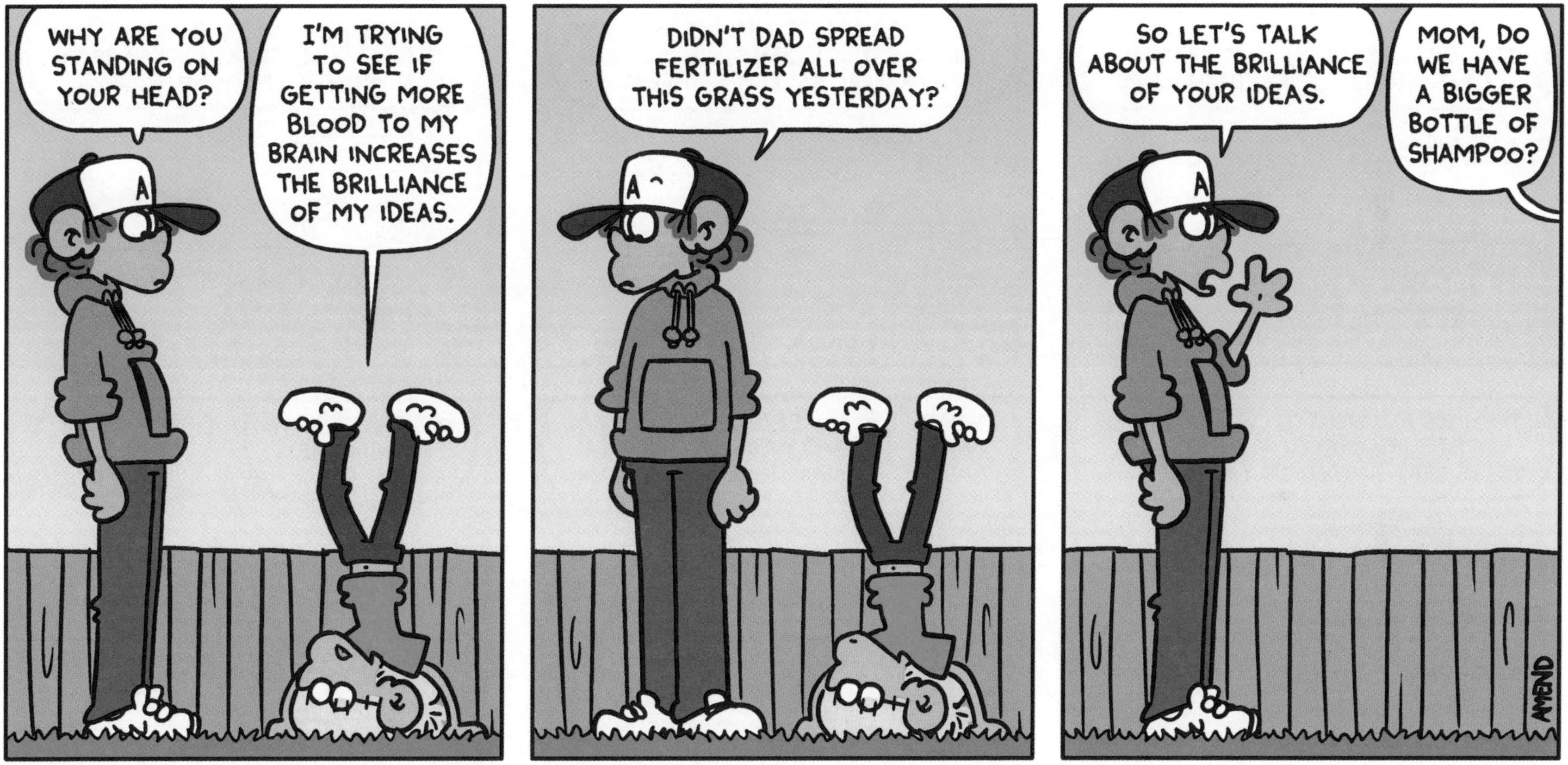
WHY ARE YOU STANDING ON YOUR HEAD?
I'M TRYING TO SEE IF GETTING MORE BLOOD TO MY BRAIN INCREASES THE BRILLIANCE OF MY IDEAS.
DIDN'T DAD SPREAD FERTILIZER ALL OVER THIS GRASS YESTERDAY?
SO LET'S TALK ABOUT THE BRILLIANCE OF YOUR IDEAS.
MOM, DO WE HAVE A BIGGER BOTTLE OF SHAMPOO?
AMEND

Impossible Dream

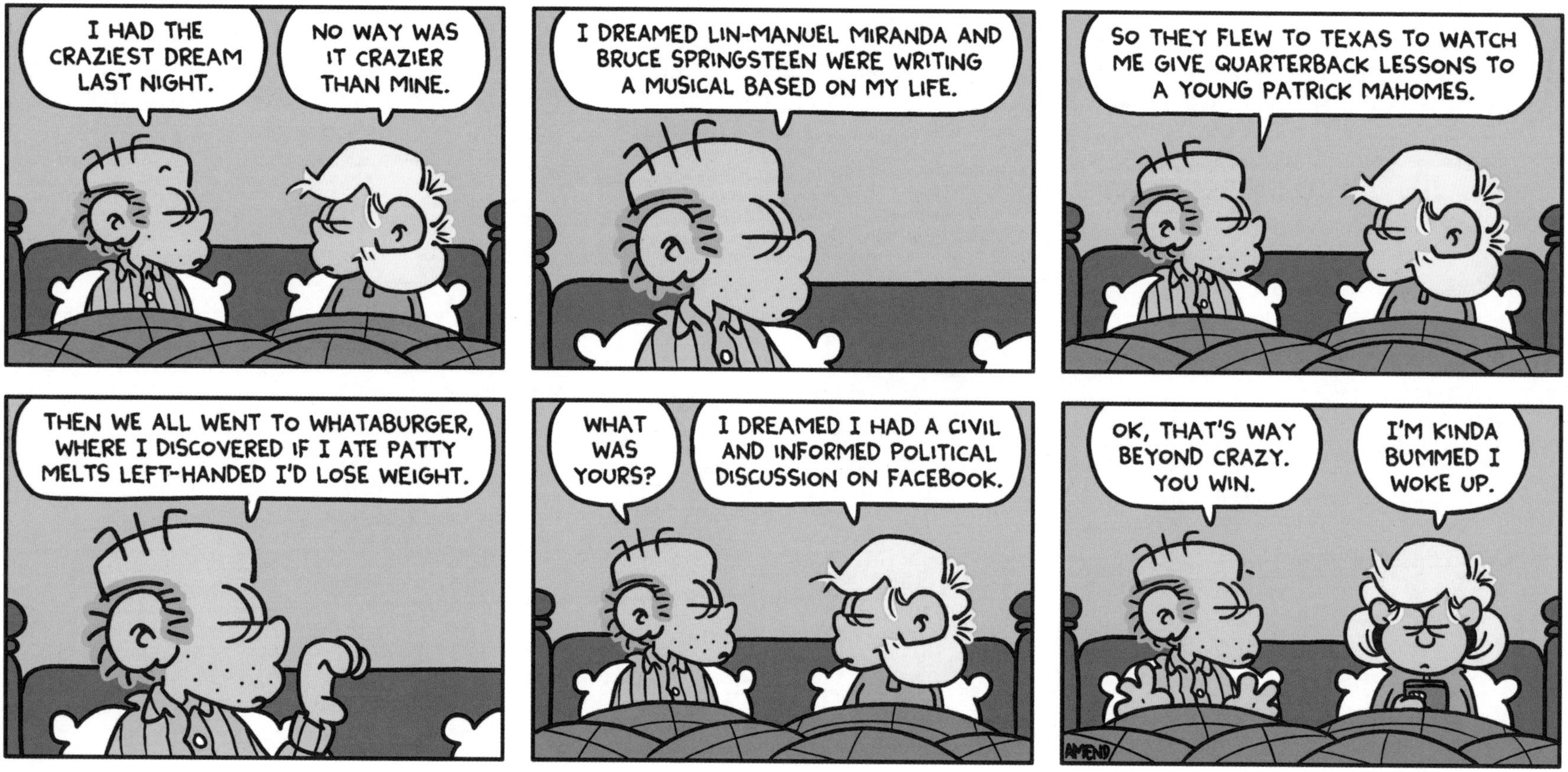
I HAD THE CRAZIEST DREAM LAST NIGHT.
NO WAY WAS IT CRAZIER THAN MINE.
I DREAMED LIN-MANUEL MIRANDA AND BRUCE SPRINGSTEEN WERE WRITING A MUSICAL BASED ON MY LIFE.
SO THEY FLEW TO TEXAS TO WATCH ME GIVE QUARTERBACK LESSONS TO A YOUNG PATRICK MAHOMES.
THEN WE ALL WENT TO WHATABURGER, WHERE I DISCOVERED IF I ATE PATTY MELTS LEFT-HANDED I'D LOSE WEIGHT.
WHAT WAS YOURS?
I DREAMED I HAD A CIVIL AND INFORMED POLITICAL DISCUSSION ON FACEBOOK.
OK, THAT'S WAY BEYOND CRAZY. YOU WIN.
I'M KINDA BUMMED I WOKE UP.
AMEND

Iguanoman 2020

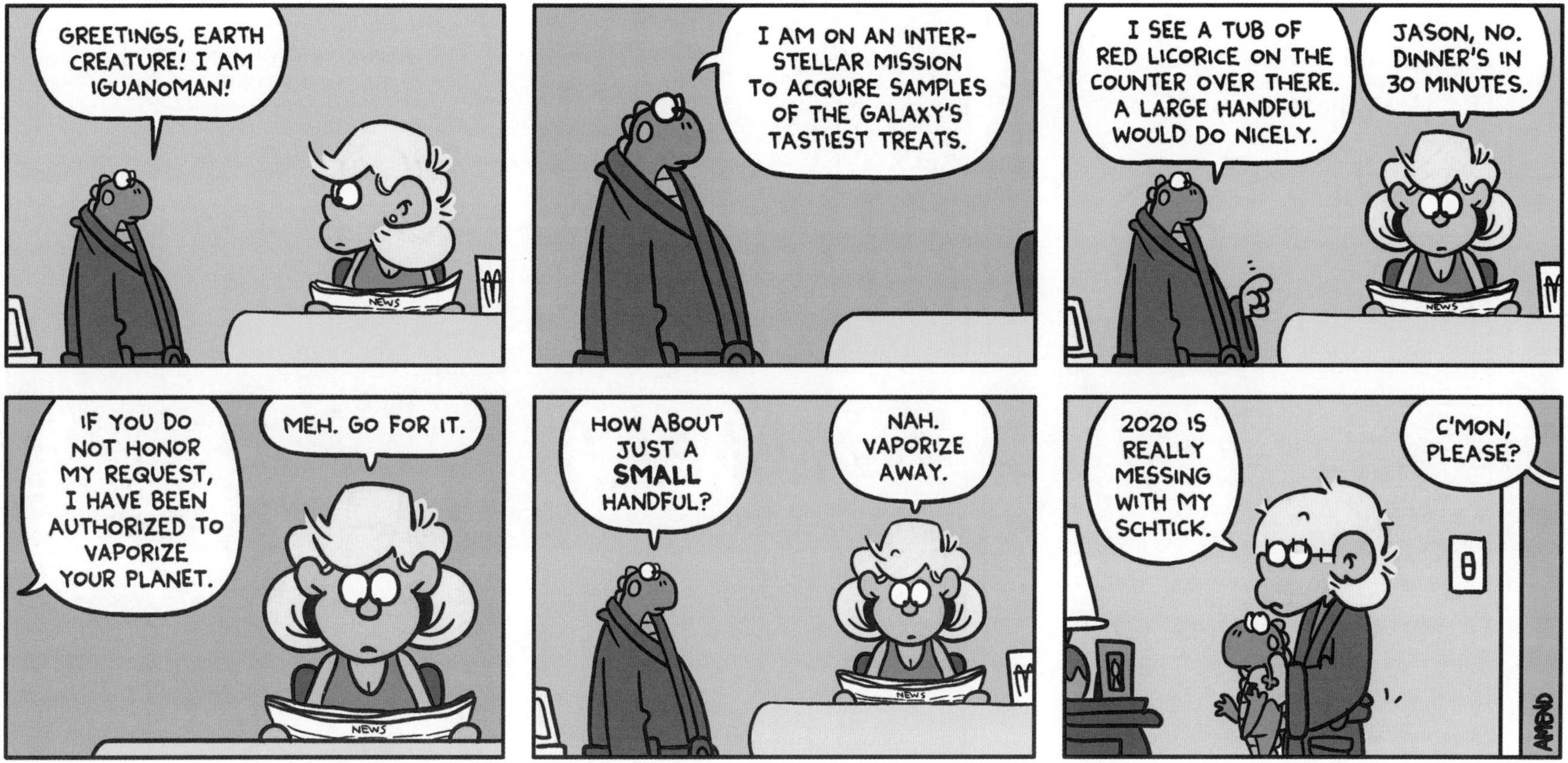
GREETINGS, EARTH CREATURE! I AM IGUANOMAN!
NEWS
I AM ON AN INTER-STELLAR MISSION TO ACQUIRE SAMPLES OF THE GALAXY'S TASTIEST TREATS.
I SEE A TUB OF RED LICORICE ON THE COUNTER OVER THERE. A LARGE HANDFUL WOULD DO NICELY.
JASON, NO. DINNER'S IN 30 MINUTES.
NEWS
IF YOU DO NOT HONOR MY REQUEST, I HAVE BEEN AUTHORIZED TO VAPORIZE YOUR PLANET.
MEH. GO FOR IT.
NEWS
HOW ABOUT JUST A **SMALL** HANDFUL?
NAH. VAPORIZE AWAY.
NEWS
2020 IS REALLY MESSING WITH MY SCHTICK.
C'MON, PLEASE?
AMEND

Midsummer Meltdown

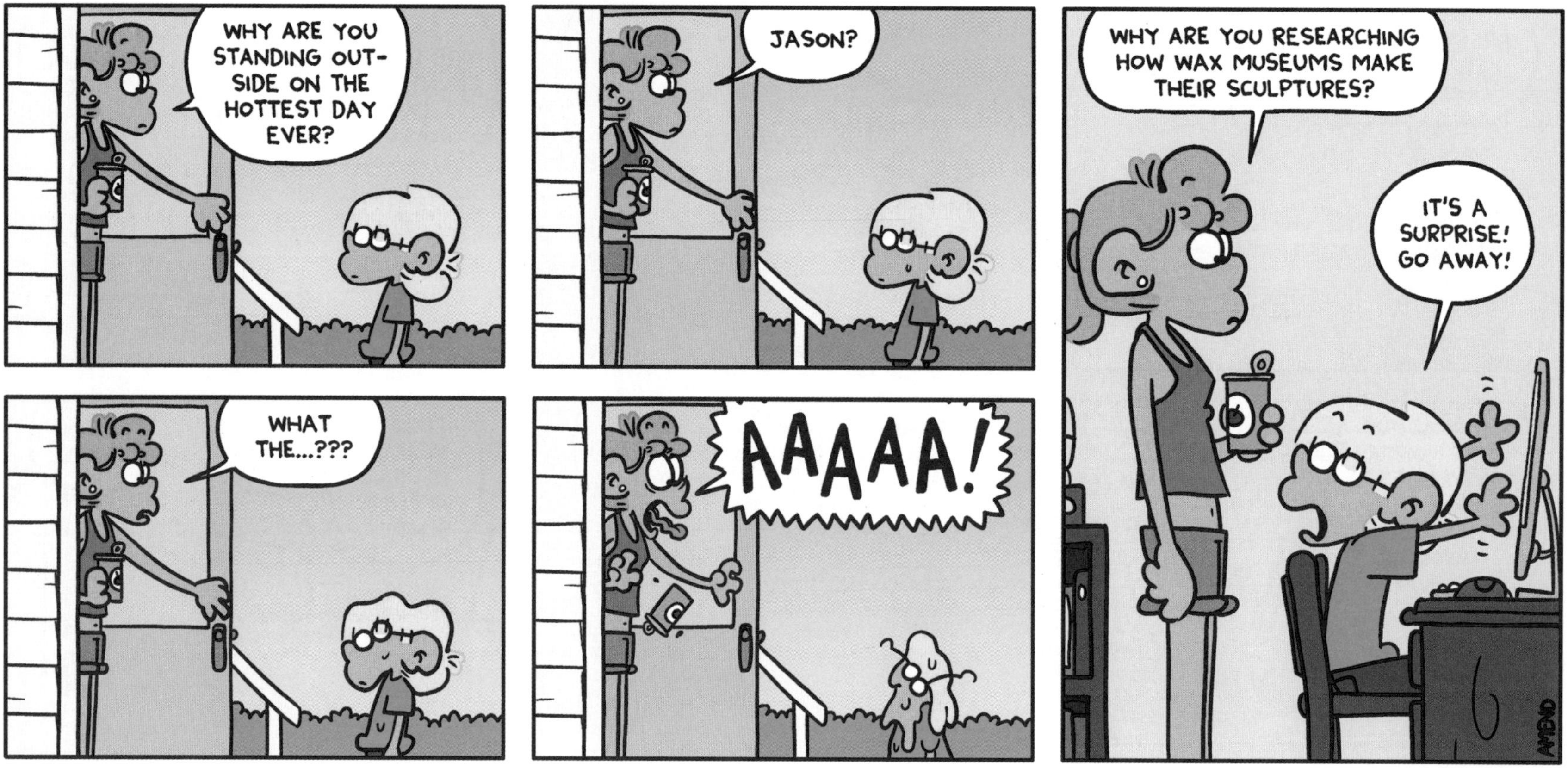
WHY ARE YOU STANDING OUT-SIDE ON THE HOTTEST DAY EVER?
JASON?
WHAT THE...???
AAAAA!
WHY ARE YOU RESEARCHING HOW WAX MUSEUMS MAKE THEIR SCULPTURES?
IT'S A SURPRISE! GO AWAY!
AMEND

Centripizzal

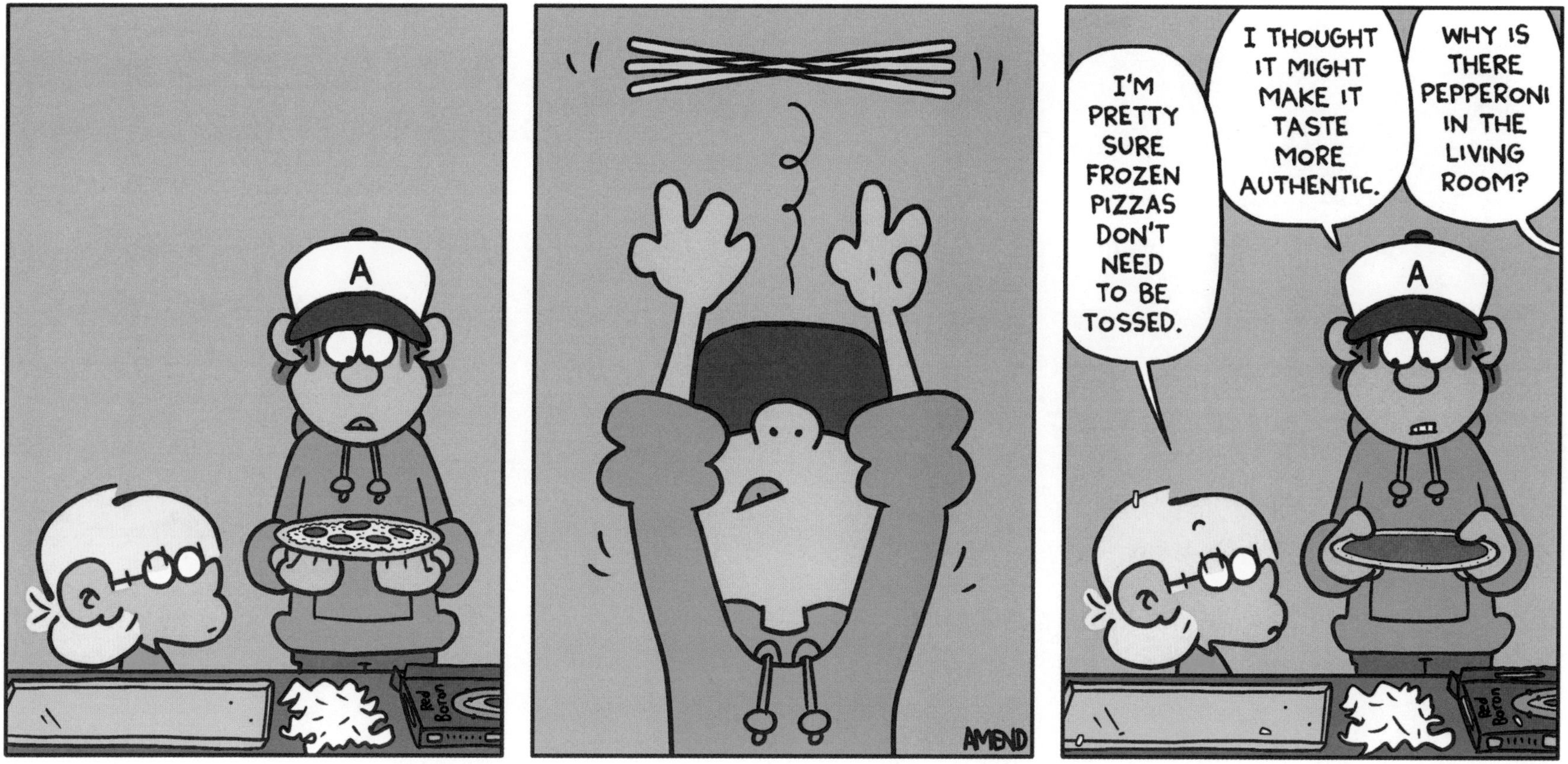
Red Baron
I'M PRETTY SURE FROZEN PIZZAS DON'T NEED TO BE TOSSED.
I THOUGHT IT MIGHT MAKE IT TASTE MORE AUTHENTIC.
WHY IS THERE PEPPERONI IN THE LIVING ROOM?
AMEND

Firestarter

SQUIRT
SQUIRT
SQUIRT

ALL RIGHT, JASON, YOU'RE UP.

DRACARYS!

IT'S OK, SON, I'VE GOT MATCHES.

QUINCY, C'MON, WE **PRACTICED** THIS!

Peachy

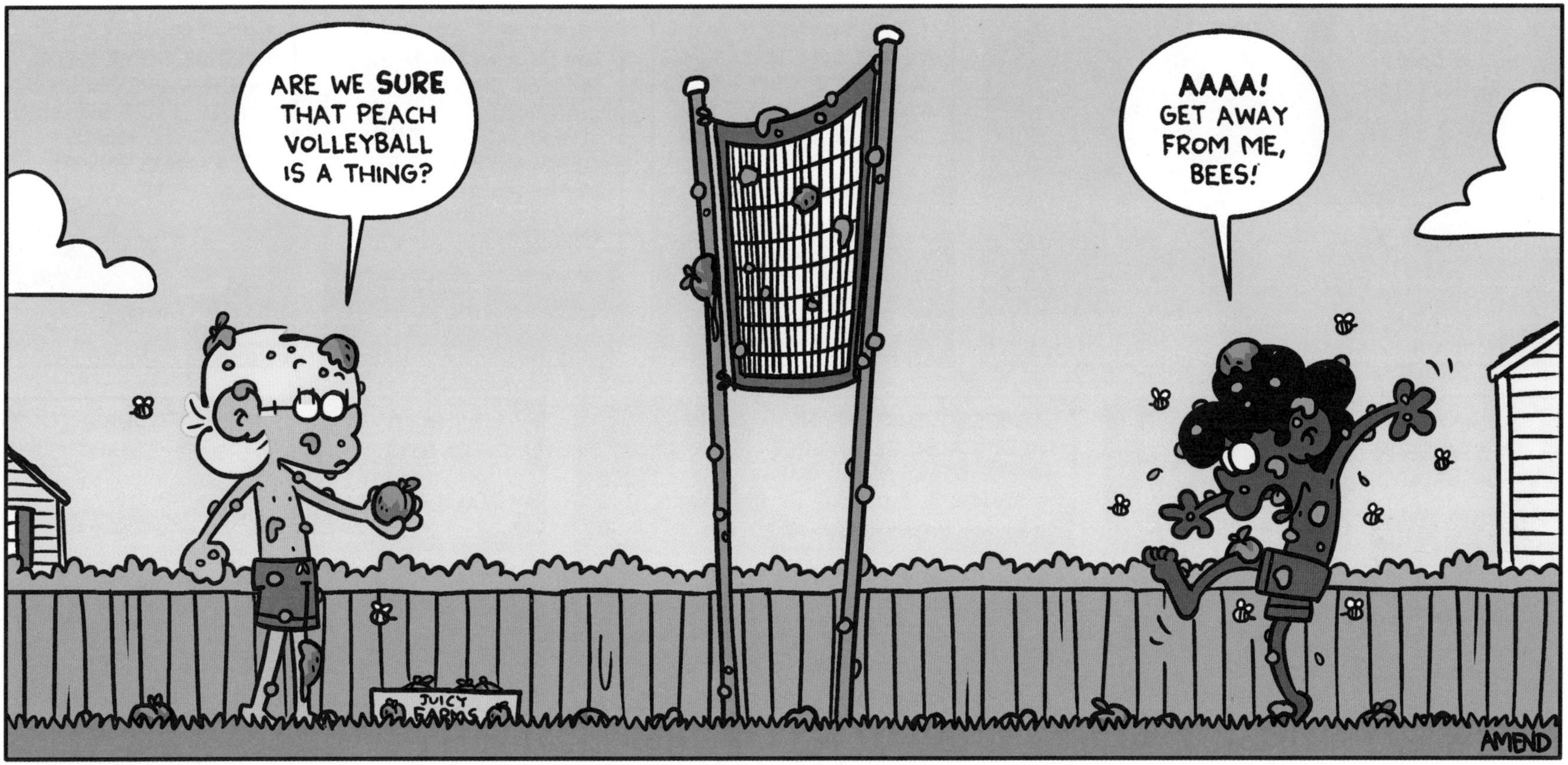

ARE WE **SURE** THAT PEACH VOLLEYBALL IS A THING?
AAAA! GET AWAY FROM ME, BEES!
JUICY FARMS
AMEND

Constellation Realizations

I JUST HAD A COOL REALIZATION.

ABOUT WHAT?

AS YOU PROBABLY KNOW, ALL THE CONSTELLATIONS WE SEE ARE DETERMINED BY OUR VANTAGE POINT IN SPACE RELATIVE TO VISIBLE STARS.

SINCE THERE ARE ESSENTIALLY A NEAR-INFINITE NUMBER OF STARS AND VANTAGE POINTS OUT THERE, IT STANDS TO REASON THERE'D BE A NEAR-INFINITE VARIETY OF POSSIBLE CONSTELLATIONS AS WELL.

WHICH MEANS IT'S LIKELY THAT **SOMEWHERE** IN THE UNIVERSE, YOU CAN SEE STARS SPELLING OUT THE WORDS "JASON IS GREAT."

MAN, I WANT A SPACESHIP SO BADLY.

DOESN'T THAT MEAN THERE'D ALSO BE A PLACE WHERE STARS SPELL OUT "JASON IS A DWEEB"?

I NEED TO STOP SHARING MY REALIZATIONS.

NOW **I** WANT A SPACESHIP.

Sweet Teeth

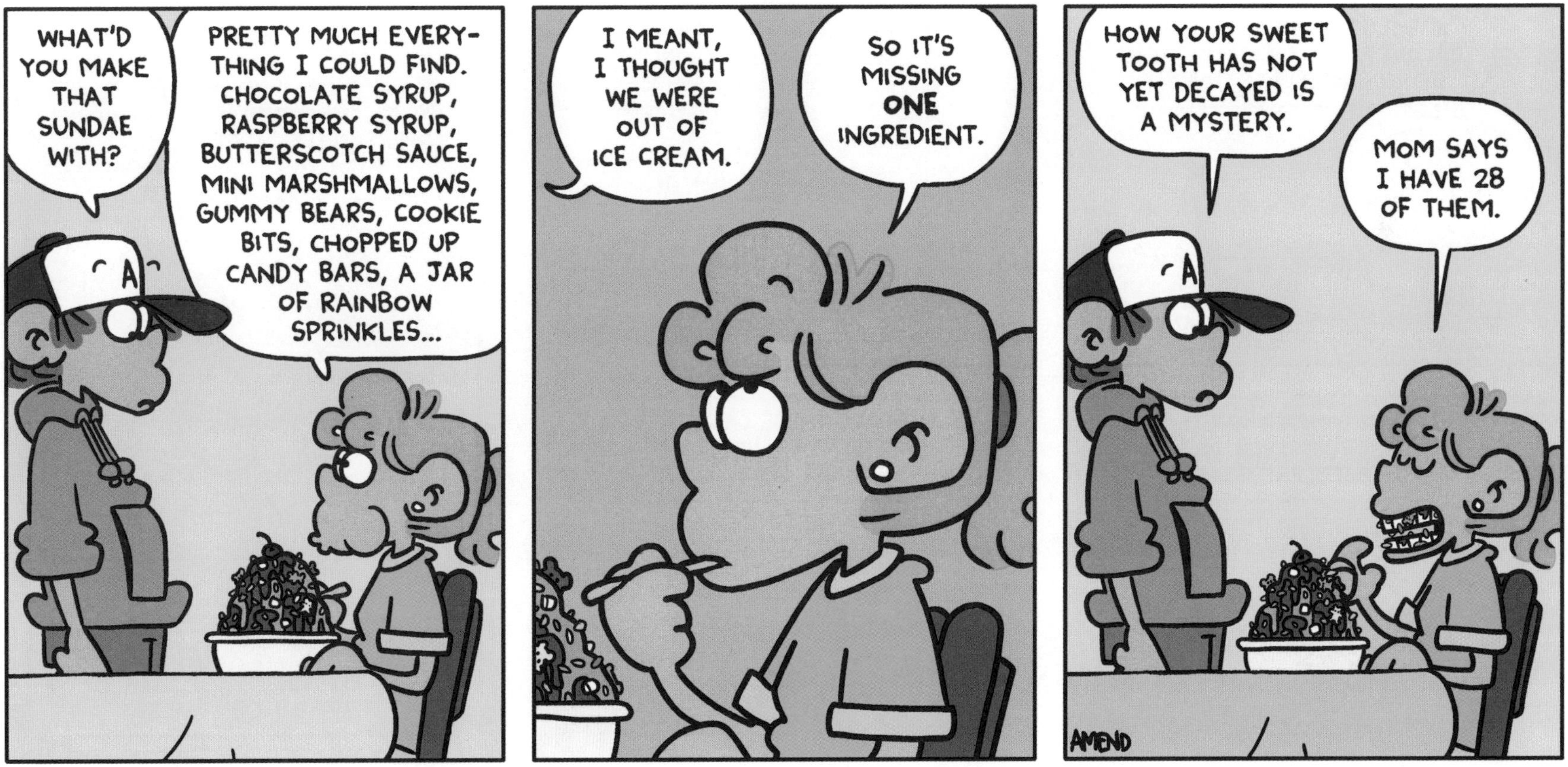
WHAT'D YOU MAKE THAT SUNDAE WITH?
PRETTY MUCH EVERYTHING I COULD FIND. CHOCOLATE SYRUP, RASPBERRY SYRUP, BUTTERSCOTCH SAUCE, MINI MARSHMALLOWS, GUMMY BEARS, COOKIE BITS, CHOPPED UP CANDY BARS, A JAR OF RAINBOW SPRINKLES...
I MEANT, I THOUGHT WE WERE OUT OF ICE CREAM.
SO IT'S MISSING **ONE** INGREDIENT.
HOW YOUR SWEET TOOTH HAS NOT YET DECAYED IS A MYSTERY.
MOM SAYS I HAVE 28 OF THEM.
AMEND

Remotely Annoying

IF BOLOGNA IS PRONOUNCED "BALONEY," WHY ISN'T LASAGNA PRONOUNCED "LASAHNEY"?
IF I DRINK HALF THIS GLASS OF WHOLE MILK, WOULD YOU SAY IT'S STILL WHOLE?
EVER WONDER WHERE THEY GET THE SEEDS TO PLANT SEEDLESS GRAPES?
WHY ARE THESE CALLED PEANUT BUTTER CUPS, WHEN THE CUP IS MADE OF CHOCOLATE?
FOR WHAT IT'S WORTH, JASON, REMOTE LUNCH-TIME WITH YOU IS EVERY BIT AS ANNOYING AS IN-PERSON LUNCHTIME WITH YOU.
PHEW! THANKS! I WAS WORRIED!
AMEND

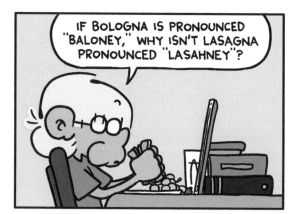

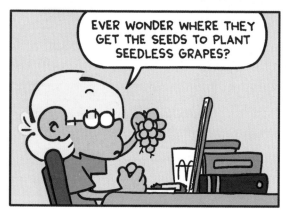

Alarming

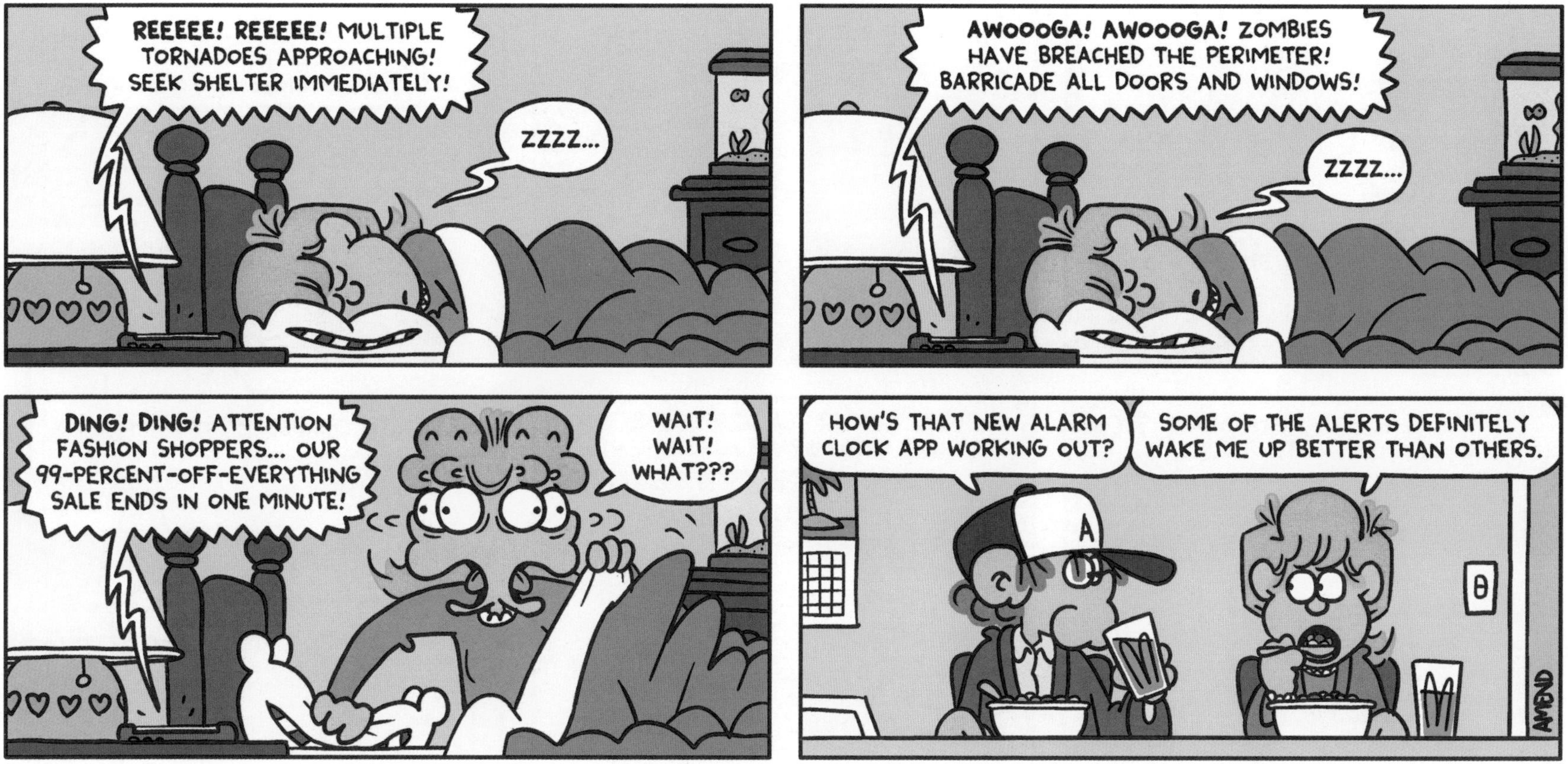
REEEEE! REEEEE! MULTIPLE TORNADOES APPROACHING! SEEK SHELTER IMMEDIATELY!
ZZZZ...
AWOOOGA! AWOOOGA! ZOMBIES HAVE BREACHED THE PERIMETER! BARRICADE ALL DOORS AND WINDOWS!
ZZZZ...
DING! DING! ATTENTION FASHION SHOPPERS... OUR 99-PERCENT-OFF-EVERYTHING SALE ENDS IN ONE MINUTE!
WAIT! WAIT! WHAT???
HOW'S THAT NEW ALARM CLOCK APP WORKING OUT?
SOME OF THE ALERTS DEFINITELY WAKE ME UP BETTER THAN OTHERS.
AMEND

Pacing Oneself

HOW'S "FIFTH GRADE FROM HOME" WORKING OUT?

IT WORKED OUT REALLY WELL.

"WORKED"? PAST-TENSE?

YEAH.

MY TEACHER SAID WE CAN STUDY AT OUR OWN PACE WHILE THE SCHOOL IRONS OUT ALL THE DISTANCE-LEARNING KINKS.

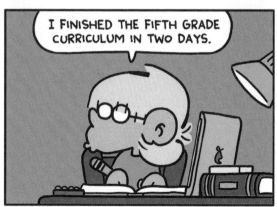

I FINISHED THE FIFTH GRADE CURRICULUM IN TWO DAYS.

SO WHAT'S YOUR TEACHER HAVING YOU DO NOW? SIXTH GRADE ASSIGNMENTS?

SEVENTH GRADE?

HI JASON, I'M LOOPING IN PROFESSOR STARR FROM CALTECH...

At Least There Aren't Snakes

HE'S BEEN INVITED TO A PARTY AND NO ONE IS WEARING A MASK...

AND EVERYONE IS STANDING CLOSER THAN SIX FEET APART...

AND THE CHILDREN HAVE BEEN ATTENDING SCHOOL FOR NEARLY A MONTH...

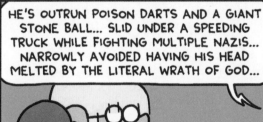

HE'S OUTRUN POISON DARTS AND A GIANT STONE BALL... SLID UNDER A SPEEDING TRUCK WHILE FIGHTING MULTIPLE NAZIS... NARROWLY AVOIDED HAVING HIS HEAD MELTED BY THE LITERAL WRATH OF GOD...

BUT WILL HE SURVIVE THIS?!?

I REALLY MISS THE OLD FORMS OF DANGER.

"INDIANA JONES AND THE GRAND-DAUGHTER'S BIRTHDAY"!

Zwoooon

NICOLE! NICOLE! YOU WON'T BELIEVE IT!

WHAT? WHAT?

THERE WAS A MOMENT IN ENGLISH CLASS TODAY WHERE SUPER-CUTE BILLY HEINZ, KIRK RICKMAN AND STEVIE SAPTIS WERE ALL LOOKING RIGHT AT ME AND SMILING!

THE THREE HOTTEST BOYS IN OUR GRADE, AND THEY WERE ALL LOOKING AND SMILING AT **MEEEEEE!!!**

MY HEART IS STILL RACING! IT WAS ONE OF THE TOP 10 MOMENTS OF MY LIFE!

PAIGE, OUR CLASSES ARE ZOOM CALLS. YOU DO REALIZE THAT EVERYONE IS LOOKING AT **EVERYONE**, RIGHT?

DUH.

IT WAS STILL A TOP-10 MOMENT.

OK, JUST MAKING SURE.

Starving Art

Burritoes

Burritoga

Burritowtruck

Burritollbooth

Burritoblerone

Burritotoro

YOU CAN ALWAYS SPOT THE WORK OF A STARVING ARTIST.

MOM, CAN YOU CALL PETER? HE WAS SUPPOSED TO BE BACK WITH LUNCH OVER AN HOUR AGO!

AMEND

Growing Pains

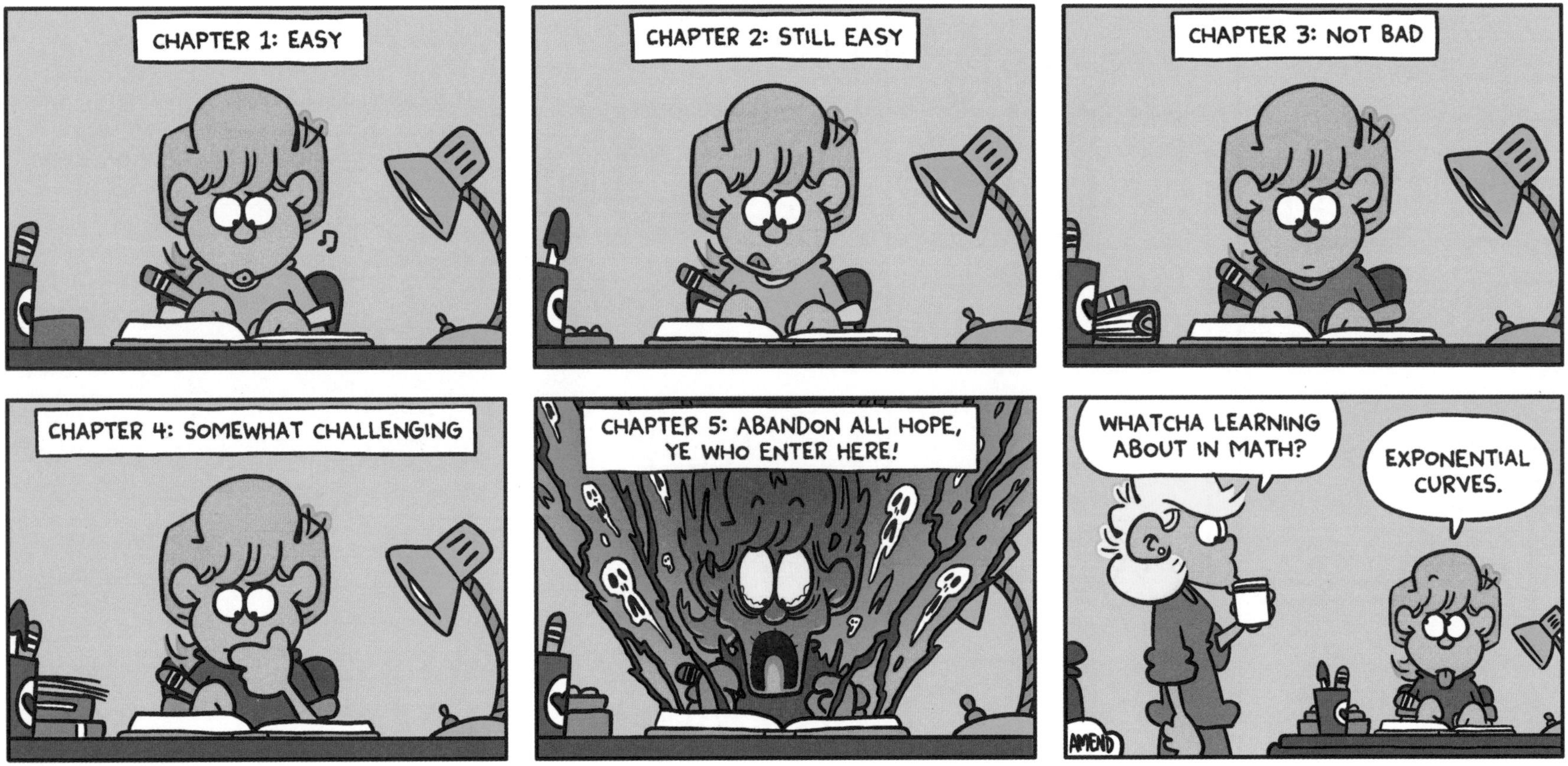
CHAPTER 1: EASY
CHAPTER 2: STILL EASY
CHAPTER 3: NOT BAD
CHAPTER 4: SOMEWHAT CHALLENGING
CHAPTER 5: ABANDON ALL HOPE, YE WHO ENTER HERE!
WHATCHA LEARNING ABOUT IN MATH?
EXPONENTIAL CURVES.
AMEND

Trick Plays

WANNA GO TO THE PARK AND HELP ME PRACTICE THE TRICK PLAY I JUST INVENTED?

NOT REALLY.

JASON, C'MON, IT'S THE BEST PLAY EVER! IT STARTS WITH A HANDOFF TO YOU, THEN YOU FLEA-FLICK IT BACK TO ME...

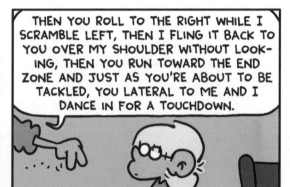

THEN YOU ROLL TO THE RIGHT WHILE I SCRAMBLE LEFT, THEN I FLING IT BACK TO YOU OVER MY SHOULDER WITHOUT LOOKING, THEN YOU RUN TOWARD THE END ZONE AND JUST AS YOU'RE ABOUT TO BE TACKLED, YOU LATERAL TO ME AND I DANCE IN FOR A TOUCHDOWN.

THINK YOU CAN DO IT?

BACK UP. YOU LOST ME.

AT WHAT PART?

WHAT'S A HANDOFF?

AND THAT, LADIES AND GENTLEMEN, WAS **MY** TRICK PLAY.

PAIGE, C'MON, PLEASE??

PETER, NO! I HATE FOOTBALL!

Fright Night

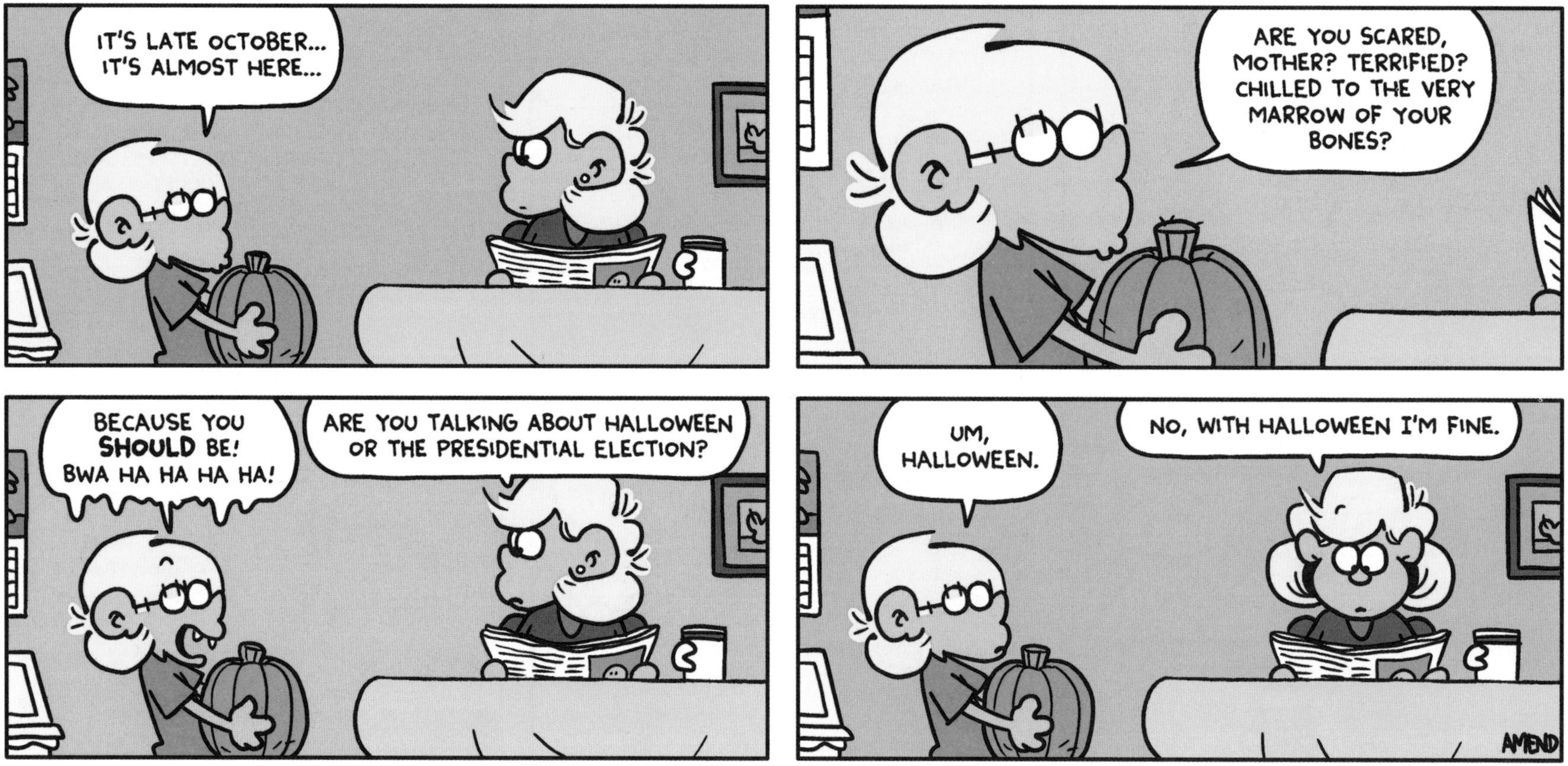
IT'S LATE OCTOBER... IT'S ALMOST HERE...
ARE YOU SCARED, MOTHER? TERRIFIED? CHILLED TO THE VERY MARROW OF YOUR BONES?
BECAUSE YOU SHOULD BE! BWA HA HA HA HA!
ARE YOU TALKING ABOUT HALLOWEEN OR THE PRESIDENTIAL ELECTION?
UM, HALLOWEEN.
NO, WITH HALLOWEEN I'M FINE.
AMEND

Rabbit Rabbit

RABBIT RABBIT.

WEIRDO.

WHAT? IT'S A GOOD LUCK THING.

SUPPOSEDLY, IF YOU SAY "RABBIT RABBIT" AT THE START OF A MONTH, IT BRINGS YOU GOOD LUCK. I HAVE A BIG HISTORY TEST THIS WEEK AND NEED ALL THE LUCK I CAN GET.

WHATEVER. IT'S STILL WEIRD.

HEY, IT'S NOT AS WEIRD AS SOME OF THE STUFF **JASON** DOES.

RIBBIT RIBBIT.

THAT'S NOT EXACTLY A HIGH BAR TO CLEAR.

I WONDER IF EATING TRIX TODAY IS ALSO LUCKY.

AMEND

Whoop$ies

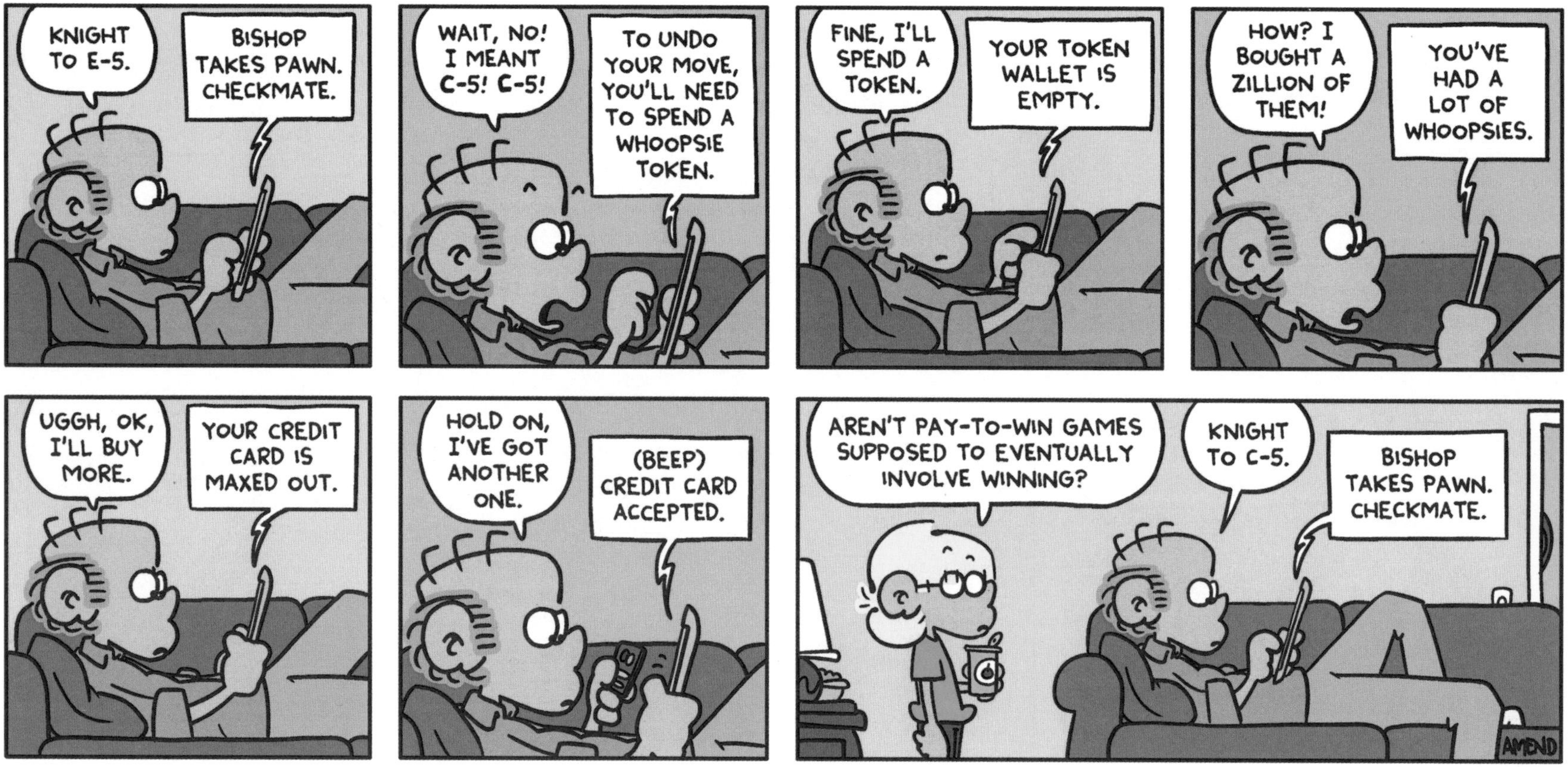

KNIGHT TO E-5.
BISHOP TAKES PAWN. CHECKMATE.
WAIT, NO! I MEANT C-5! C-5!
TO UNDO YOUR MOVE, YOU'LL NEED TO SPEND A WHOOPSIE TOKEN.
FINE, I'LL SPEND A TOKEN.
YOUR TOKEN WALLET IS EMPTY.
HOW? I BOUGHT A ZILLION OF THEM!
YOU'VE HAD A LOT OF WHOOPSIES.
UGGH, OK, I'LL BUY MORE.
YOUR CREDIT CARD IS MAXED OUT.
HOLD ON, I'VE GOT ANOTHER ONE.
(BEEP) CREDIT CARD ACCEPTED.
AREN'T PAY-TO-WIN GAMES SUPPOSED TO EVENTUALLY INVOLVE WINNING?
KNIGHT TO C-5.
BISHOP TAKES PAWN. CHECKMATE.
AMEND

The Way

DON'T START YET, PAIGE! I CAN'T FIND QUINCY'S EARS!

THEY WERE ON MY DESK AND NOW THEY'RE GONE!

WHERE ARE QUINCY'S EARS?!? AAAAAA!

OH, WAIT. NEVER MIND. FOUND THEM.

IS THERE A **REASON** WHY YOU HAVE TO DRESS UP FOR EVERY STUPID EPISODE?

THIS IS THE WAY.

Playing It Safe

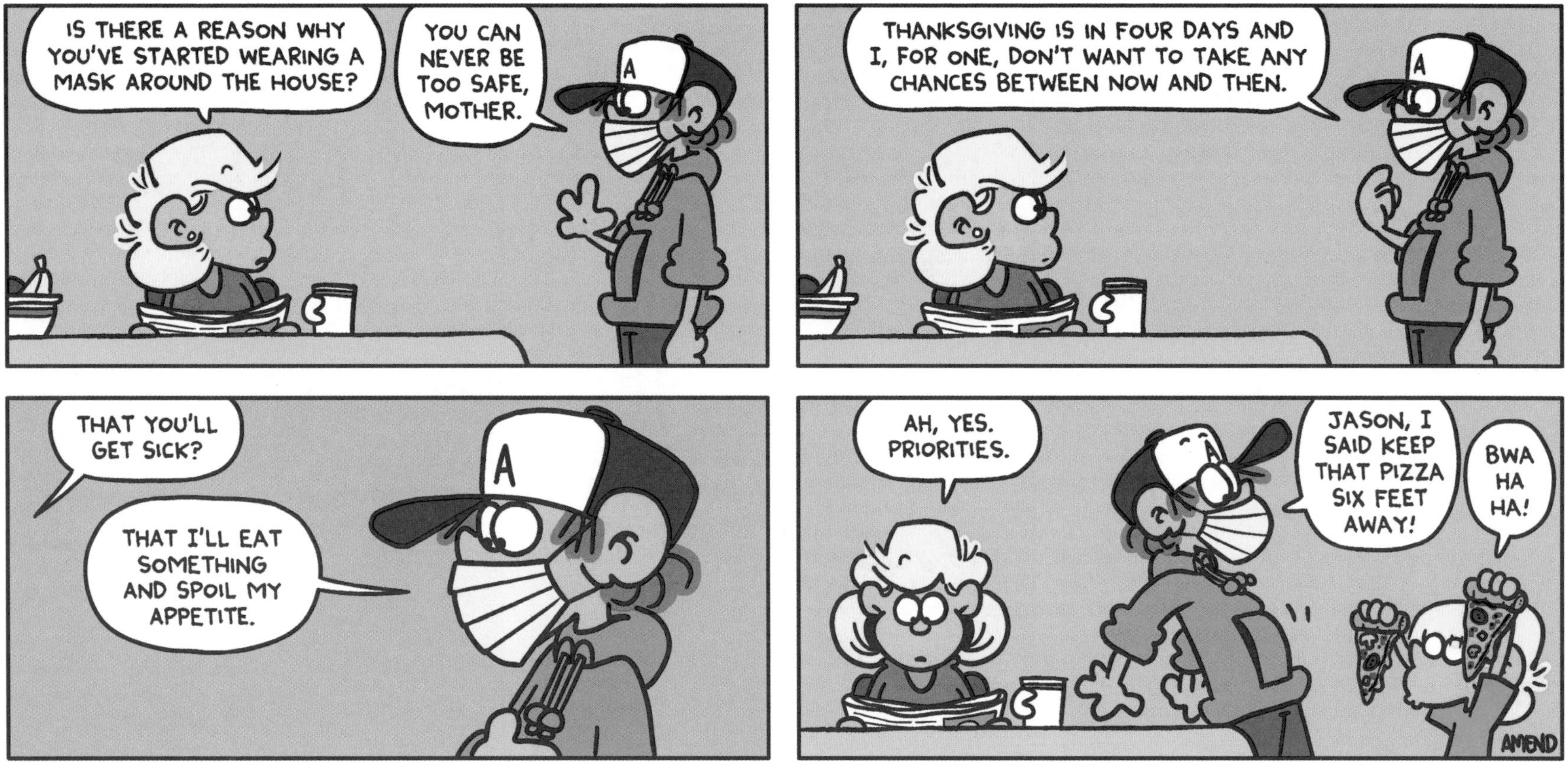
IS THERE A REASON WHY YOU'VE STARTED WEARING A MASK AROUND THE HOUSE?
YOU CAN NEVER BE TOO SAFE, MOTHER.
THANKSGIVING IS IN FOUR DAYS AND I, FOR ONE, DON'T WANT TO TAKE ANY CHANCES BETWEEN NOW AND THEN.
THAT YOU'LL GET SICK?
THAT I'LL EAT SOMETHING AND SPOIL MY APPETITE.
AH, YES. PRIORITIES.
JASON, I SAID KEEP THAT PIZZA SIX FEET AWAY!
BWA HA HA!
AMEND

The Horror

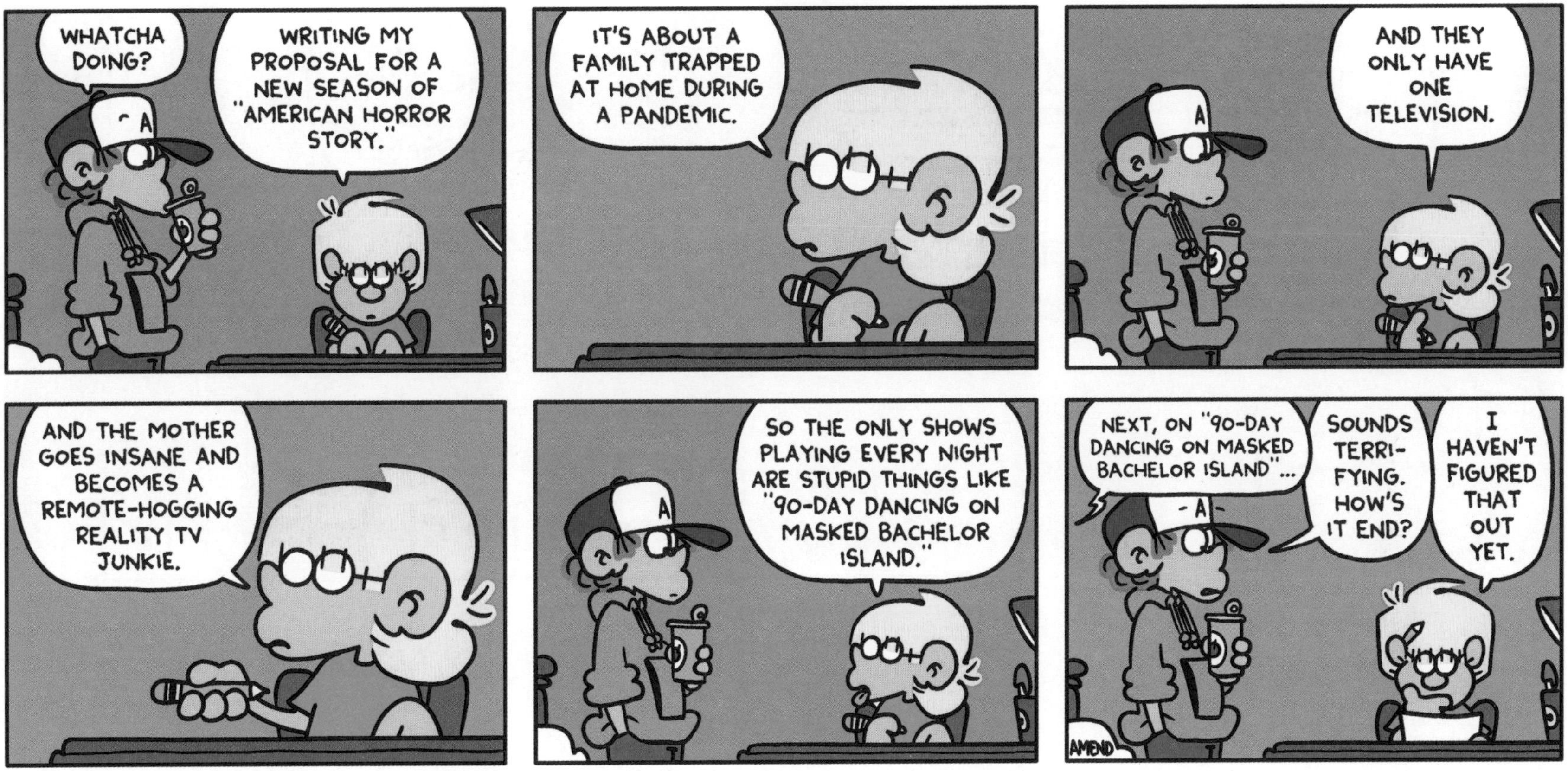
WHATCHA DOING?
WRITING MY PROPOSAL FOR A NEW SEASON OF "AMERICAN HORROR STORY."
IT'S ABOUT A FAMILY TRAPPED AT HOME DURING A PANDEMIC.
AND THEY ONLY HAVE ONE TELEVISION.
AND THE MOTHER GOES INSANE AND BECOMES A REMOTE-HOGGING REALITY TV JUNKIE.
SO THE ONLY SHOWS PLAYING EVERY NIGHT ARE STUPID THINGS LIKE "90-DAY DANCING ON MASKED BACHELOR ISLAND."
NEXT, ON "90-DAY DANCING ON MASKED BACHELOR ISLAND"...
SOUNDS TERRI-FYING. HOW'S IT END?
I HAVEN'T FIGURED THAT OUT YET.
AMEND

Coffee <3

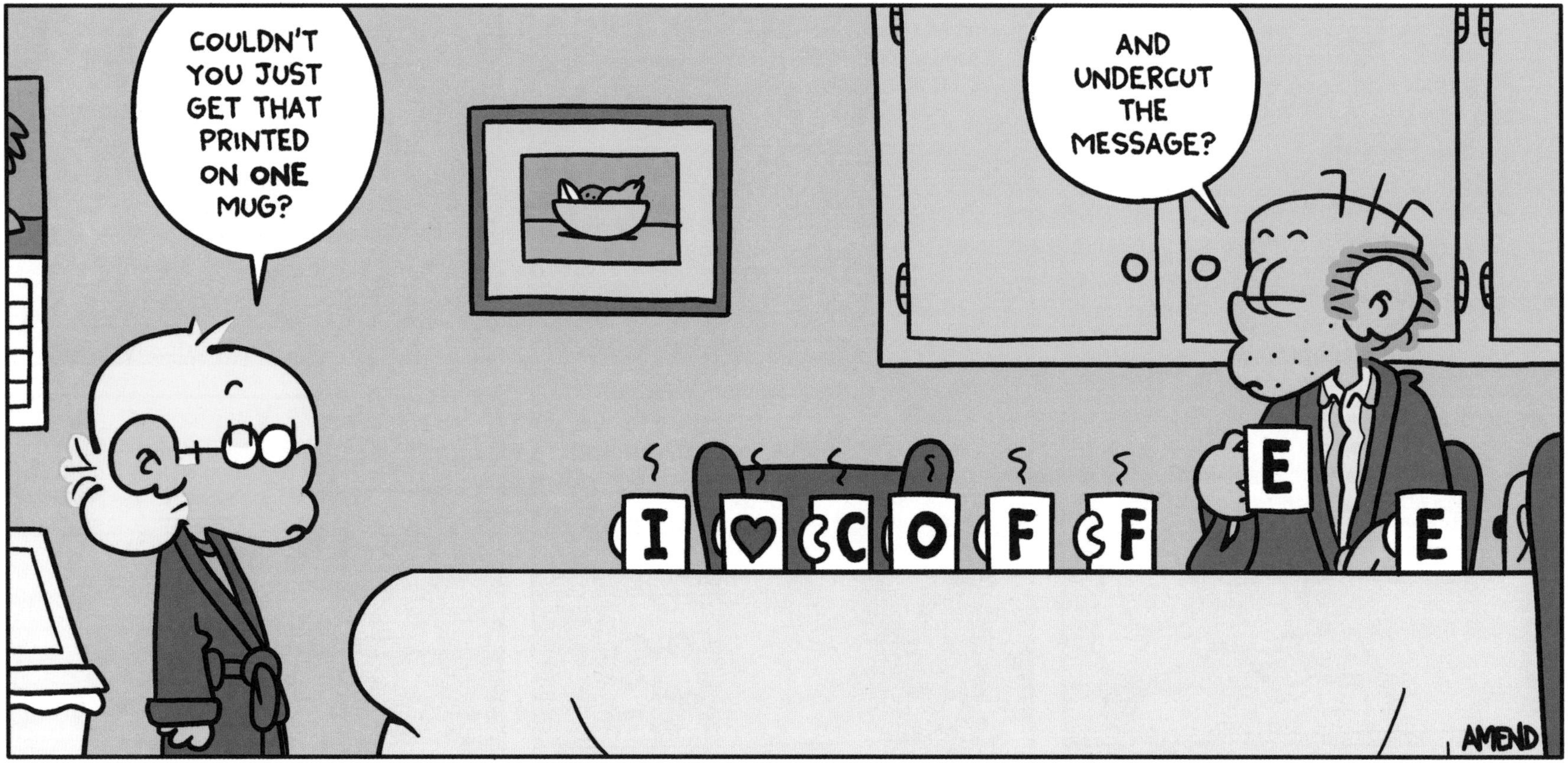
COULDN'T YOU JUST GET THAT PRINTED ON ONE MUG?
I ♥ C O F F E E
AND UNDERCUT THE MESSAGE?
AMEND

Santa Questions

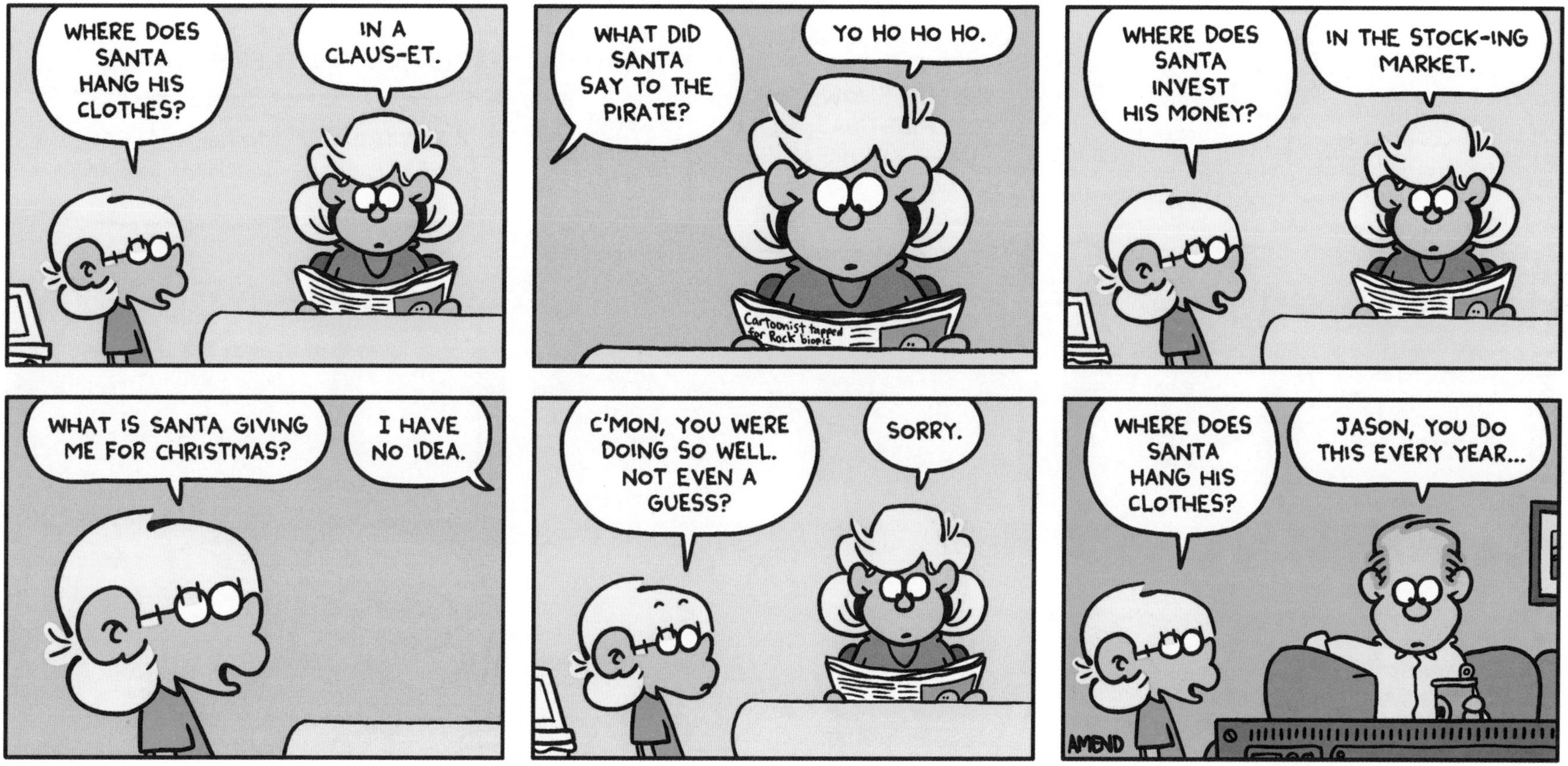
WHERE DOES SANTA HANG HIS CLOTHES?
IN A CLAUS-ET.
WHAT DID SANTA SAY TO THE PIRATE?
YO HO HO HO.
Cartoonist tapped for Rock biopic
WHERE DOES SANTA INVEST HIS MONEY?
IN THE STOCK-ING MARKET.
WHAT IS SANTA GIVING ME FOR CHRISTMAS?
I HAVE NO IDEA.
C'MON, YOU WERE DOING SO WELL. NOT EVEN A GUESS?
SORRY.
WHERE DOES SANTA HANG HIS CLOTHES?
JASON, YOU DO THIS EVERY YEAR...
AMEND

Qudolph

SAY HELLO TO QUDOLPH, THE RED-NOSED IGUANA!

CUTE.

CUTE **AND** FUNCTIONAL! IN THE EVENT OF AN INDOOR SNOWSTORM ON CHRISTMAS, HE'LL LIGHT UP HIS NOSE AND GUIDE ME SAFELY TO MY PRESENTS!

INDOOR SNOW-STORMS AREN'T A THING, YOU DWEEB.

WHICH ONE OF YOU KIDS RAISED THE THERMOSTAT?!

BETTER SAFE THAN SORRY.

MOTHER, PLEASE! I COULD SEE MY BREATH!

AMEND

Roger's Gambit

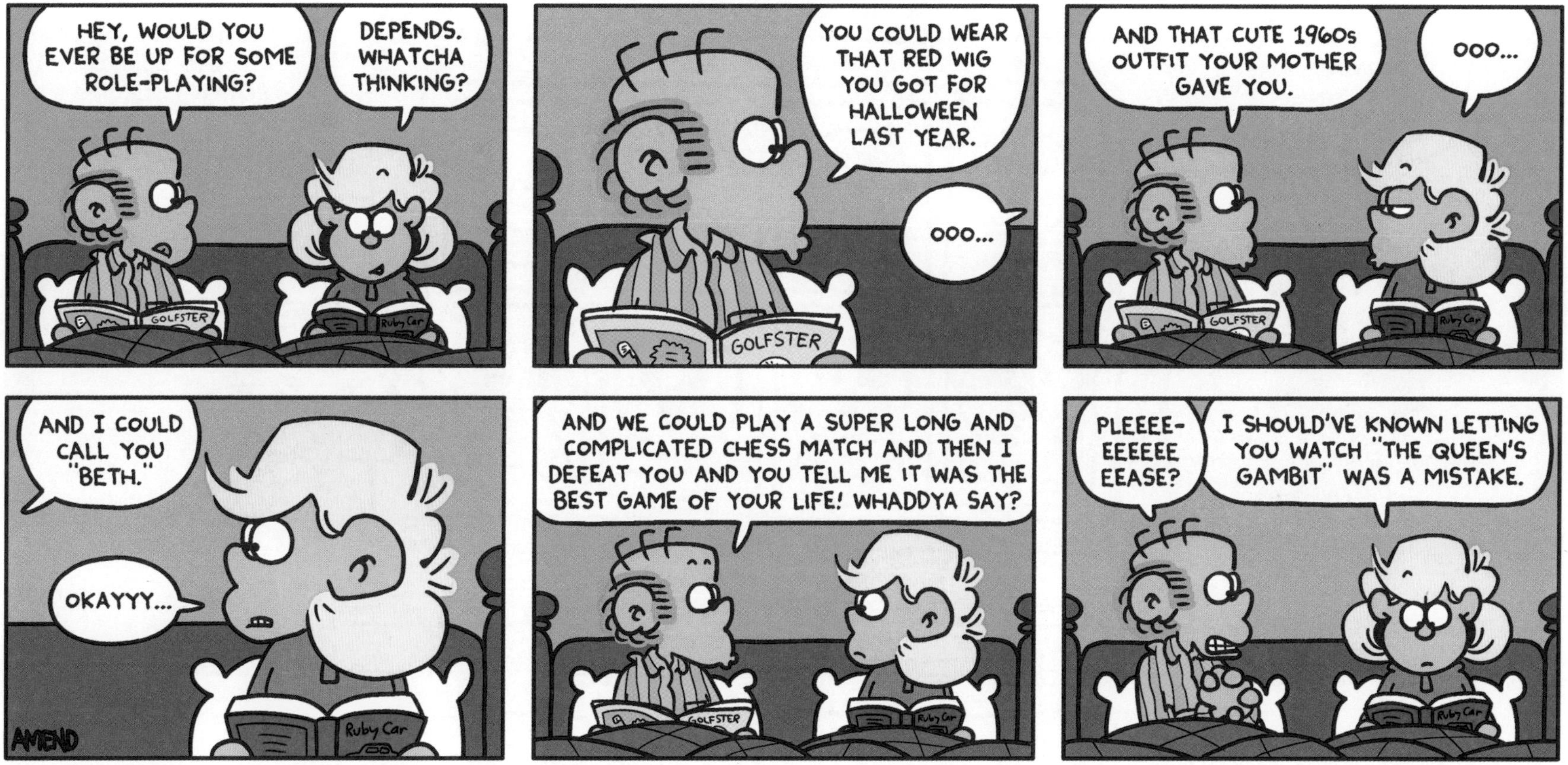
HEY, WOULD YOU EVER BE UP FOR SOME ROLE-PLAYING?
DEPENDS. WHATCHA THINKING?
GOLFSTER
Ruby Car
YOU COULD WEAR THAT RED WIG YOU GOT FOR HALLOWEEN LAST YEAR.
OOO...
GOLFSTER
AND THAT CUTE 1960s OUTFIT YOUR MOTHER GAVE YOU.
OOO...
AND I COULD CALL YOU "BETH."
OKAYYY...
AMEND
Ruby Car
AND WE COULD PLAY A SUPER LONG AND COMPLICATED CHESS MATCH AND THEN I DEFEAT YOU AND YOU TELL ME IT WAS THE BEST GAME OF YOUR LIFE! WHADDYA SAY?
PLEEEE-EEEEEE EEASE?
I SHOULD'VE KNOWN LETTING YOU WATCH "THE QUEEN'S GAMBIT" WAS A MISTAKE.

Computer Issues

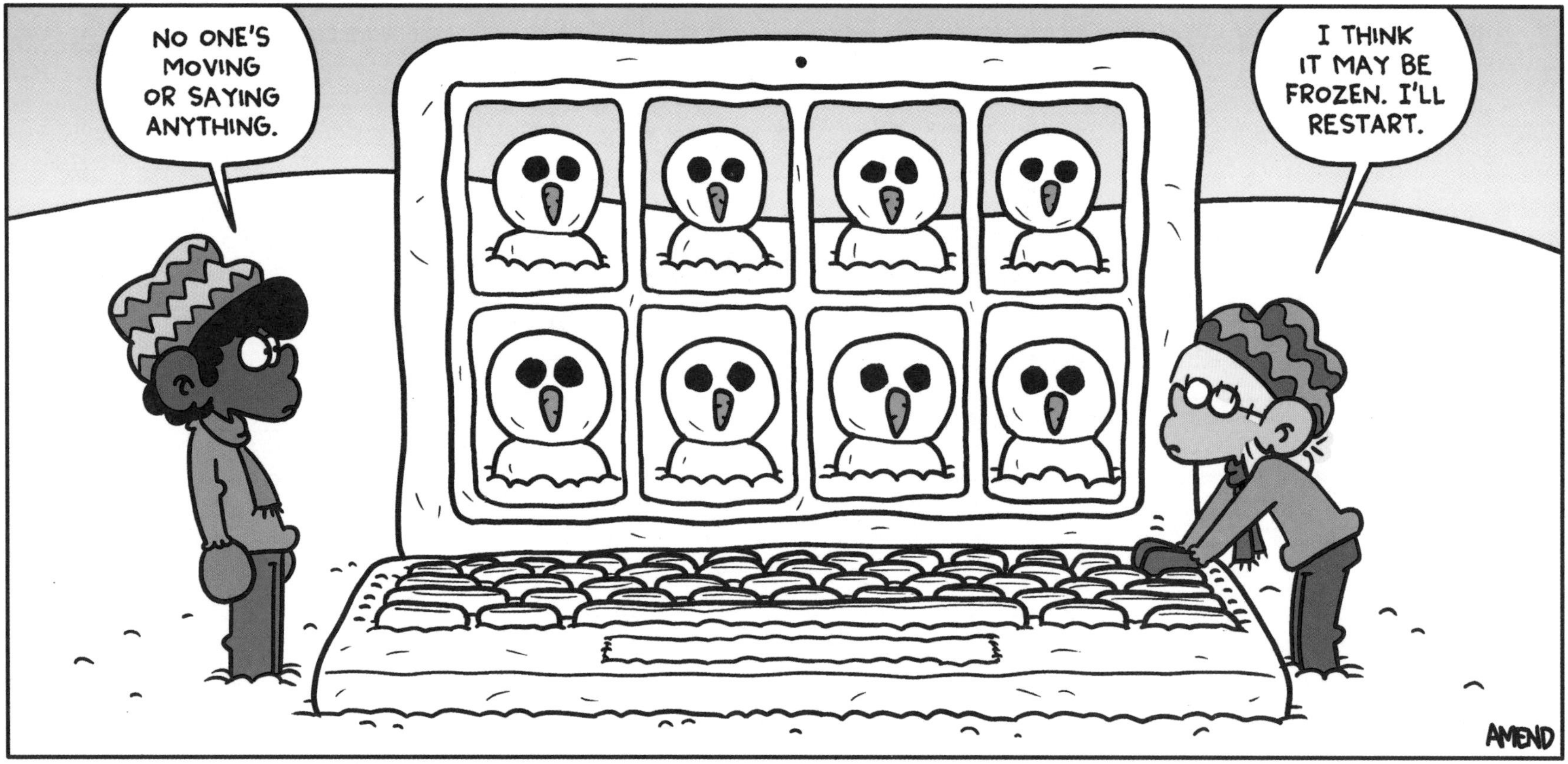
NO ONE'S MOVING OR SAYING ANYTHING.
I THINK IT MAY BE FROZEN. I'LL RESTART.
AMEND

HELLO PETER

WHAT ON EARTH ARE YOU SCREAMING ABOUT?

LOOK AT MY CEREAL!

I SWEAR I DIDN'T DO THIS! IT FORMED THE WORDS ON ITS OWN!

HELLO PETER

IT'S LIKE A GREETING FROM THE SPIRIT WORLD!

GHOSTS ARE REAL! GHOSTS ARE REAL! AAAAAA!

AMEND

CALM DOWN. RANDOM LETTERS ARE BOUND TO FORM WORDS NOW AND THEN.

BUT "**HELLO PETER**"?! THAT'S LIKE ONE IN A GAZILLION!

PETER, THINK ABOUT HOW MANY BOWLS OF CEREAL YOU EAT IN A WEEK.

OK, GOOD POINT.

Death Breath

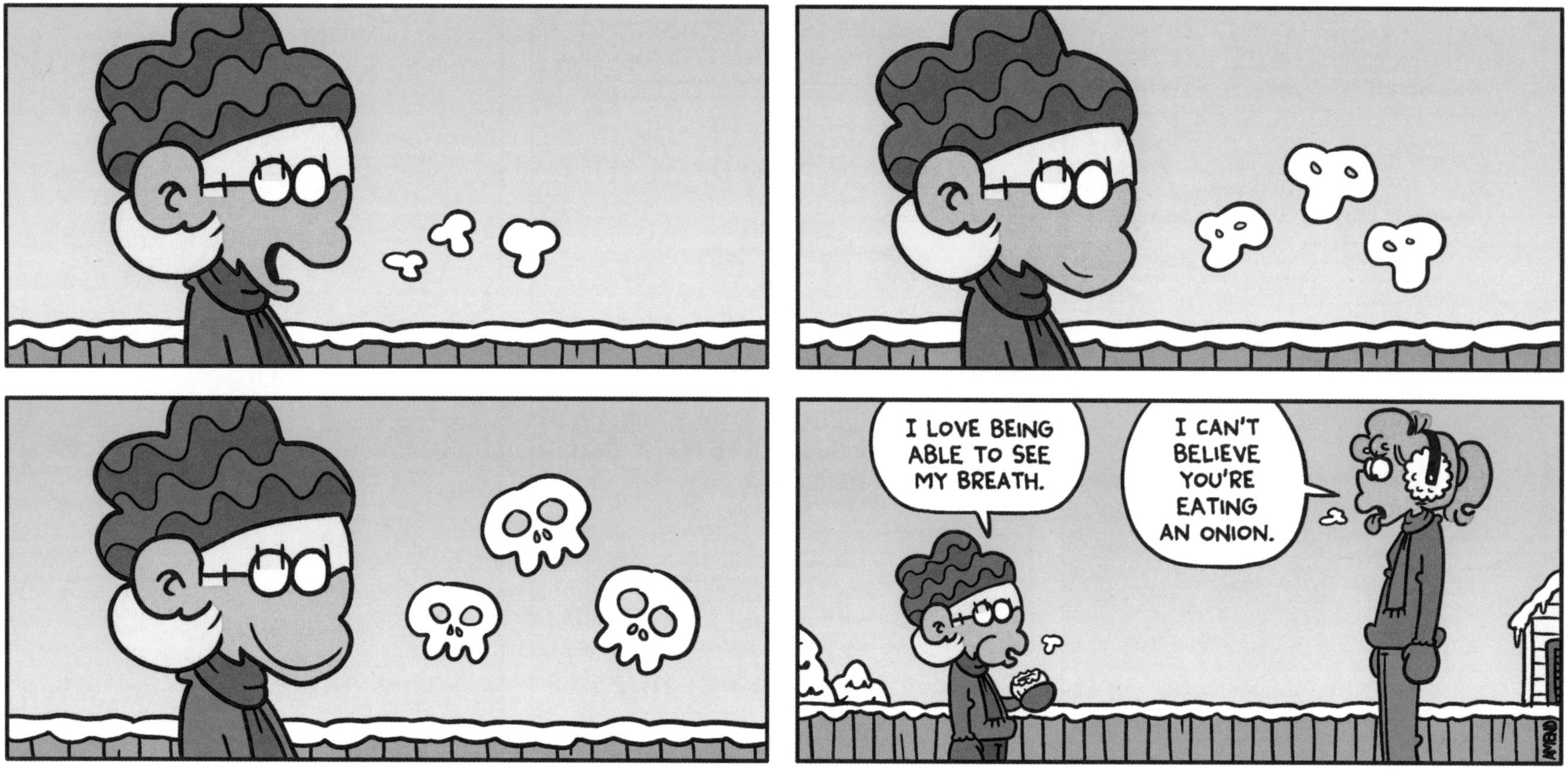
I LOVE BEING ABLE TO SEE MY BREATH.
I CAN'T BELIEVE YOU'RE EATING AN ONION.

Puzzle Killer

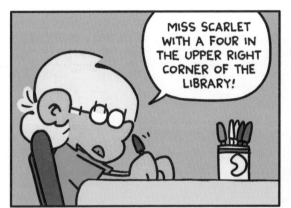

MISS SCARLET WITH A FOUR IN THE UPPER RIGHT CORNER OF THE LIBRARY!

COLONEL MUSTARD WITH A SEVEN IN THE BOTTOM CENTER SQUARE IN THE BILLIARD ROOM!

"SUDOCLUE" IS NEVER GOING TO CATCH ON, JASON.

MOM, ANY WORD FROM HASBRO YET?

BUT WHAT'S THIS?! PROFESSOR PLUM WITH A ONE-EIGHT-NINE COMBO IN THE CONSERVATORY TO FINISH IT OUT!

AND WE HAVE OUR PUZZLE KILLER! CONGRATULATIONS, PROFESSOR!

AMEND

Pre-Gaming

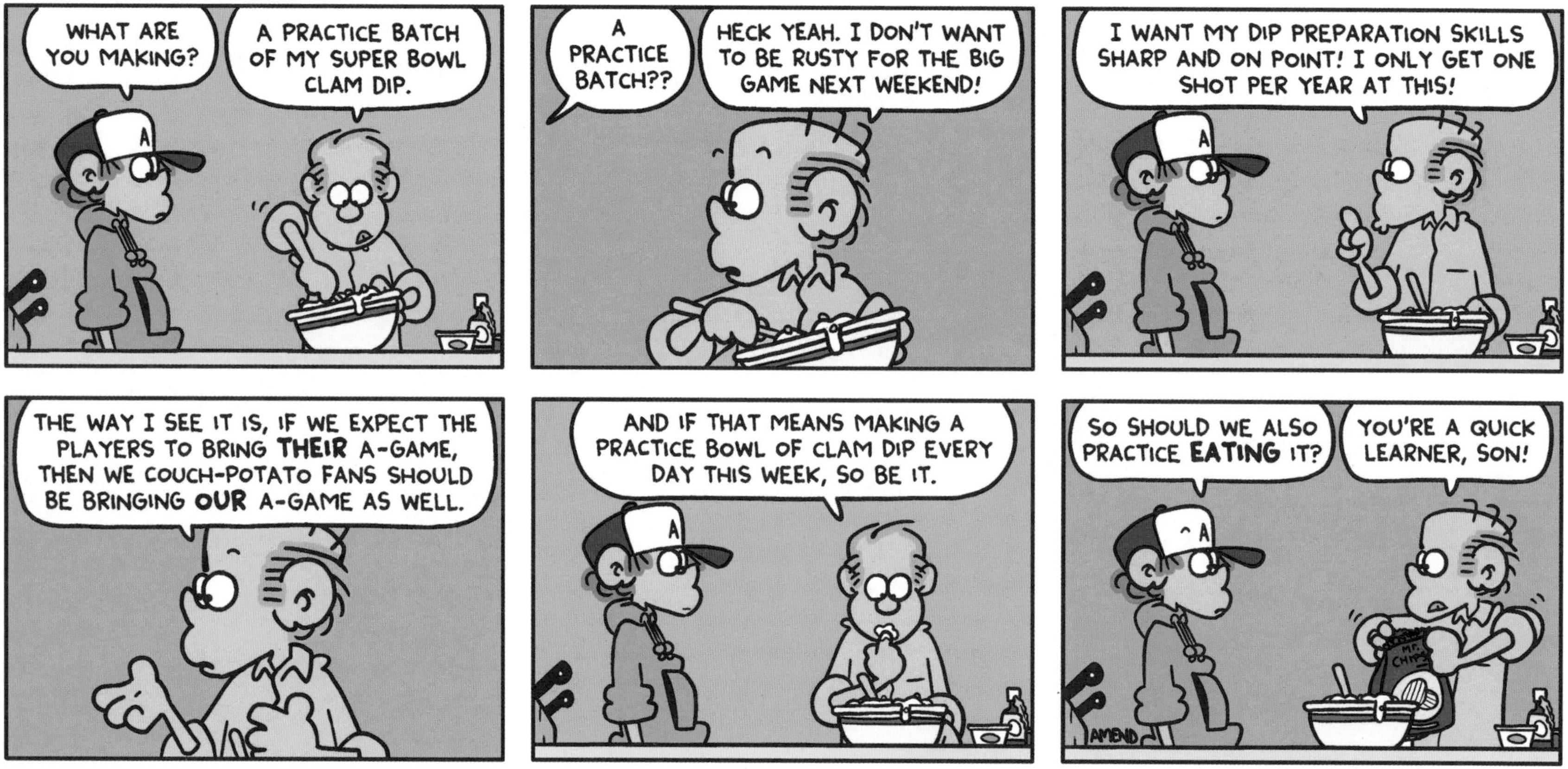
WHAT ARE YOU MAKING?
A PRACTICE BATCH OF MY SUPER BOWL CLAM DIP.
A PRACTICE BATCH??
HECK YEAH. I DON'T WANT TO BE RUSTY FOR THE BIG GAME NEXT WEEKEND!
I WANT MY DIP PREPARATION SKILLS SHARP AND ON POINT! I ONLY GET ONE SHOT PER YEAR AT THIS!
THE WAY I SEE IT IS, IF WE EXPECT THE PLAYERS TO BRING **THEIR** A-GAME, THEN WE COUCH-POTATO FANS SHOULD BE BRINGING **OUR** A-GAME AS WELL.
AND IF THAT MEANS MAKING A PRACTICE BOWL OF CLAM DIP EVERY DAY THIS WEEK, SO BE IT.
SO SHOULD WE ALSO PRACTICE **EATING** IT?
YOU'RE A QUICK LEARNER, SON!
AMEND

Six Foot Ball

LET ME TRY PUNTING IT.

HAVING TO STAND SIX FEET APART IS MAKING THIS WAY HARDER THAN USUAL.

Jowlentine's Day

HAPPY JOWLENTINE'S DAY!

WHAT'S THAT?

I MADE IT UP. THINK OF IT AS A MORE PLEASANT ALTERNATIVE TO VALENTINE'S DAY.

RATHER THAN BEING ABOUT ICKY THINGS LIKE LOVE AND ROMANCE, JOWLENTINE'S DAY IS ALL ABOUT HOW MANY CANDY HEARTS YOU CAN CRAM INTO YOUR CHEEKS.

GACK! GACK! COUGH!

DANG. I KEEP CHOKING ON THESE THINGS.

ANYWAY, IT'S STILL MORE PLEASANT AND LESS ICKY.

YOU HAVE GREEN DROOL ON YOUR CHIN, BY THE WAY.

AMEND

Party Time

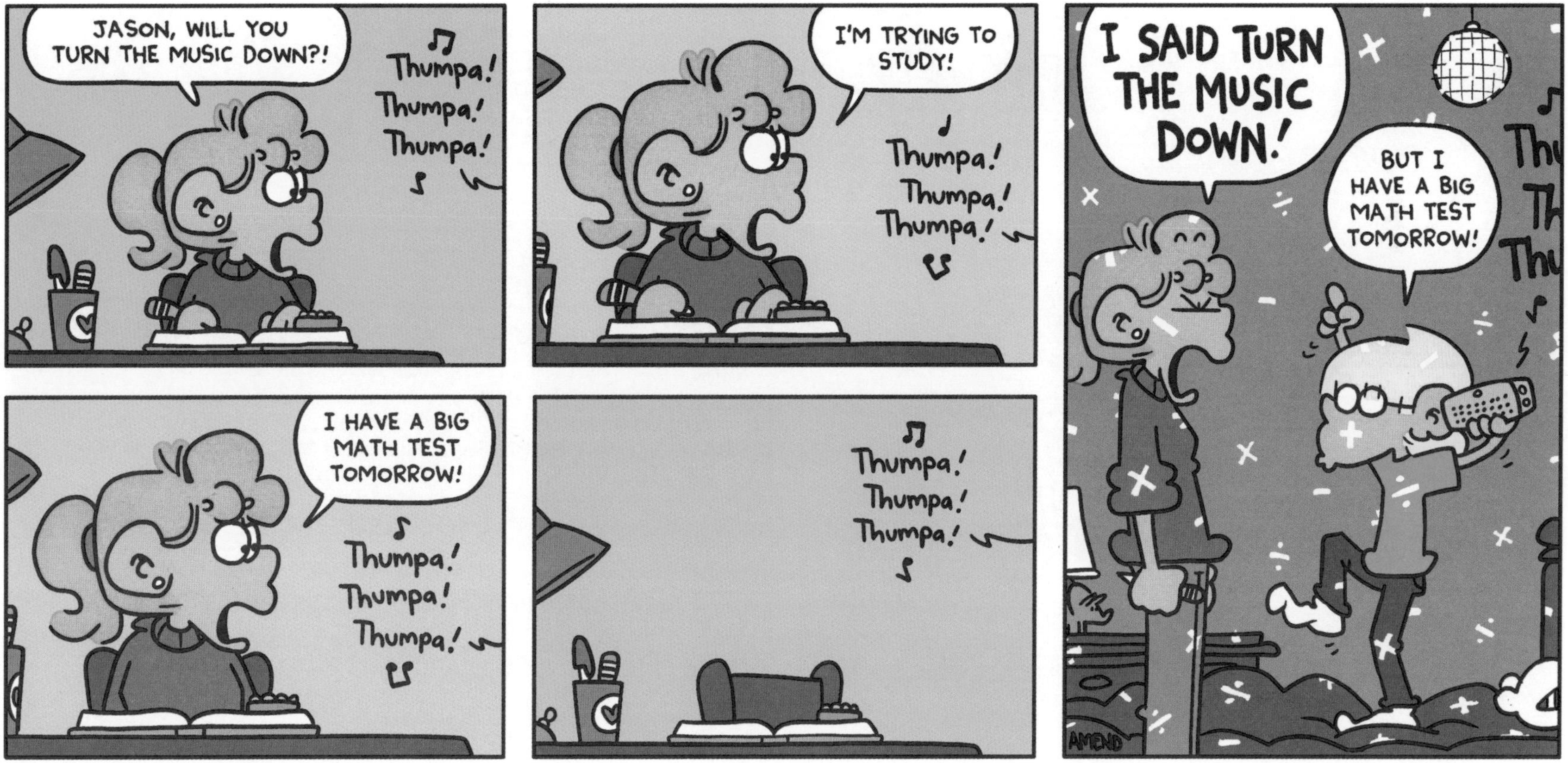

JASON, WILL YOU TURN THE MUSIC DOWN?!
Thumpa! Thumpa! Thumpa!
I'M TRYING TO STUDY!
Thumpa! Thumpa! Thumpa!
I HAVE A BIG MATH TEST TOMORROW!
Thumpa! Thumpa! Thumpa!
Thumpa! Thumpa! Thumpa!
I SAID TURN THE MUSIC DOWN!
BUT I HAVE A BIG MATH TEST TOMORROW!
AMEND

Pizzics

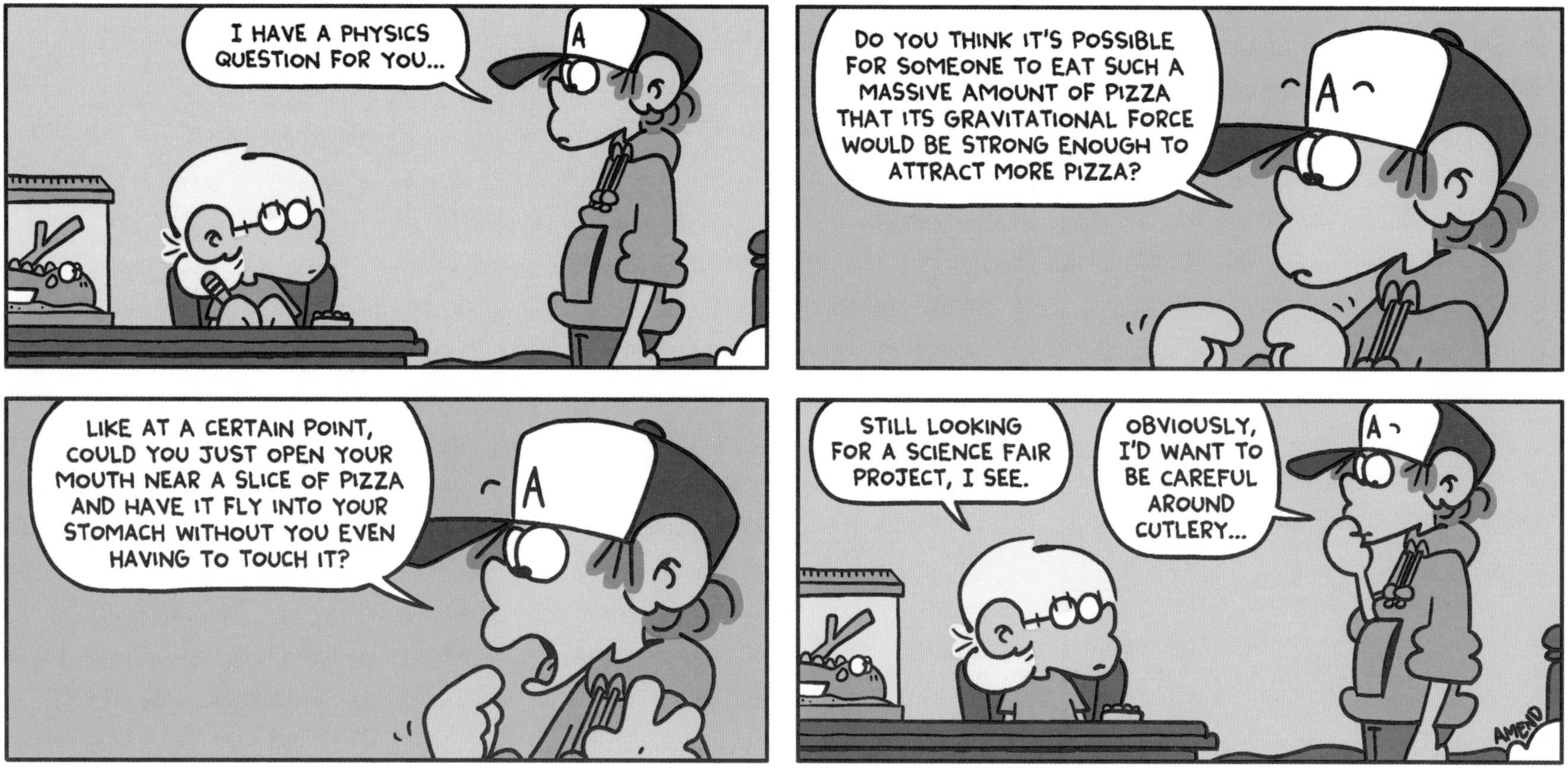
I HAVE A PHYSICS QUESTION FOR YOU...
DO YOU THINK IT'S POSSIBLE FOR SOMEONE TO EAT SUCH A MASSIVE AMOUNT OF PIZZA THAT ITS GRAVITATIONAL FORCE WOULD BE STRONG ENOUGH TO ATTRACT MORE PIZZA?
LIKE AT A CERTAIN POINT, COULD YOU JUST OPEN YOUR MOUTH NEAR A SLICE OF PIZZA AND HAVE IT FLY INTO YOUR STOMACH WITHOUT YOU EVEN HAVING TO TOUCH IT?
STILL LOOKING FOR A SCIENCE FAIR PROJECT, I SEE.
OBVIOUSLY, I'D WANT TO BE CAREFUL AROUND CUTLERY...
AMEND

Studybait

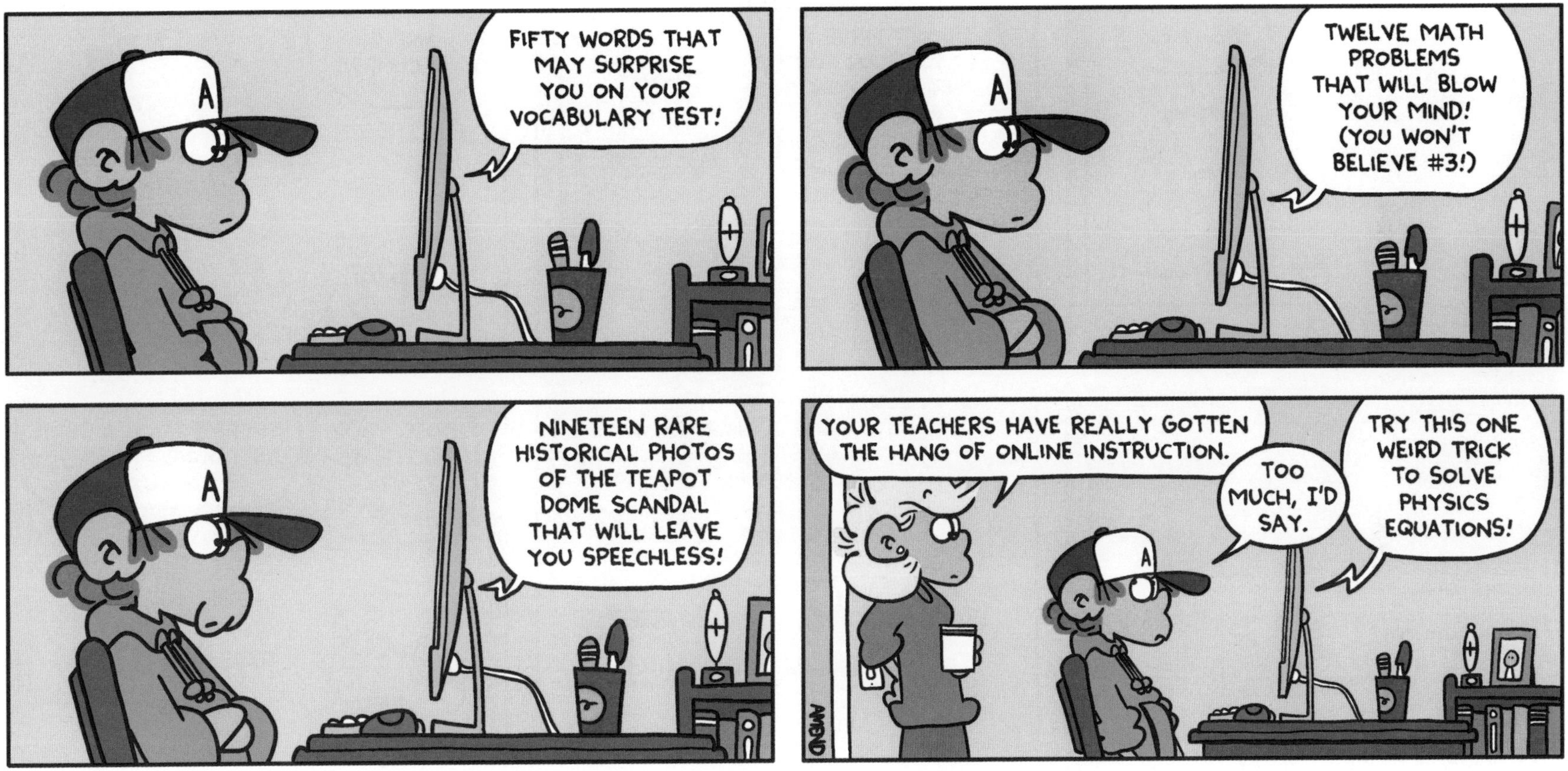

FIFTY WORDS THAT MAY SURPRISE YOU ON YOUR VOCABULARY TEST!
TWELVE MATH PROBLEMS THAT WILL BLOW YOUR MIND! (YOU WON'T BELIEVE #3!)
NINETEEN RARE HISTORICAL PHOTOS OF THE TEAPOT DOME SCANDAL THAT WILL LEAVE YOU SPEECHLESS!
YOUR TEACHERS HAVE REALLY GOTTEN THE HANG OF ONLINE INSTRUCTION.
TOO MUCH, I'D SAY.
TRY THIS ONE WEIRD TRICK TO SOLVE PHYSICS EQUATIONS!
AMEND

3-14

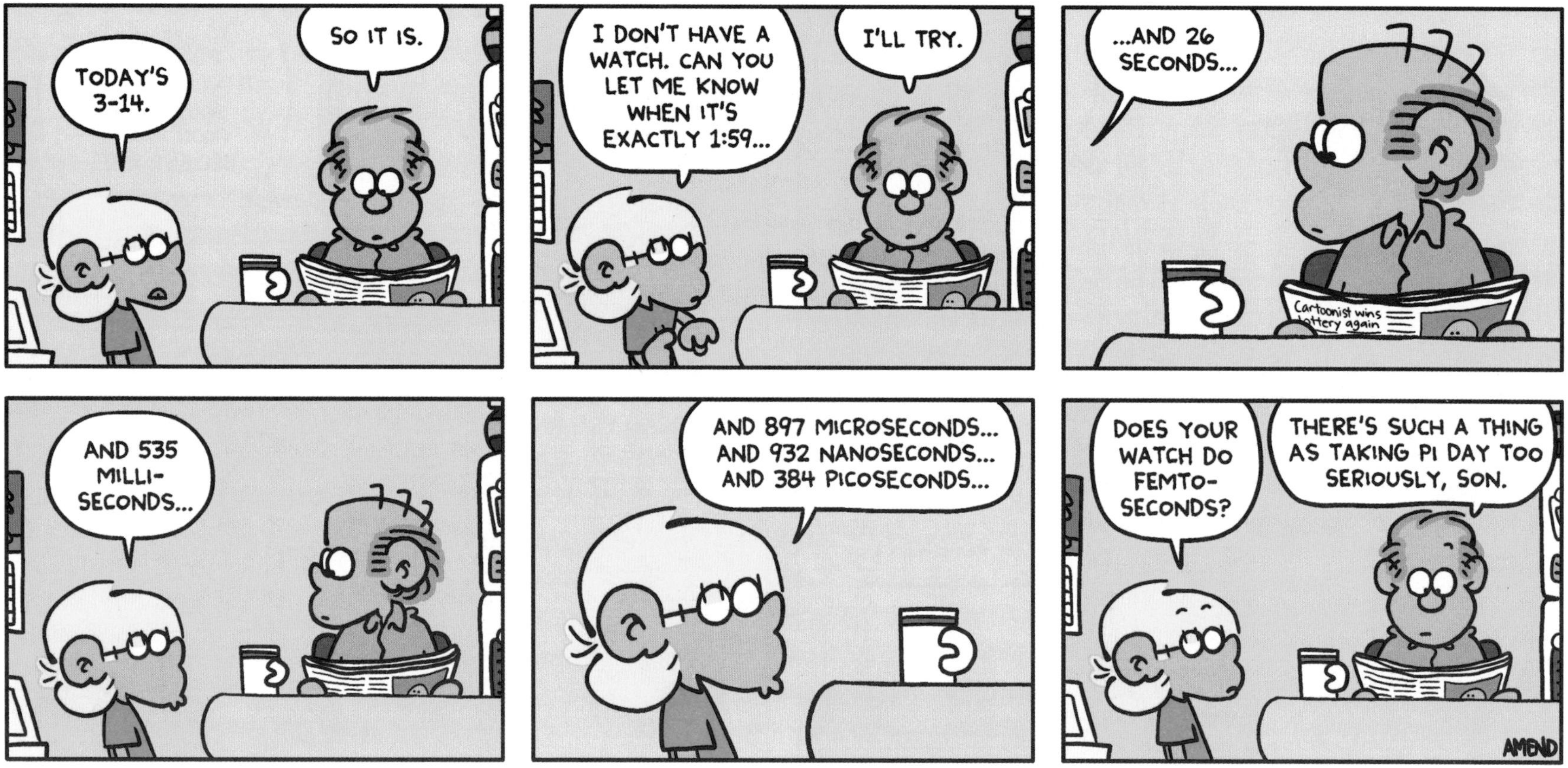
TODAY'S 3-14.
SO IT IS.
I DON'T HAVE A WATCH. CAN YOU LET ME KNOW WHEN IT'S EXACTLY 1:59...
I'LL TRY.
...AND 26 SECONDS...
Cartoonist wins lottery again
AND 535 MILLI-SECONDS...
AND 897 MICROSECONDS... AND 932 NANOSECONDS... AND 384 PICOSECONDS...
DOES YOUR WATCH DO FEMTO-SECONDS?
THERE'S SUCH A THING AS TAKING PI DAY TOO SERIOUSLY, SON.
AMEND

Shell Game

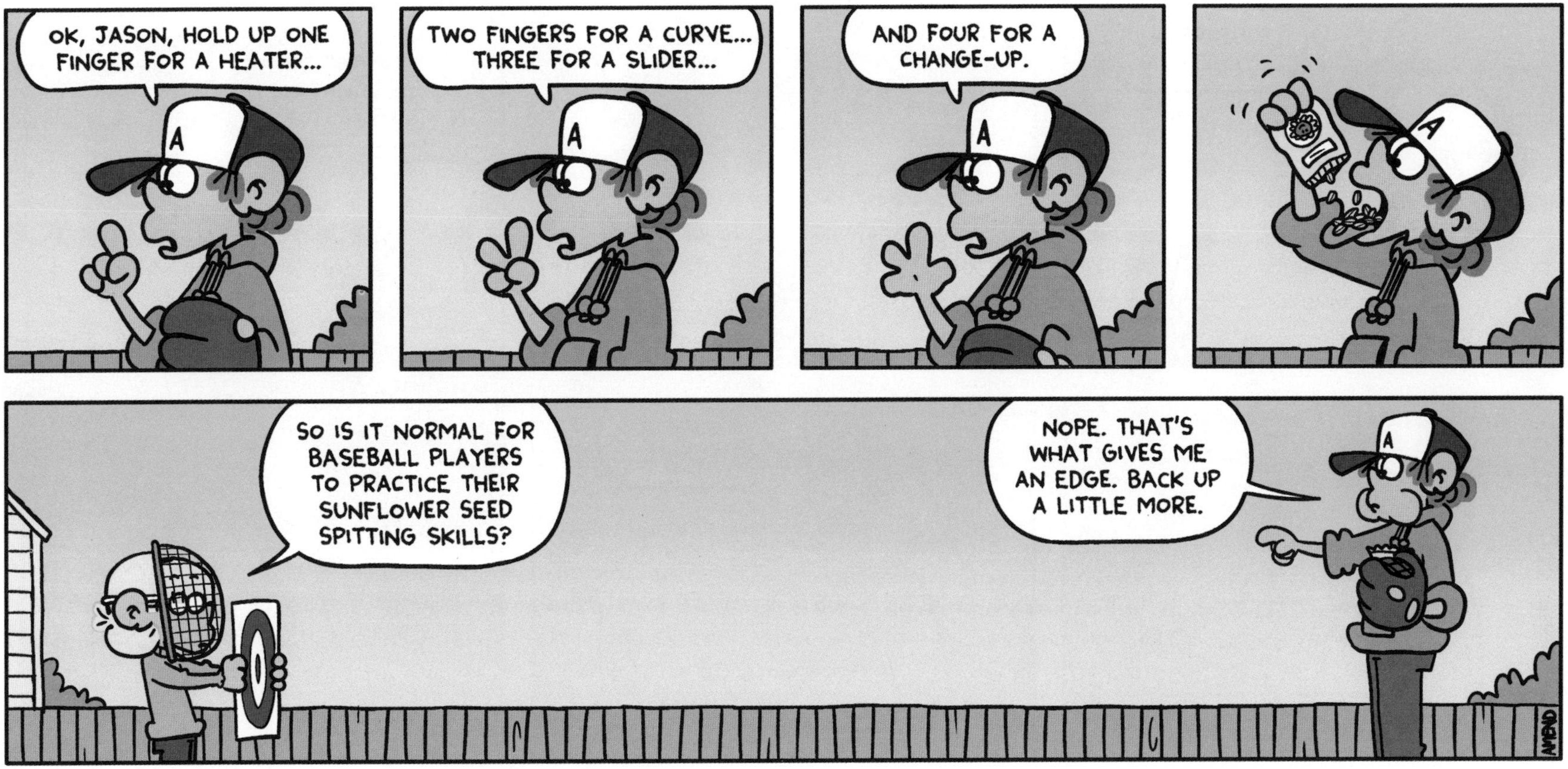

OK, JASON, HOLD UP ONE FINGER FOR A HEATER...
TWO FINGERS FOR A CURVE... THREE FOR A SLIDER...
AND FOUR FOR A CHANGE-UP.
SO IS IT NORMAL FOR BASEBALL PLAYERS TO PRACTICE THEIR SUNFLOWER SEED SPITTING SKILLS?
NOPE. THAT'S WHAT GIVES ME AN EDGE. BACK UP A LITTLE MORE.
AMEND

Island Girl

SUNSCREEN... CHECK.

SUNGLASSES... CHECK.

"ANIMAL CROSSING" AS SPRING BREAK DESTINATION. INTERESTING.

AAA! IT'S RAINING! NOOOO!

BEACH TOWEL... CHECK.

TROPICAL ISLAND...

AMEND

The Easter Chicken

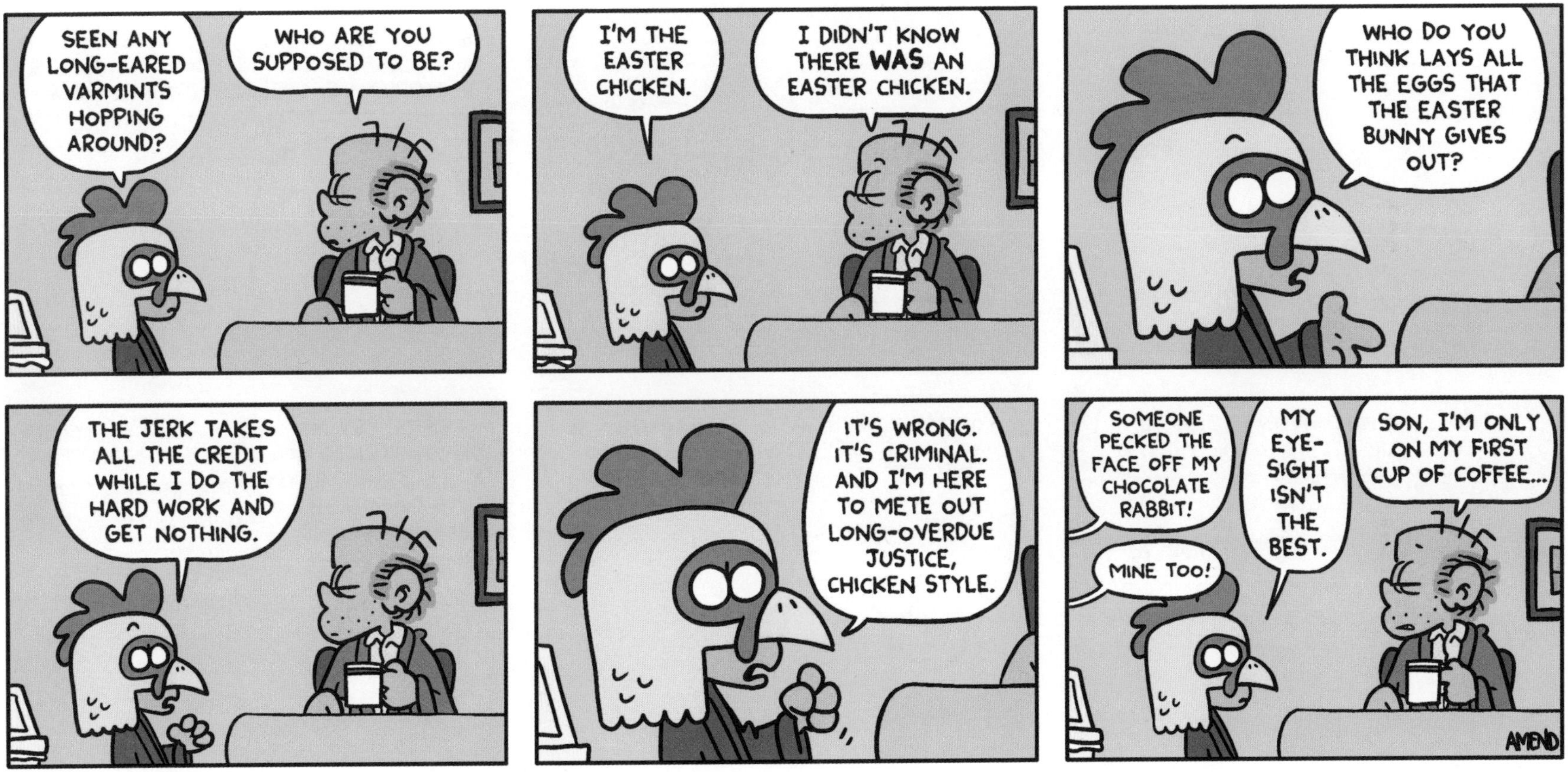
SEEN ANY LONG-EARED VARMINTS HOPPING AROUND?
WHO ARE YOU SUPPOSED TO BE?
I'M THE EASTER CHICKEN.
I DIDN'T KNOW THERE **WAS** AN EASTER CHICKEN.
WHO DO YOU THINK LAYS ALL THE EGGS THAT THE EASTER BUNNY GIVES OUT?
THE JERK TAKES ALL THE CREDIT WHILE I DO THE HARD WORK AND GET NOTHING.
IT'S WRONG. IT'S CRIMINAL. AND I'M HERE TO METE OUT LONG-OVERDUE JUSTICE, CHICKEN STYLE.
SOMEONE PECKED THE FACE OFF MY CHOCOLATE RABBIT!
MINE TOO!
MY EYE-SIGHT ISN'T THE BEST.
SON, I'M ONLY ON MY FIRST CUP OF COFFEE...
AMEND

Jason-Minus

WANNA SUBSCRIBE TO JASON-MINUS?

JASON-MINUS?

IT'S MY NEW VIDEO STREAMING SERVICE.

FOR ONLY $5.99 A MONTH, YOU GET SPECIAL VIP ACCESS TO ALL THE HOME VIDEOS I'VE RECORDED AND UPLOADED TO THE CLOUD.

DUDE, I'M NOT PAYING $5.99 TO WATCH YOUR STUPID HOME VIDEOS.

YOU MISUNDERSTAND... STREAMING THE VIDEOS IS FREE. IT'S THE ABILITY TO **DELETE** THEM THAT COSTS $5.99.

HERE, LET ME DEMONSTRATE WITH A CLIP FROM "PETER SAYS GOODNIGHT TO HIS GIRLFRIEND"...

YOU HID A CAMERA IN THE CAR?!

Ben iFranklins

DANG, YOU'D THINK IT'D BE CHARGING BY NOW.
ARE WE 100 PERCENT CERTAIN YOUR BROTHER'S PHONE IS WATERPROOF?
AMEND

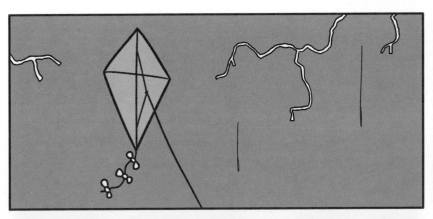

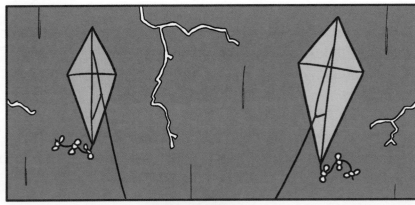

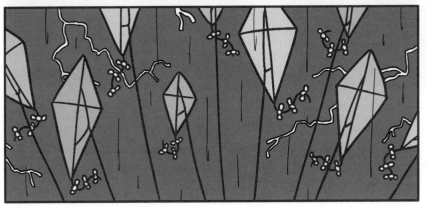

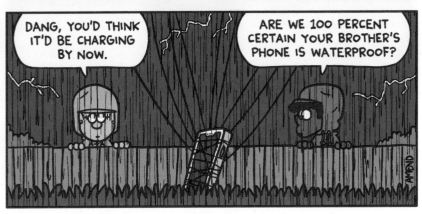

Acid Redux

WAIT... IS THAT YOUR HOMEMADE WINE?

IT IS! GOOD MEMORY!

THAT STUFF WAS NASTY. I THOUGHT YOU TOSSED IT ALL.

I SAVED ONE BOTTLE AS AN EXPERIMENT.

Cartoonist Saves Planet

SINCE WINE GETS BETTER WITH AGE, I FIGURED MAYBE AFTER A FEW YEARS IT MIGHT BE MORE DRINKABLE.

C'MON, WHADDYA SAY WE UNCORK IT AND GIVE CLOS DU ROGER ANOTHER TRY?

HOW ABOUT WE WAIT A FEW **MORE** YEARS, JUST TO BE SAFE?

I DON'T THINK WE CAN DO THAT.

WHY NOT?

IT'S STARTING TO EAT THROUGH THE GLASS.

Week Off

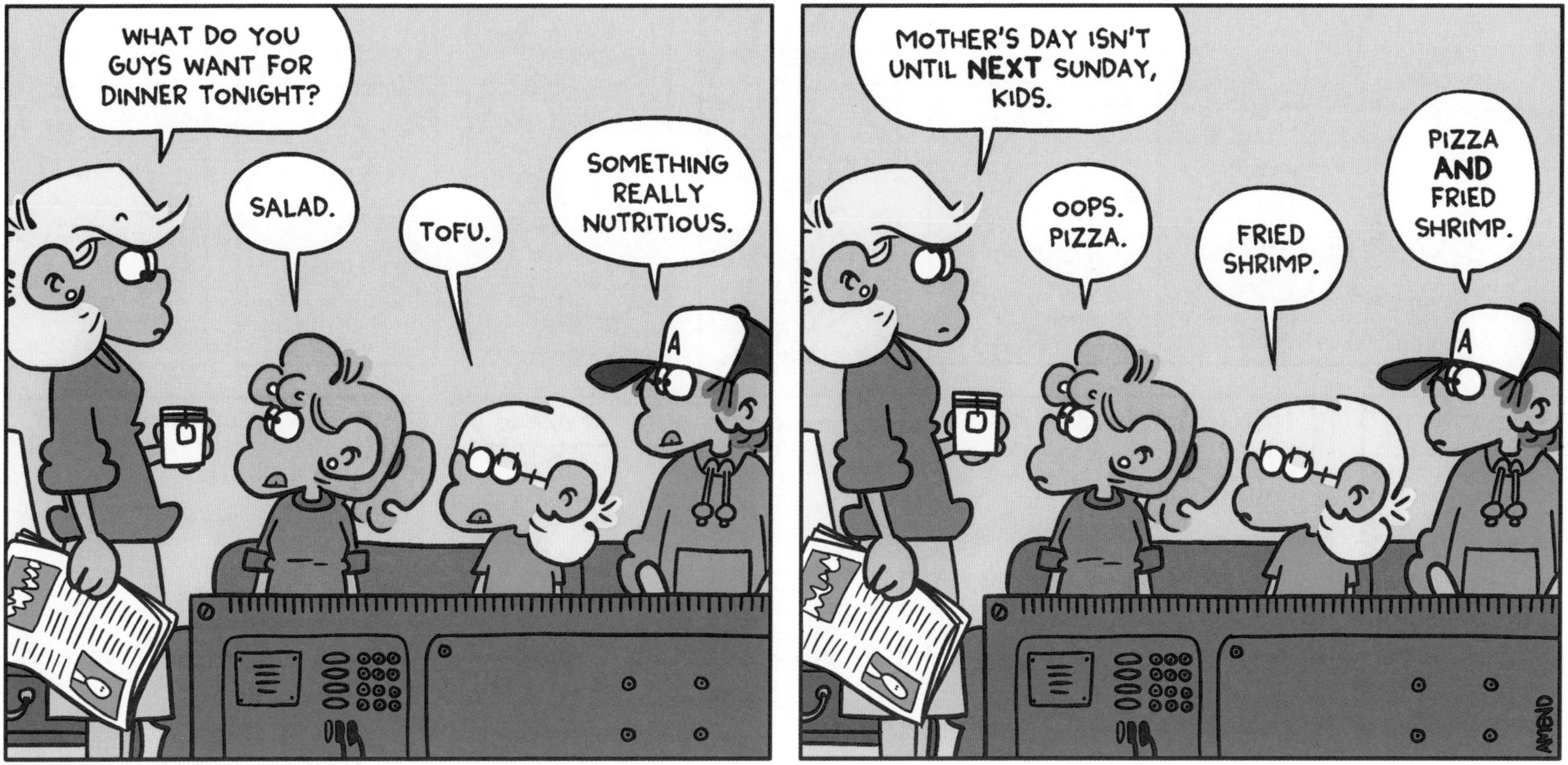
WHAT DO YOU GUYS WANT FOR DINNER TONIGHT?
SALAD.
TOFU.
SOMETHING REALLY NUTRITIOUS.
MOTHER'S DAY ISN'T UNTIL **NEXT** SUNDAY, KIDS.
OOPS. PIZZA.
FRIED SHRIMP.
PIZZA **AND** FRIED SHRIMP.
AMEND

Unpsychic

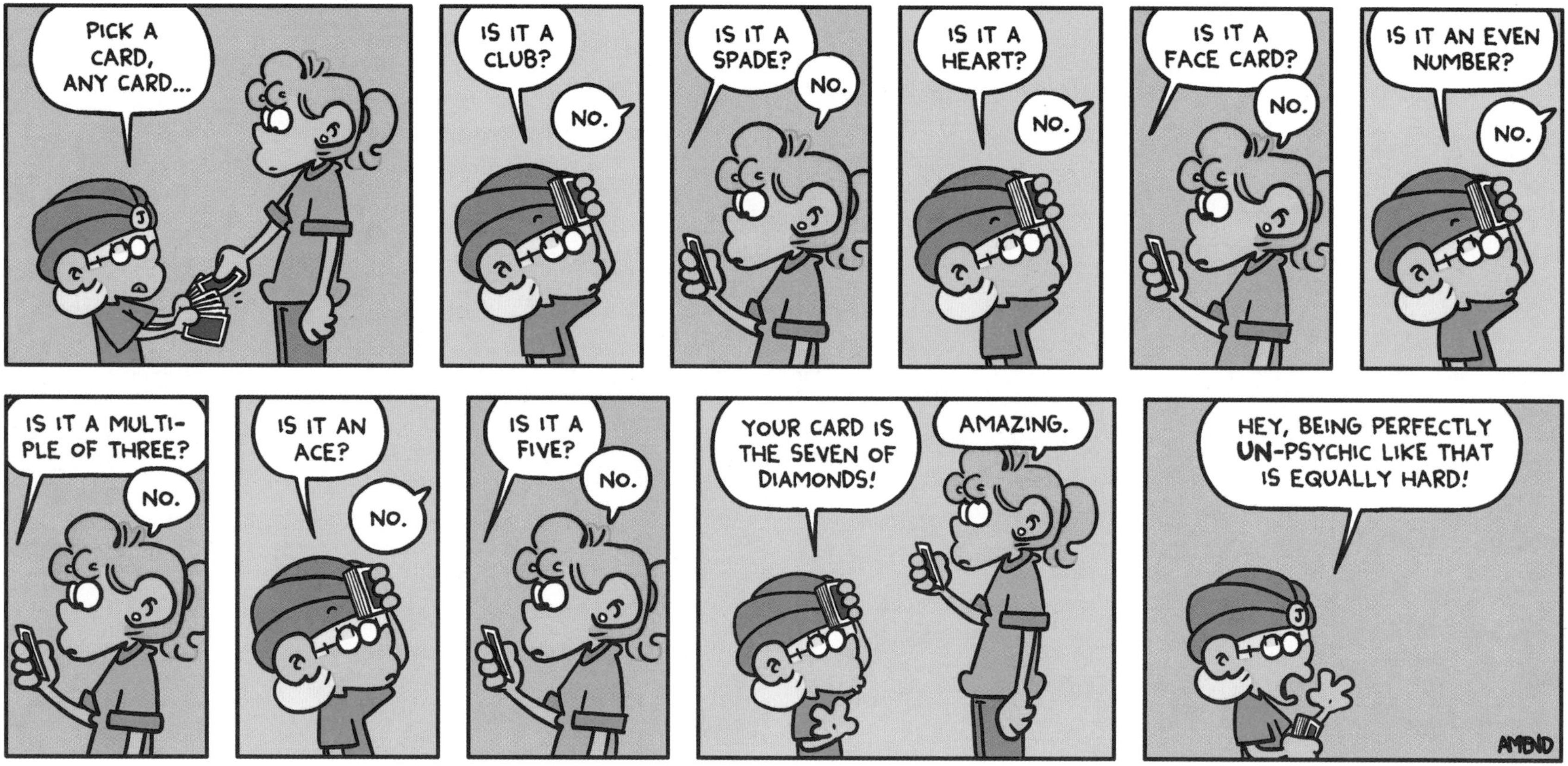
PICK A CARD, ANY CARD...
IS IT A CLUB?
NO.
IS IT A SPADE?
NO.
IS IT A HEART?
NO.
IS IT A FACE CARD?
NO.
IS IT AN EVEN NUMBER?
NO.
IS IT A MULTI-PLE OF THREE?
NO.
IS IT AN ACE?
NO.
IS IT A FIVE?
NO.
YOUR CARD IS THE SEVEN OF DIAMONDS!
AMAZING.
HEY, BEING PERFECTLY UN-PSYCHIC LIKE THAT IS EQUALLY HARD!
AMEND

enohP pilF

SO I'M THINKING ABOUT TRIMMING MY BANGS.

SHOULD I DO IT?

OOPS. ONE SEC.

SORRY ABOUT THAT.

SO I'M THINKING ABOUT TRIMMING MY BANGS...

I ALWAYS FORGET THAT THE CAMERA IN THIS APP FLIPS EVERYTHING.

I JUST TALK LIKE THIS.

AMEND

Finals Drama

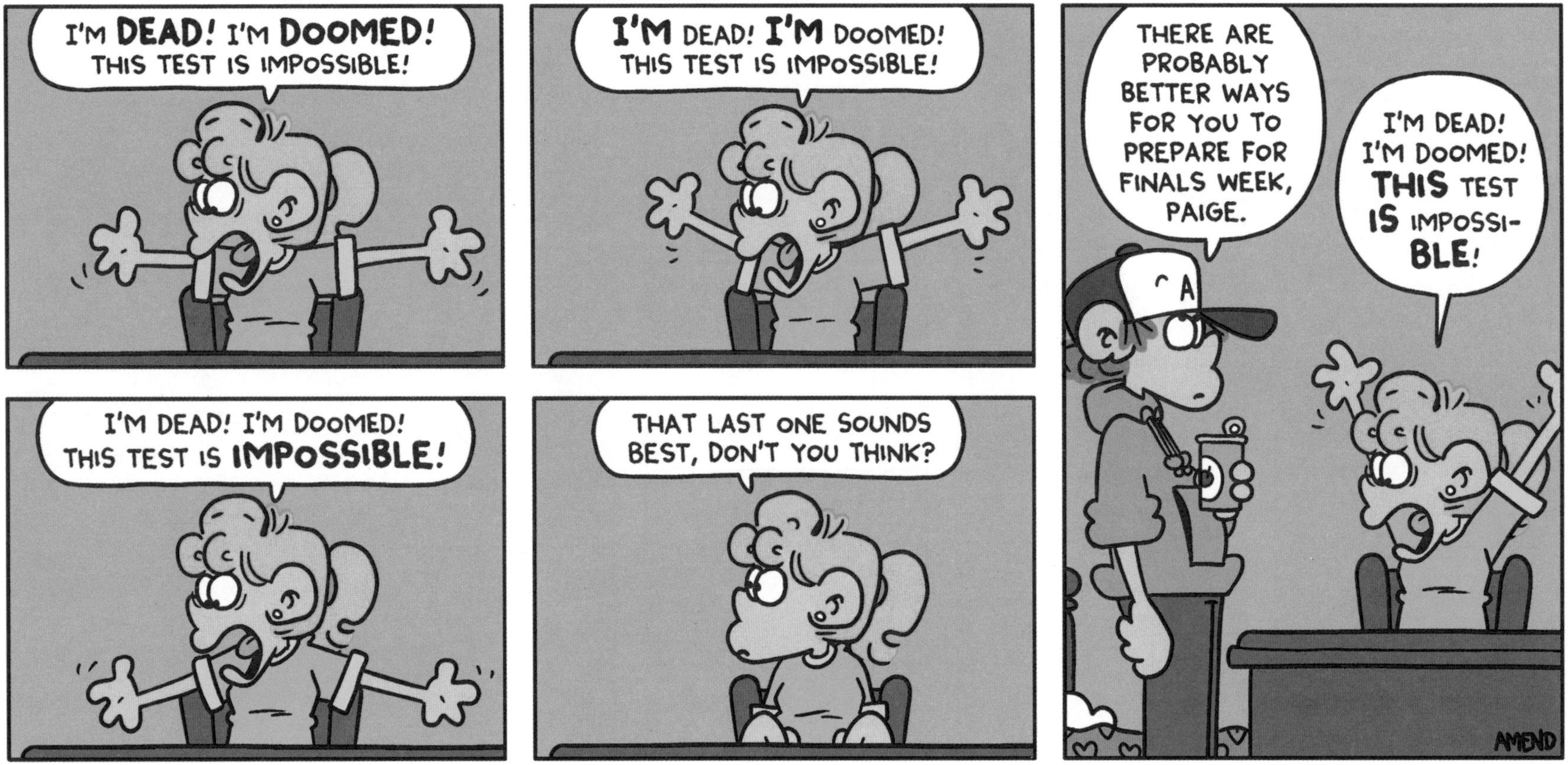
I'M DEAD! I'M DOOMED! THIS TEST IS IMPOSSIBLE!
I'M DEAD! I'M DOOMED! THIS TEST IS IMPOSSIBLE!
I'M DEAD! I'M DOOMED! THIS TEST IS IMPOSSIBLE!
THAT LAST ONE SOUNDS BEST, DON'T YOU THINK?
THERE ARE PROBABLY BETTER WAYS FOR YOU TO PREPARE FOR FINALS WEEK, PAIGE.
I'M DEAD! I'M DOOMED! THIS TEST IS IMPOSSI-BLE!
A
AMEND

Continental Breakfast

Caution Is Warranted

WHAT ARE YOU DOING?

UPLOADING VIDEOS FROM THE D&D CAMPAIGN I JUST FINISHED HOSTING.

"THE PARTY DEBATES ENTERING JASON'S DUNGEON (PART 1)."

"THE PARTY DEBATES ENTERING JASON'S DUNGEON (PART 2)."

"THE PARTY DEBATES ENTERING JASON'S DUNGEON (PART 3)."

"(PART 4)"... "(PART 5)"... "(PART 6)"...

MY FRIENDS ARE VERY CAUTIOUS PLAYERS.

AND EACH VIDEO IS TWO HOURS LONG?!?

THE LAST VIDEO IS ONLY 15 SECONDS.

"THE PARTY ENTERS JASON'S DUNGEON AND DIES."

OBVIOUSLY, THEY WEREN'T CAUTIOUS **ENOUGH.**

AMEND

Superaccuweather

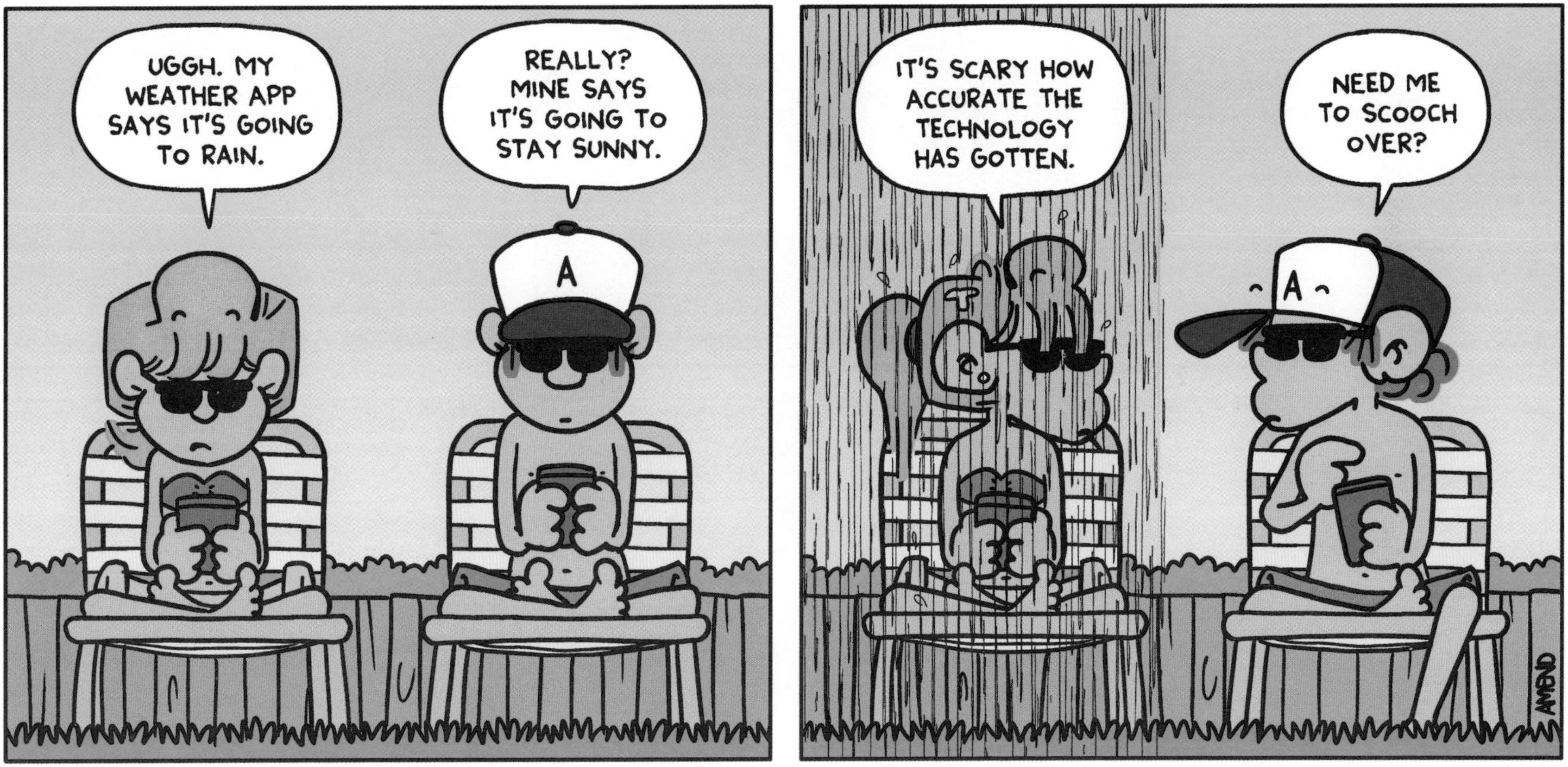

UGGH. MY WEATHER APP SAYS IT'S GOING TO RAIN.
REALLY? MINE SAYS IT'S GOING TO STAY SUNNY.
IT'S SCARY HOW ACCURATE THE TECHNOLOGY HAS GOTTEN.
NEED ME TO SCOOCH OVER?
AMEND

Can't Win

WOOHOO! CHECKMATE! I WIN!

WAIT A MINUTE... THAT WAS ALMOST **TOO** EASY.

YOU DIDN'T INTENTIONALLY LOSE JUST BECAUSE IT'S FATHER'S DAY, DID YOU??

YOU DID! I CAN SEE IT IN YOUR EYES!

THAT DOES IT... WE'RE STARTING OVER! AND THIS TIME YOU HAVE TO REALLY TRY TO WIN! NO HOLDING BACK!

CHECKMATE ALREADY?! YOU CAN'T CHECKMATE ME THAT QUICKLY ON FATHER'S DAY!

AMEND

Super Priorities

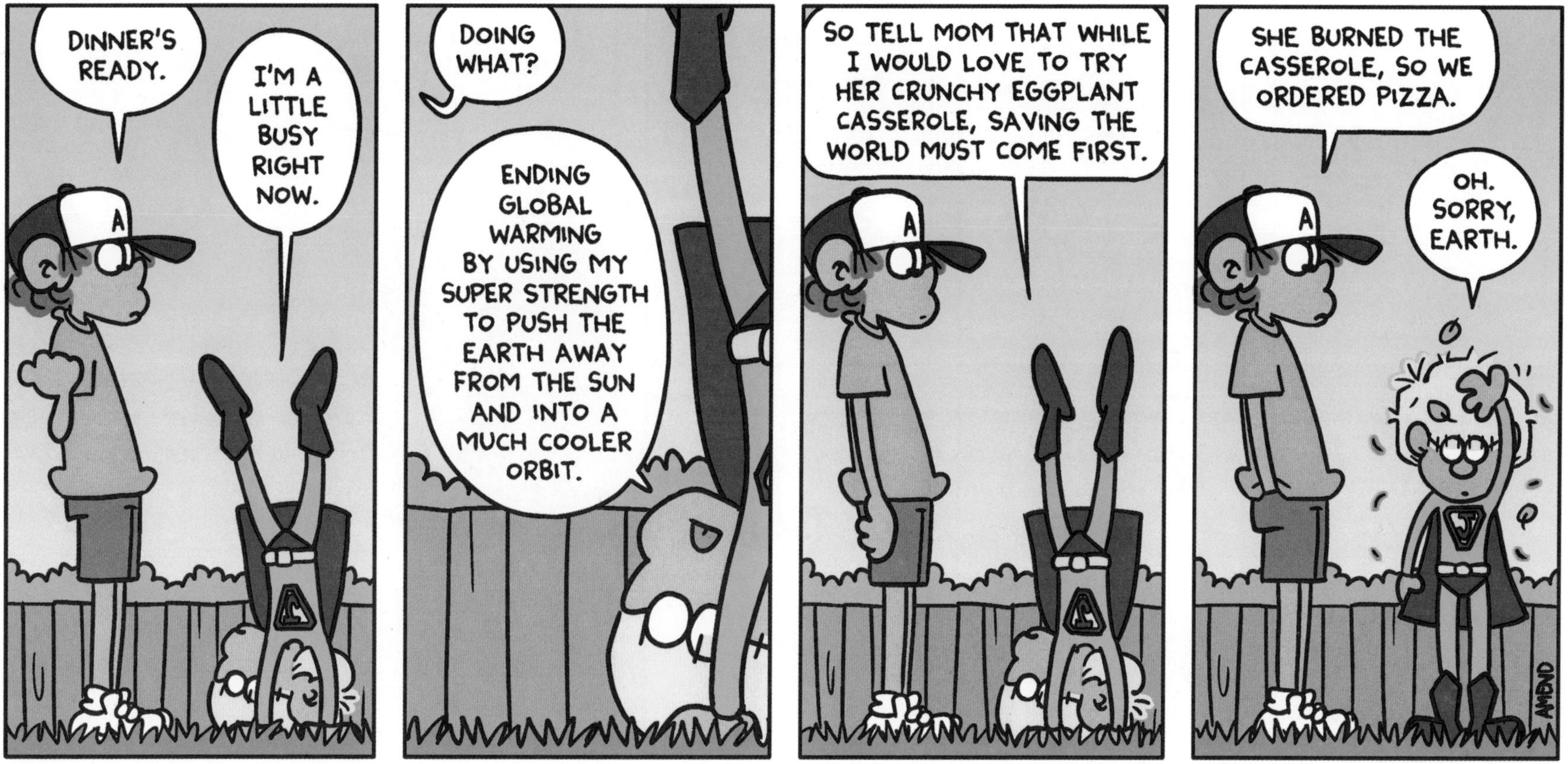
DINNER'S READY.
I'M A LITTLE BUSY RIGHT NOW.
DOING WHAT?
ENDING GLOBAL WARMING BY USING MY SUPER STRENGTH TO PUSH THE EARTH AWAY FROM THE SUN AND INTO A MUCH COOLER ORBIT.
SO TELL MOM THAT WHILE I WOULD LOVE TO TRY HER CRUNCHY EGGPLANT CASSEROLE, SAVING THE WORLD MUST COME FIRST.
SHE BURNED THE CASSEROLE, SO WE ORDERED PIZZA.
OH. SORRY, EARTH.
AMEND

Pun Dunce

American holidays that didn't make the cut...

Inde-pen-dance Day

Inde-pan-dents Day
Who dinged-up my cookware?!

Inde-pin-taunts Day
You've got a hole in your head... You've got a hole in your head... Stop needling me!

Inde-bent-tents Day
That was some gust of wind!

Inde-pint-tints Day
My 16-ounce beverage is bluish. My 16-ounce beverage is reddish.

HOW ABOUT INDE-PUN-DUNCE DAY?

I DON'T GET IT.

Tall Order

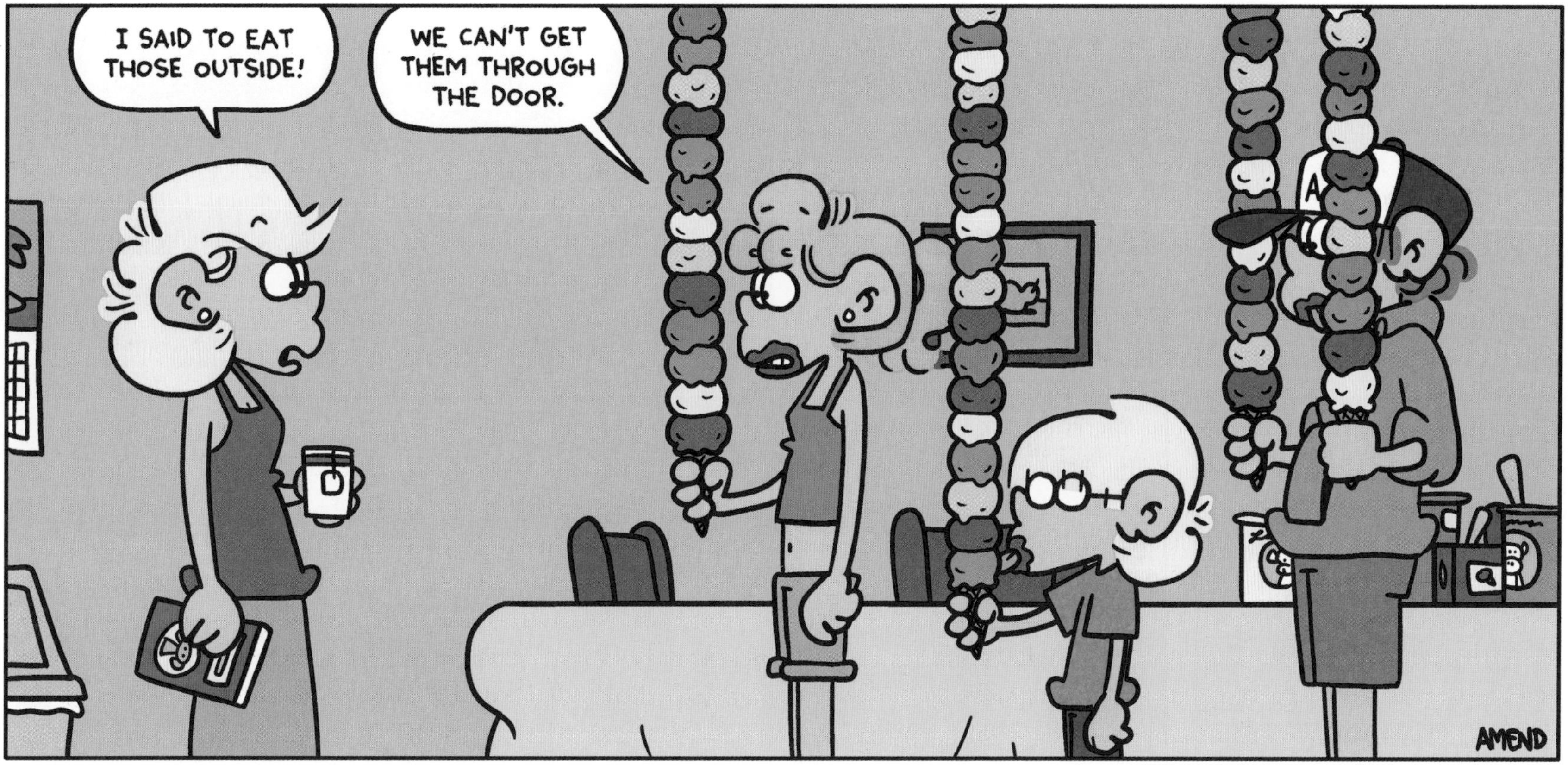
I SAID TO EAT THOSE OUTSIDE!
WE CAN'T GET THEM THROUGH THE DOOR.
AMEND

Hot/Cold Girl Summer

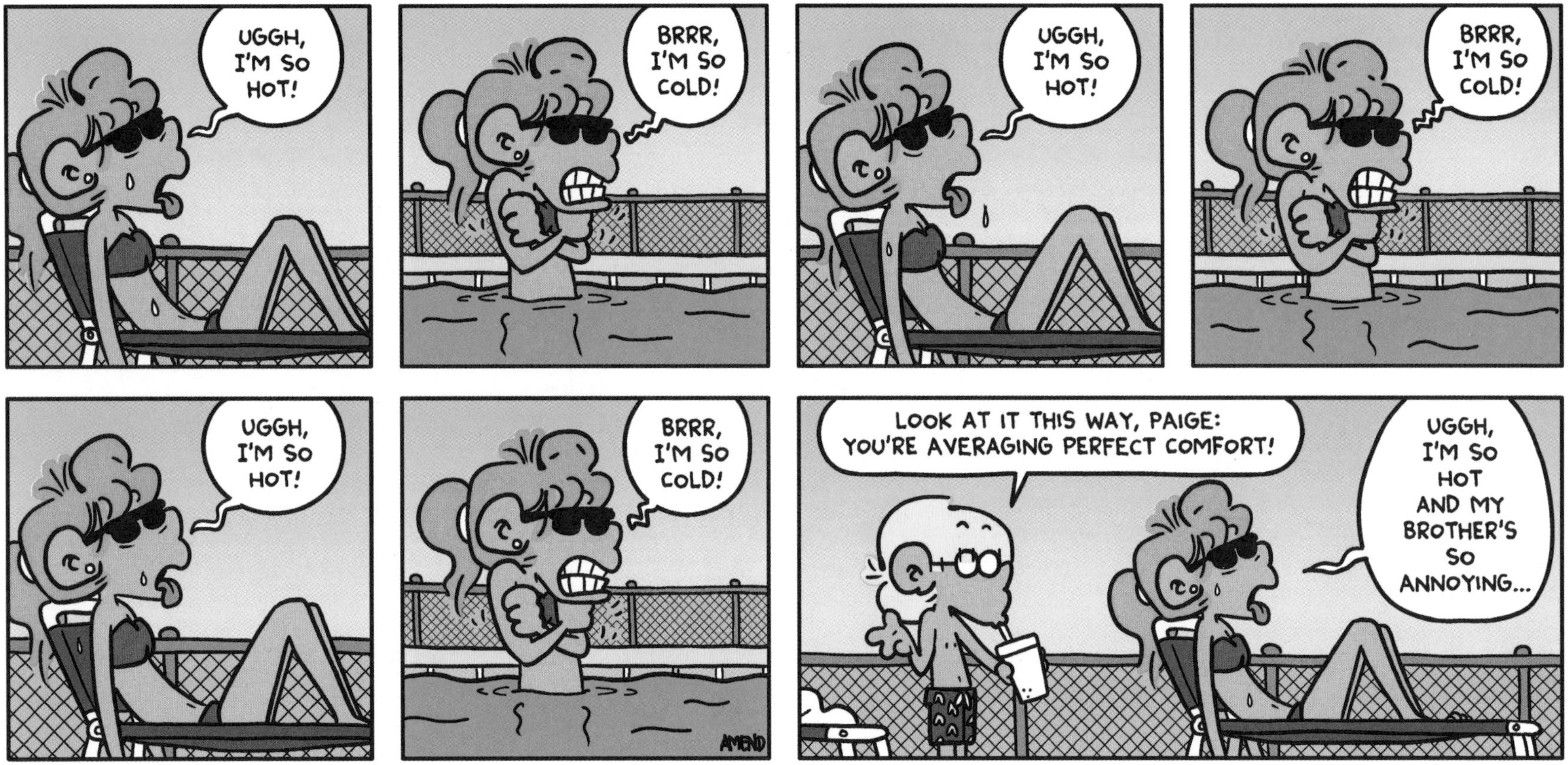
UGGH, I'M SO HOT!
BRRR, I'M SO COLD!
UGGH, I'M SO HOT!
BRRR, I'M SO COLD!
UGGH, I'M SO HOT!
BRRR, I'M SO COLD!
AMEND
LOOK AT IT THIS WAY, PAIGE: YOU'RE AVERAGING PERFECT COMFORT!
UGGH, I'M SO HOT AND MY BROTHER'S SO ANNOYING...

High-Carbon Diet

CRUNCH!

CRUNCH CRUNCH CRUNCH

MOM WAS RIGHT... I REALLY CAN'T TELL THAT THESE BURGERS ARE MEATLESS.

I'M NOT SURE THIS COUNTS AS A FAIR TEST.

WHO'S READY FOR SECONDS?

Growth Opportunity

QUINCY HAS A FAVOR TO ASK.

OH?

HE WANTS YOU TO CONTINUE BEING STINGY ABOUT RUNNING THE AIR CONDITIONER.

HE SAYS OUR HOME IS **THIS CLOSE** TO MATCHING THE HEAT AND HUMIDITY OF THE LATE CRETACEOUS ERA.

HE'S HOPING THAT'LL ACTIVATE HIS LATENT DINOSAUR GENES AND HE CAN GROW INTO A 20-FOOT-TALL T. REX.

GRANTED, HE'D THEN PROBABLY TRY TO EAT US ALL...

SHE'S STILL NOT TURNING ON THE A/C.

HOW DID THAT **NOT** WORK?? SHE'S INSANE!

AMEND

Vacation Fun

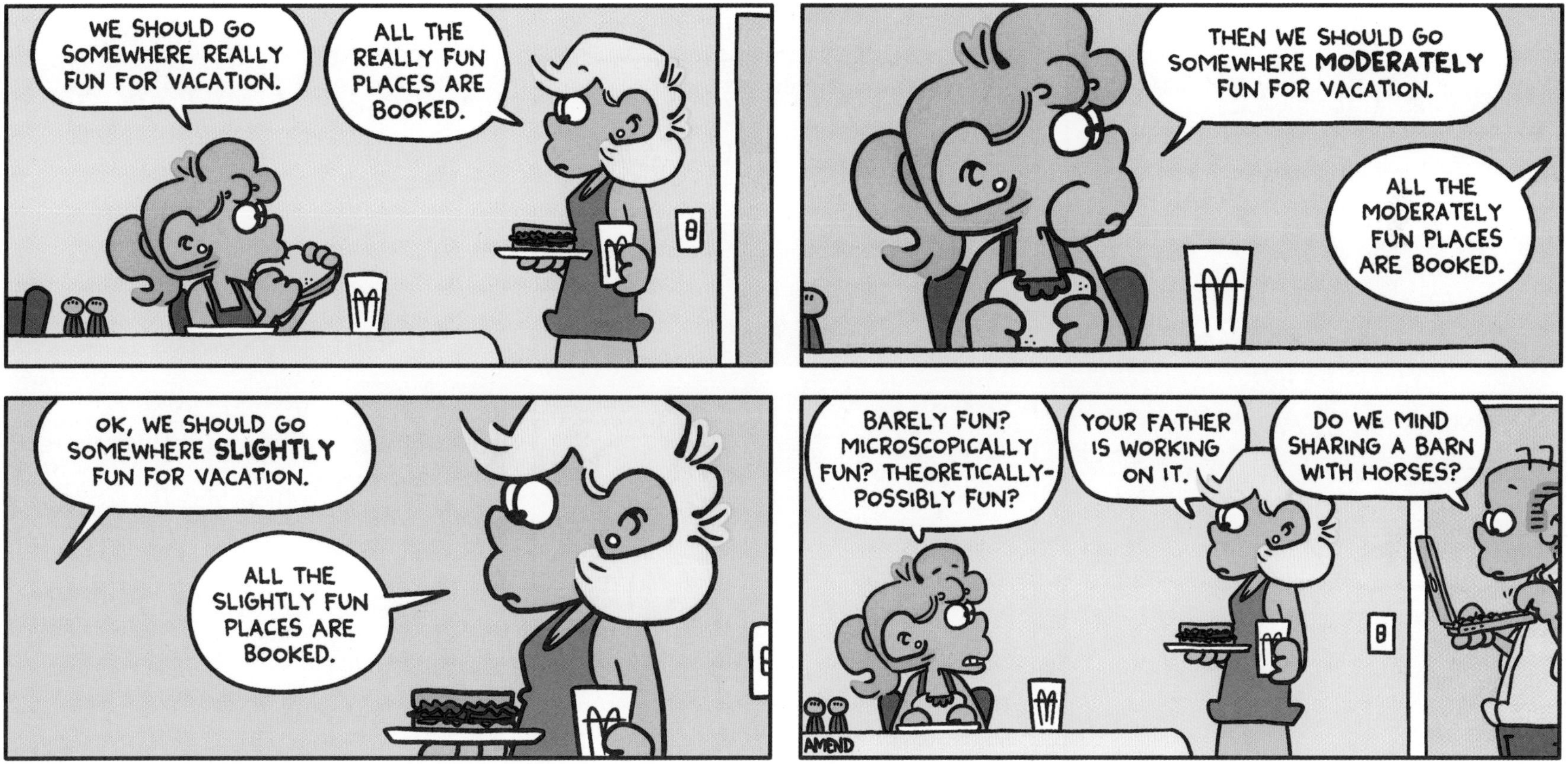
WE SHOULD GO SOMEWHERE REALLY FUN FOR VACATION.
ALL THE REALLY FUN PLACES ARE BOOKED.
THEN WE SHOULD GO SOMEWHERE MODERATELY FUN FOR VACATION.
ALL THE MODERATELY FUN PLACES ARE BOOKED.
OK, WE SHOULD GO SOMEWHERE SLIGHTLY FUN FOR VACATION.
ALL THE SLIGHTLY FUN PLACES ARE BOOKED.
BARELY FUN? MICROSCOPICALLY FUN? THEORETICALLY-POSSIBLY FUN?
YOUR FATHER IS WORKING ON IT.
DO WE MIND SHARING A BARN WITH HORSES?
AMEND

Summer Pests

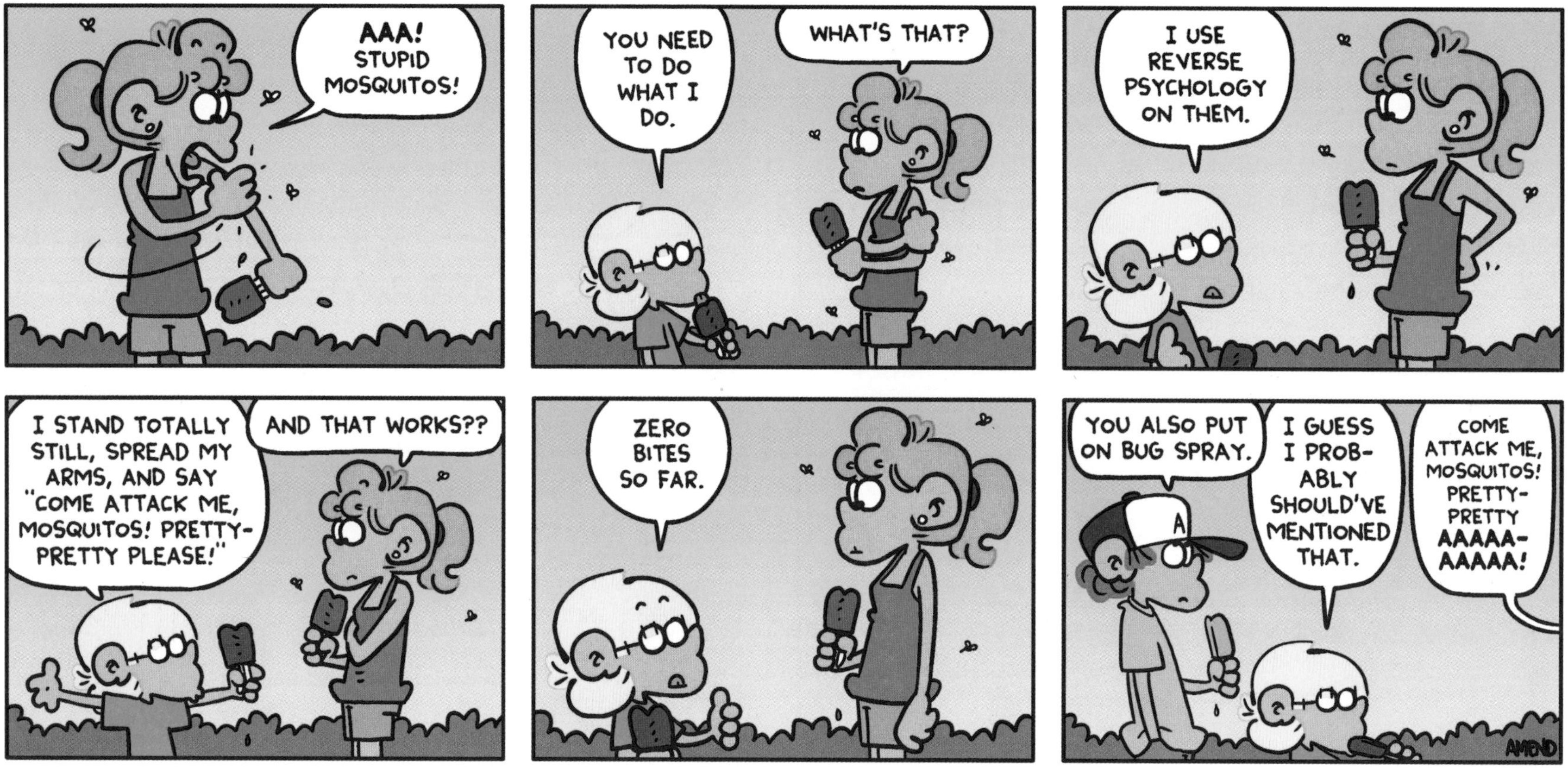
AAA! STUPID MOSQUITOS!
YOU NEED TO DO WHAT I DO.
WHAT'S THAT?
I USE REVERSE PSYCHOLOGY ON THEM.
I STAND TOTALLY STILL, SPREAD MY ARMS, AND SAY "COME ATTACK ME, MOSQUITOS! PRETTY-PRETTY PLEASE!"
AND THAT WORKS??
ZERO BITES SO FAR.
YOU ALSO PUT ON BUG SPRAY.
I GUESS I PROBABLY SHOULD'VE MENTIONED THAT.
COME ATTACK ME, MOSQUITOS! PRETTY-PRETTY AAAAA-AAAAA!
AMEND

Hard Mode

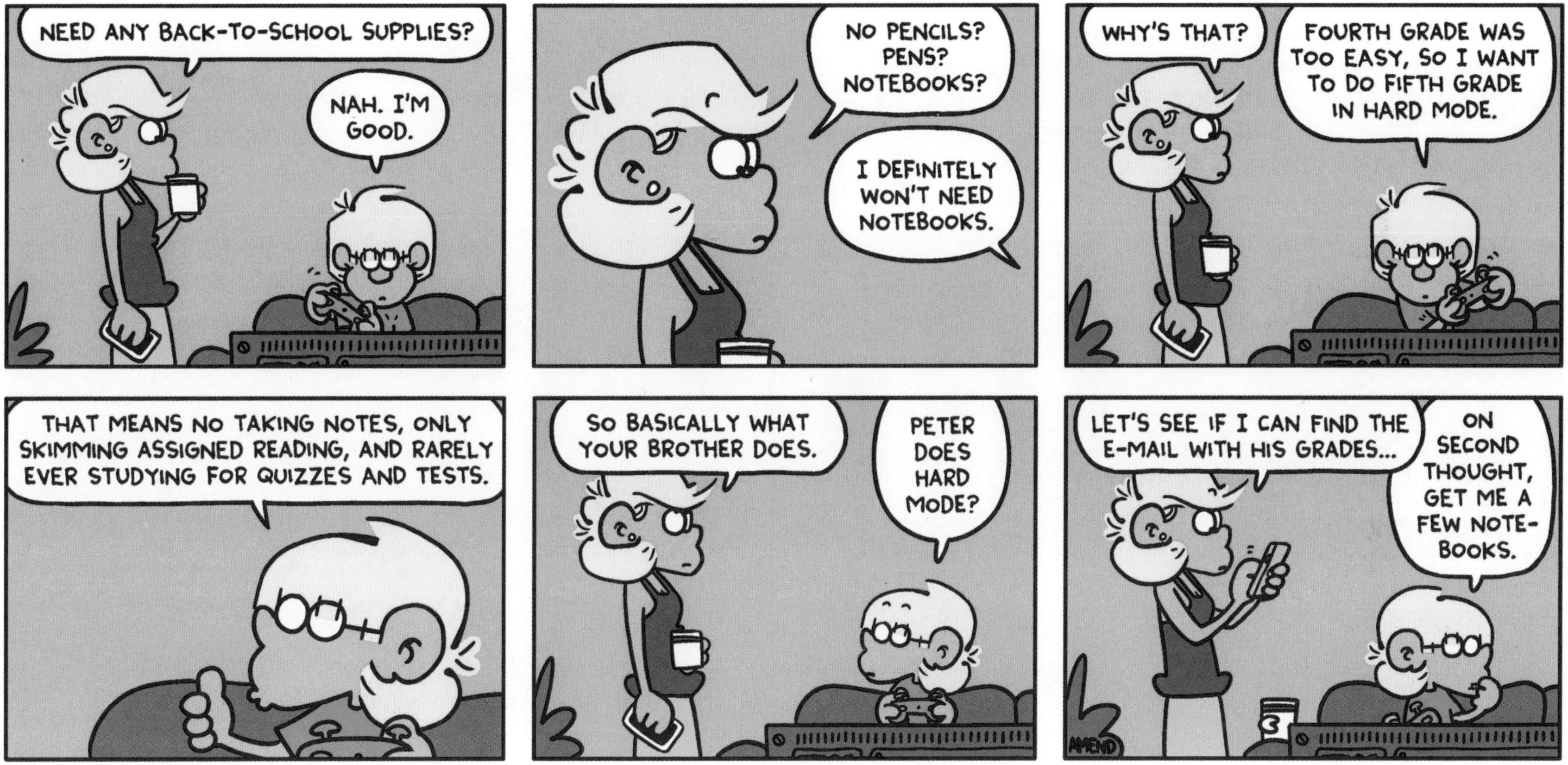

NEED ANY BACK-TO-SCHOOL SUPPLIES?
NAH. I'M GOOD.
NO PENCILS? PENS? NOTEBOOKS?
I DEFINITELY WON'T NEED NOTEBOOKS.
WHY'S THAT?
FOURTH GRADE WAS TOO EASY, SO I WANT TO DO FIFTH GRADE IN HARD MODE.
THAT MEANS NO TAKING NOTES, ONLY SKIMMING ASSIGNED READING, AND RARELY EVER STUDYING FOR QUIZZES AND TESTS.
SO BASICALLY WHAT YOUR BROTHER DOES.
PETER DOES HARD MODE?
LET'S SEE IF I CAN FIND THE E-MAIL WITH HIS GRADES...
ON SECOND THOUGHT, GET ME A FEW NOTE-BOOKS.
AMEND

Summertime Sadness

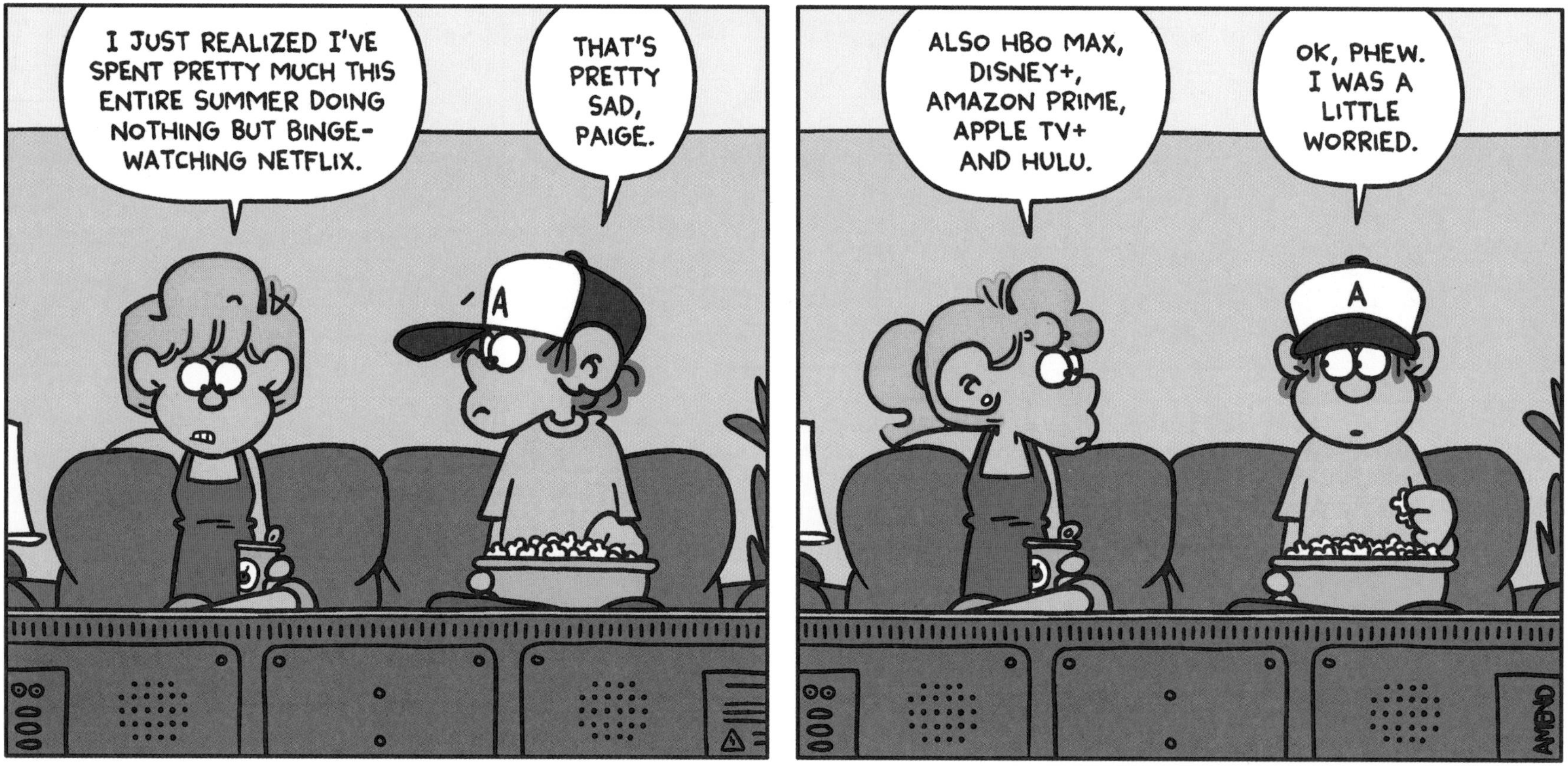
I JUST REALIZED I'VE SPENT PRETTY MUCH THIS ENTIRE SUMMER DOING NOTHING BUT BINGE-WATCHING NETFLIX.
THAT'S PRETTY SAD, PAIGE.
ALSO HBo MAX, DISNEY+, AMAZON PRIME, APPLE TV+ AND HULU.
OK, PHEW. I WAS A LITTLE WORRIED.
AMEND

Laboring Day

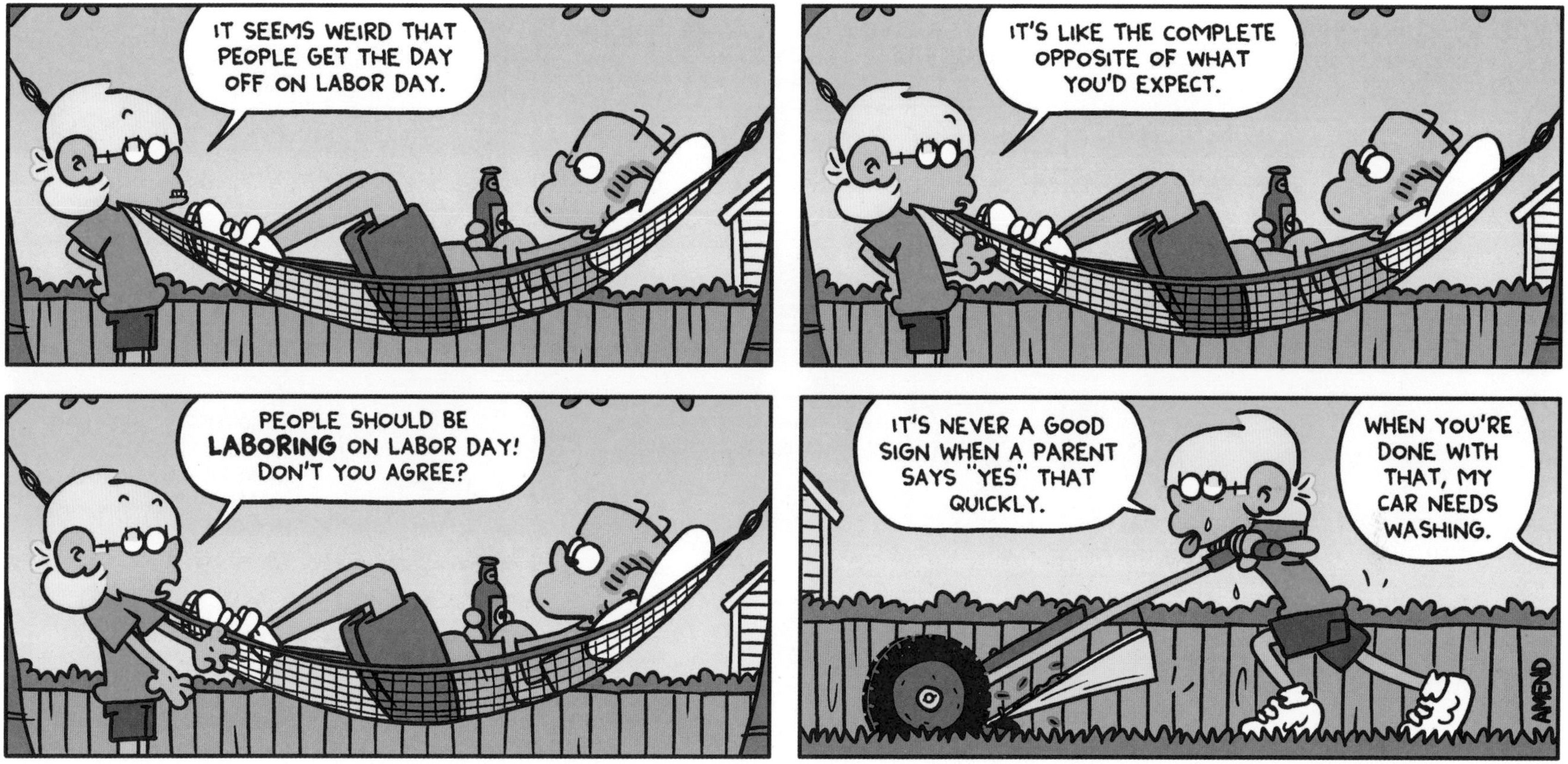
IT SEEMS WEIRD THAT PEOPLE GET THE DAY OFF ON LABOR DAY.
IT'S LIKE THE COMPLETE OPPOSITE OF WHAT YOU'D EXPECT.
PEOPLE SHOULD BE **LABORING** ON LABOR DAY! DON'T YOU AGREE?
IT'S NEVER A GOOD SIGN WHEN A PARENT SAYS "YES" THAT QUICKLY.
WHEN YOU'RE DONE WITH THAT, MY CAR NEEDS WASHING.
AMEND

High School Annoyances

HIGH SCHOOL IS A LOT HARDER THAN I THOUGHT.

HOW SO?

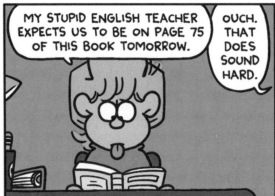

MY STUPID ENGLISH TEACHER EXPECTS US TO BE ON PAGE 75 OF THIS BOOK TOMORROW.

OUCH. THAT DOES SOUND HARD.

ANYTIME I START A BOOK, I LIKE TO READ THE WHOLE THING IN ONE SITTING.

HAVING TO STOP AT PAGE 75 WOULD BE PURE TORTURE.

OR IS THAT NOT WHAT YOU MEANT?

OUR MOTHER IS A LOT WEIRDER THAN I THOUGHT.

WELCOME TO HIGH SCHOOL.

AMEND

Finals Fantasy

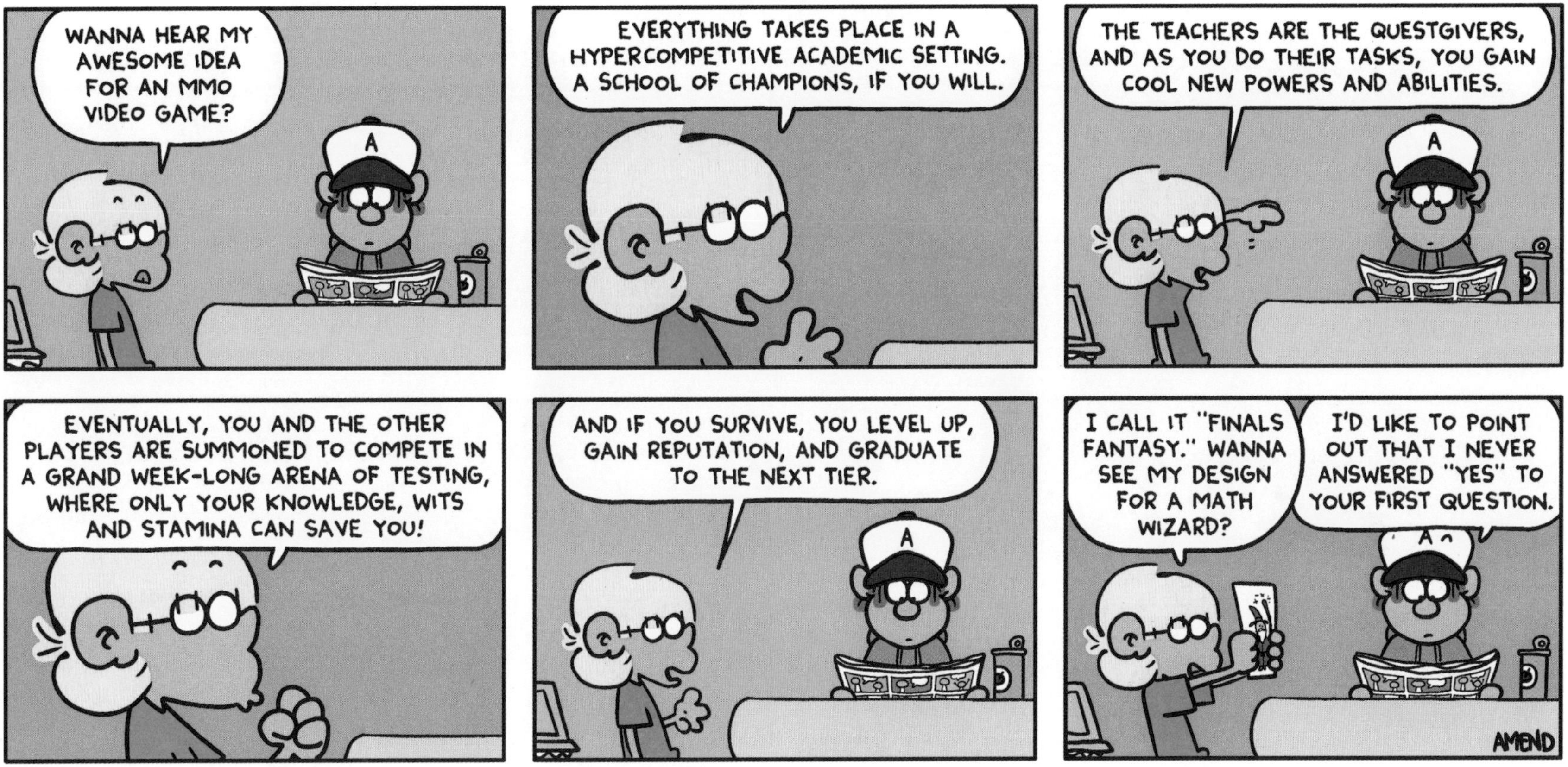
WANNA HEAR MY AWESOME IDEA FOR AN MMO VIDEO GAME?
EVERYTHING TAKES PLACE IN A HYPERCOMPETITIVE ACADEMIC SETTING. A SCHOOL OF CHAMPIONS, IF YOU WILL.
THE TEACHERS ARE THE QUESTGIVERS, AND AS YOU DO THEIR TASKS, YOU GAIN COOL NEW POWERS AND ABILITIES.
EVENTUALLY, YOU AND THE OTHER PLAYERS ARE SUMMONED TO COMPETE IN A GRAND WEEK-LONG ARENA OF TESTING, WHERE ONLY YOUR KNOWLEDGE, WITS AND STAMINA CAN SAVE YOU!
AND IF YOU SURVIVE, YOU LEVEL UP, GAIN REPUTATION, AND GRADUATE TO THE NEXT TIER.
I CALL IT "FINALS FANTASY." WANNA SEE MY DESIGN FOR A MATH WIZARD?
I'D LIKE TO POINT OUT THAT I NEVER ANSWERED "YES" TO YOUR FIRST QUESTION.
AMEND

Waterback

OK GUYS, HERE'S THE PLAY...

WETZEL, GO 10 YARDS AND CUT LEFT. O'BRIEN, GO 10 YARDS AND CUT RIGHT. BENNETT, DO A QUICK SLANT OVER THE MIDDLE.

GOT IT?

JUST GIVE US THE WATER BOTTLES, FOX!

C'MON, THIS'LL BE MORE FUN!

JUST GIVE THEM THE WATER BOTTLES, FOX!

Pizza Practice

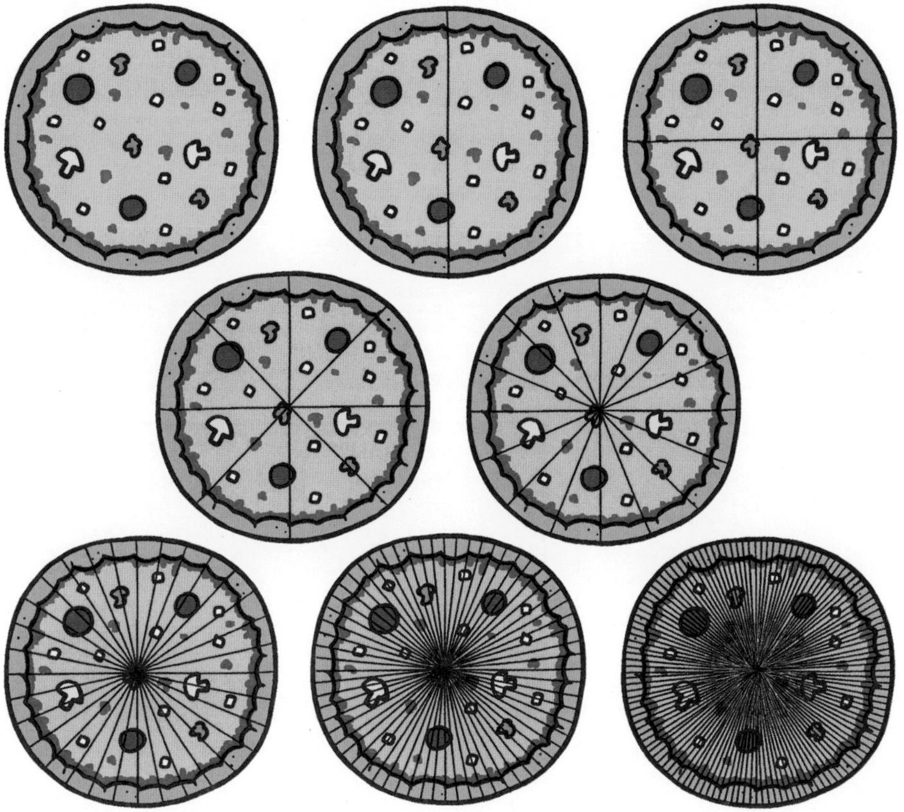

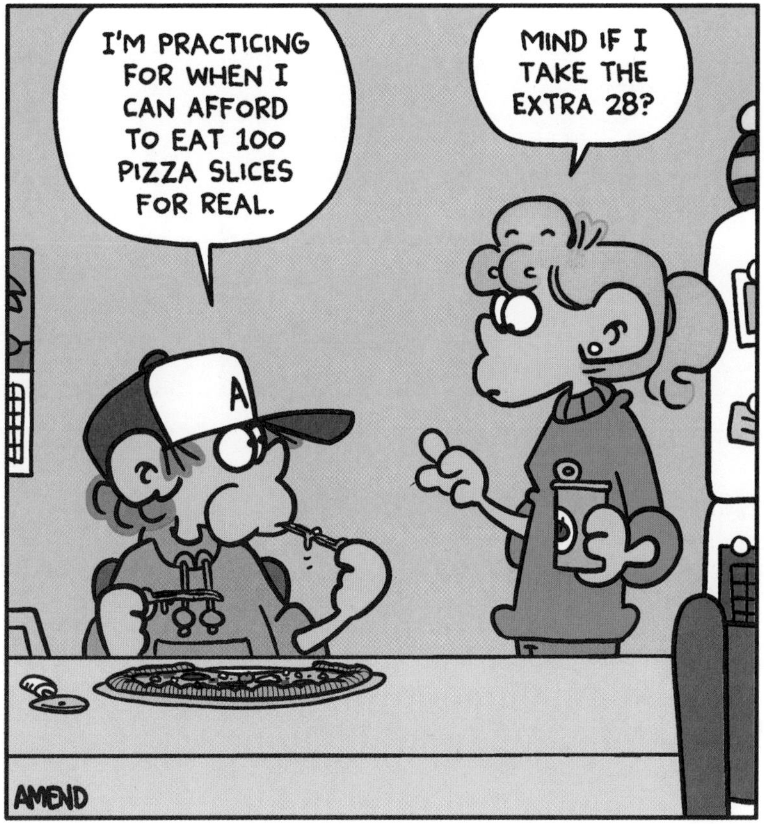
I'M PRACTICING FOR WHEN I CAN AFFORD TO EAT 100 PIZZA SLICES FOR REAL.
MIND IF I TAKE THE EXTRA 28?
A
AMEND

Personality Test

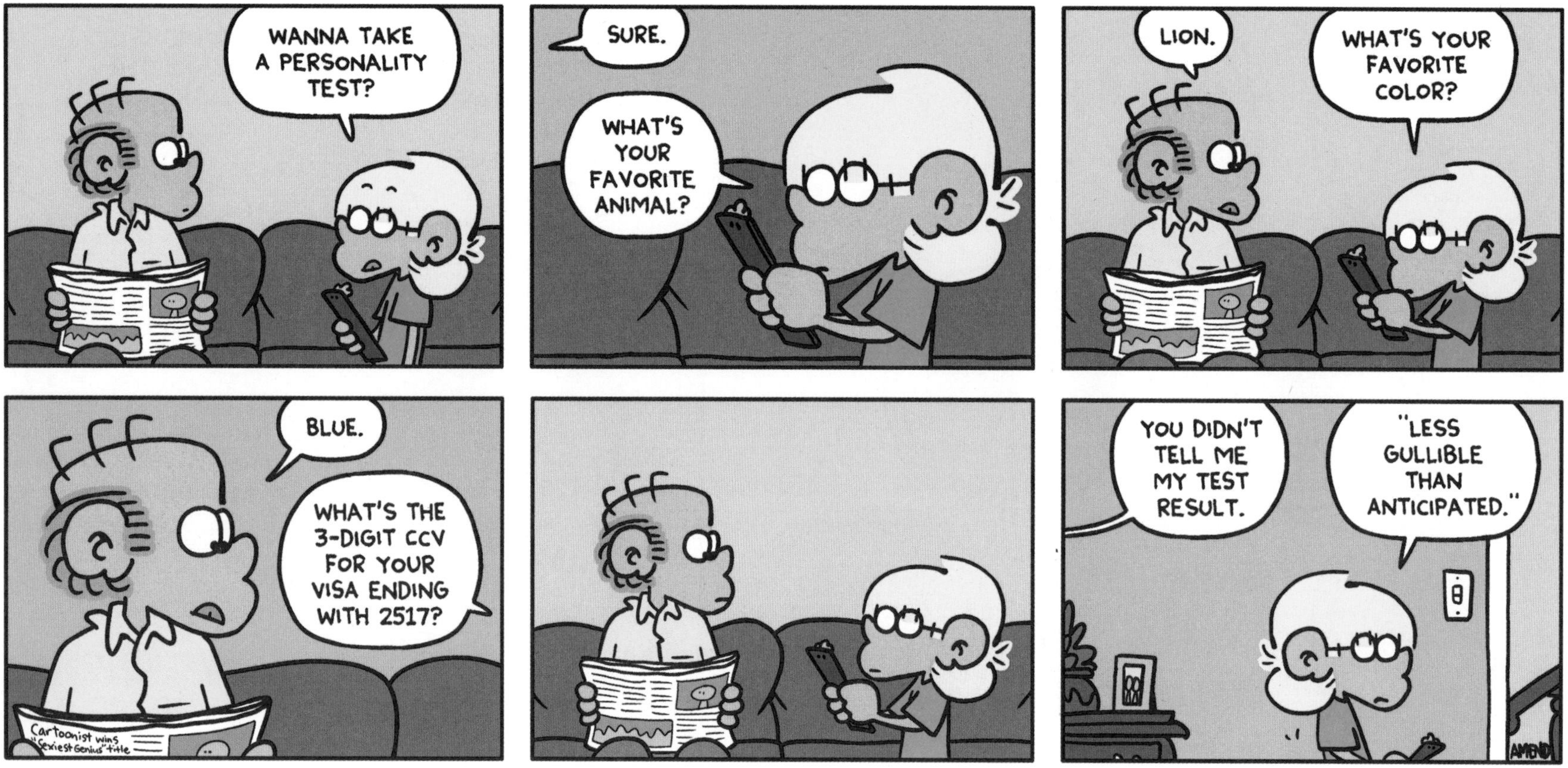
WANNA TAKE A PERSONALITY TEST?
SURE.
WHAT'S YOUR FAVORITE ANIMAL?
LION.
WHAT'S YOUR FAVORITE COLOR?
BLUE.
WHAT'S THE 3-DIGIT CCV FOR YOUR VISA ENDING WITH 2517?
Cartoonist wins "Sexiest Genius" title
YOU DIDN'T TELL ME MY TEST RESULT.
"LESS GULLIBLE THAN ANTICIPATED."
AMEND

Sweater Weather

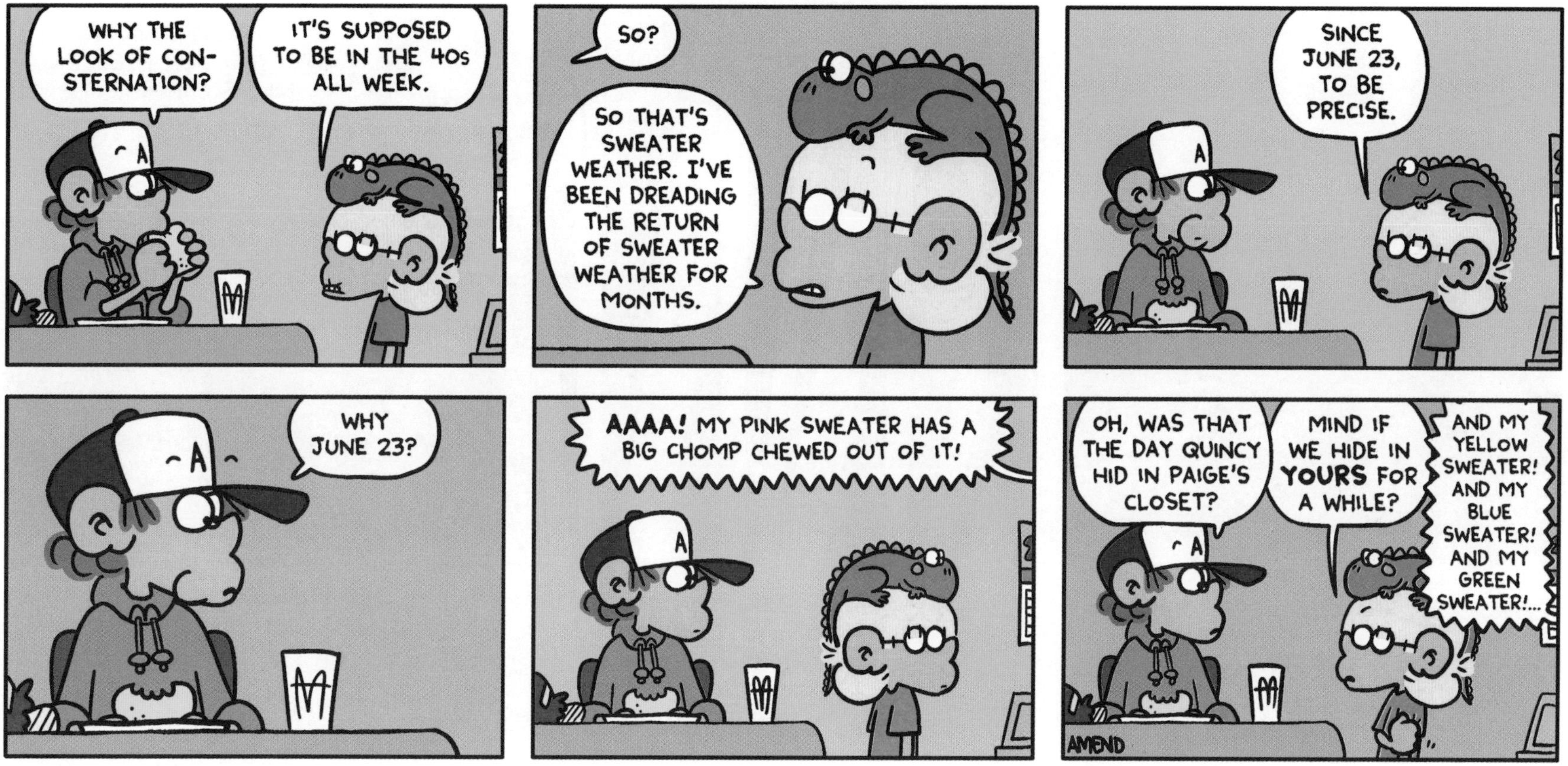
WHY THE LOOK OF CONSTERNATION?
IT'S SUPPOSED TO BE IN THE 40s ALL WEEK.
SO?
SO THAT'S SWEATER WEATHER. I'VE BEEN DREADING THE RETURN OF SWEATER WEATHER FOR MONTHS.
SINCE JUNE 23, TO BE PRECISE.
WHY JUNE 23?
AAAA! MY PINK SWEATER HAS A BIG CHOMP CHEWED OUT OF IT!
OH, WAS THAT THE DAY QUINCY HID IN PAIGE'S CLOSET?
MIND IF WE HIDE IN YOURS FOR A WHILE?
AND MY YELLOW SWEATER! AND MY BLUE SWEATER! AND MY GREEN SWEATER!...
AMEND

Jack O'Signal

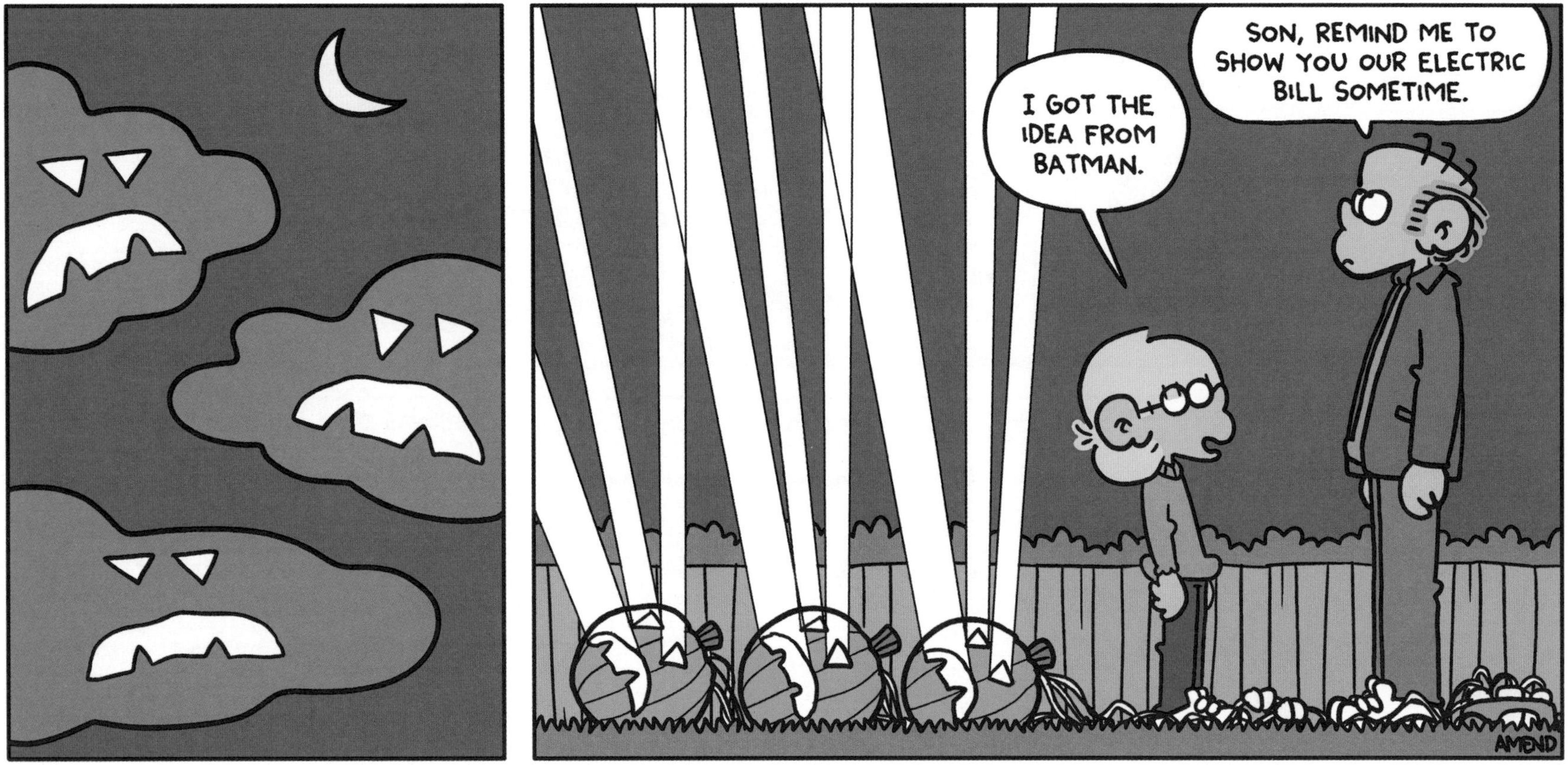
I GOT THE IDEA FROM BATMAN.
SON, REMIND ME TO SHOW YOU OUR ELECTRIC BILL SOMETIME.
AMEND

Wan-Obis

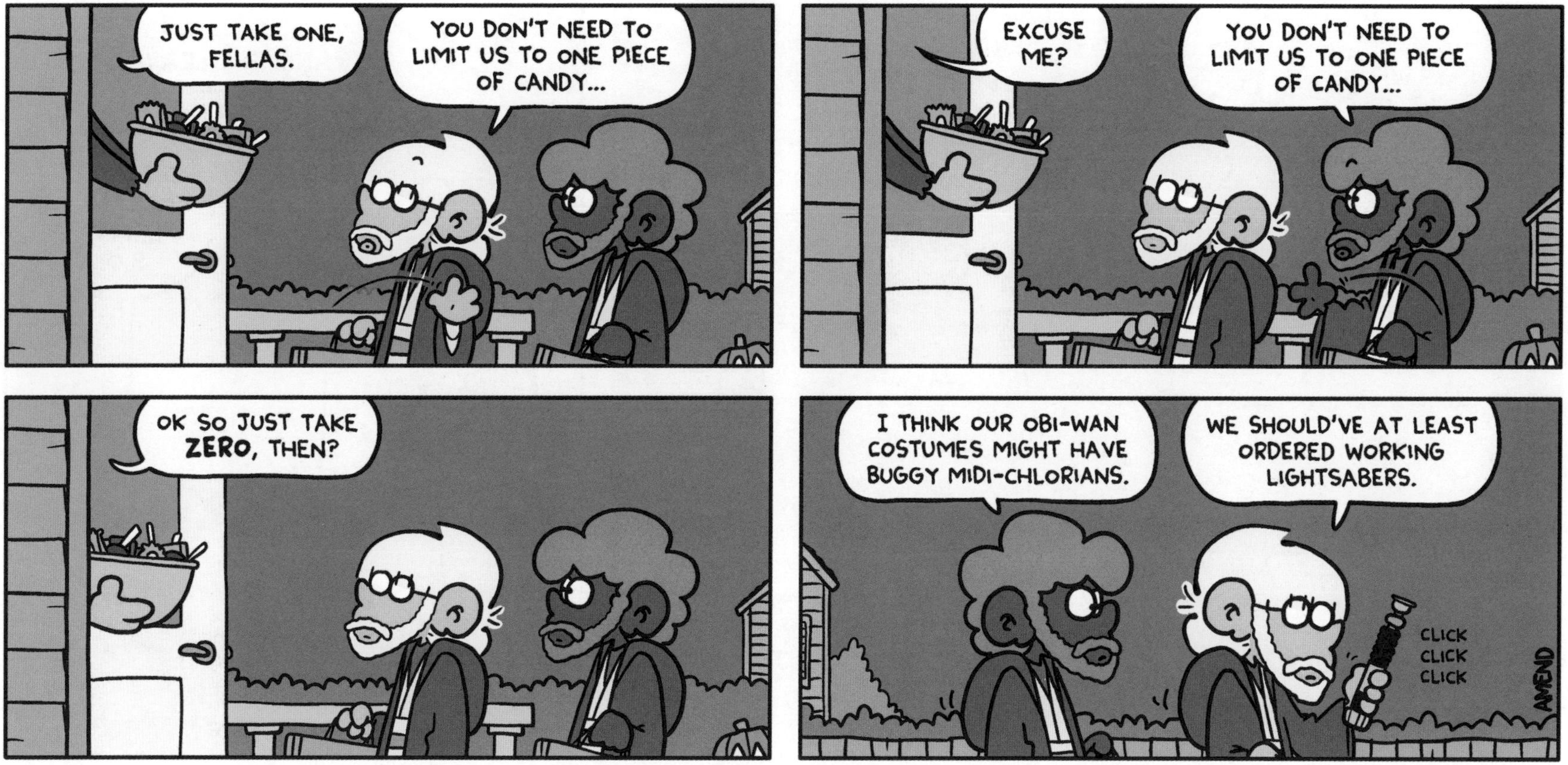

JUST TAKE ONE, FELLAS.
YOU DON'T NEED TO LIMIT US TO ONE PIECE OF CANDY...
EXCUSE ME?
YOU DON'T NEED TO LIMIT US TO ONE PIECE OF CANDY...
OK SO JUST TAKE **ZERO**, THEN?
I THINK OUR OBI-WAN COSTUMES MIGHT HAVE BUGGY MIDI-CHLORIANS.
WE SHOULD'VE AT LEAST ORDERED WORKING LIGHTSABERS.
CLICK CLICK CLICK
AMEND

Fall Ratings

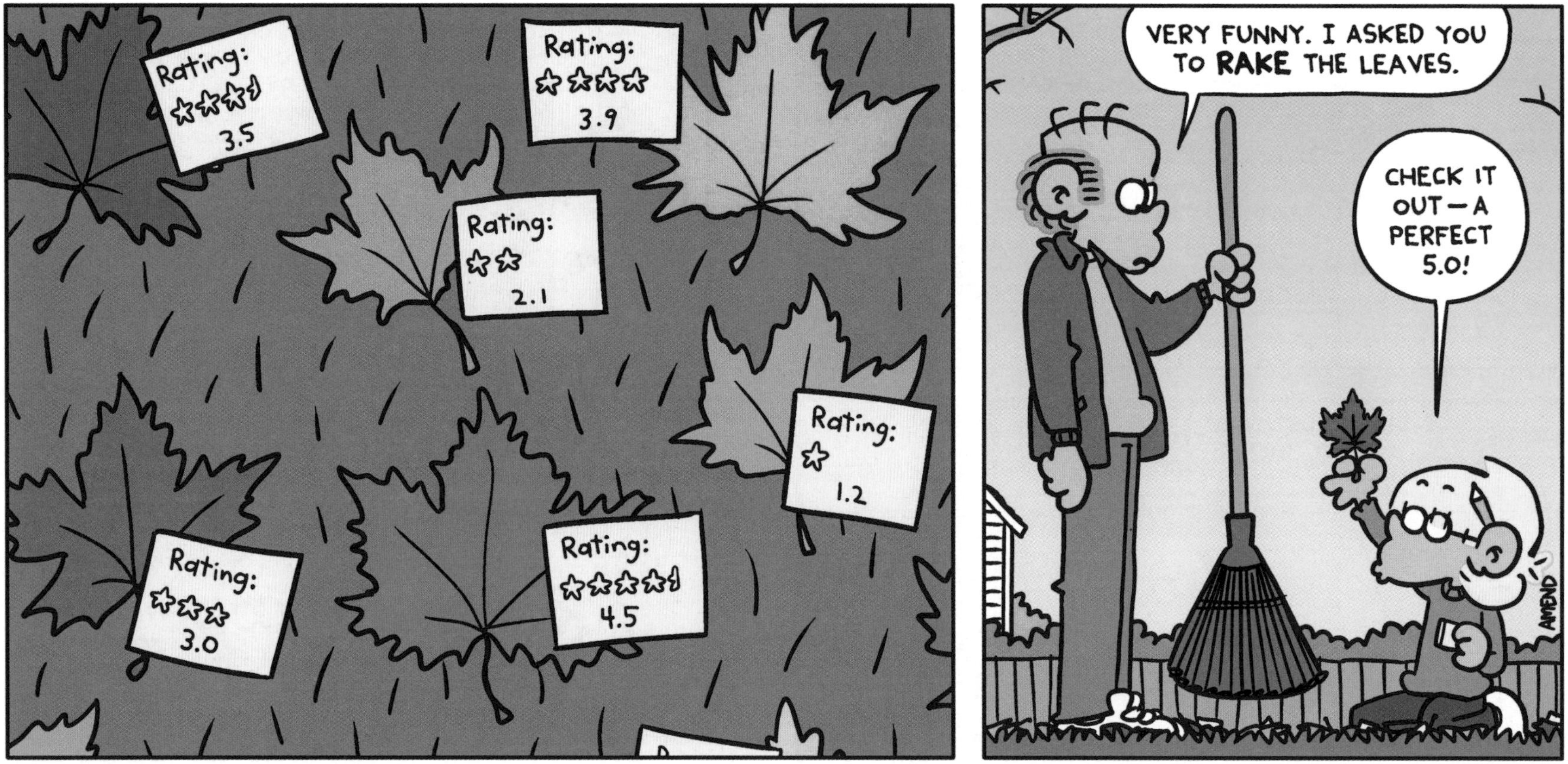
Rating: 3.5
Rating: 3.9
Rating: 2.1
Rating: 1.2
Rating: 3.0
Rating: 4.5
VERY FUNNY. I ASKED YOU TO **RAKE** THE LEAVES.
CHECK IT OUT—A PERFECT 5.0!
AMEND

Photographic Evidence

CLICK
CLICK
CLICK

I DON'T UNDERSTAND WHY YOU'RE ALWAYS TAKING PICTURES OF YOUR FOOD.

TRUST ME, PAIGE. NO ONE ON INSTA-GRAM CARES WHAT MOM MADE US FOR DINNER.

IT'S NOT FOR INSTAGRAM.

FINE, FACEBOOK.

IT'S NOT FOR FACEBOOK.

TWITTER... TIKTOK... SNAPCHAT... WHATEVER.

CHILD PROTECTIVE SERVICES.

AH, OK. THERE MIGHT BE INTEREST THERE.

WHO WANTS GRAVY FOR THEIR BEETLOAF?

AMEND

Holiday Ball

GRAW GRAW GRAW...

WHAT ON EARTH ARE YOU DOING??

BITING ON A RUBBER BALL TO STRENGTHEN MY JAW MUSCLES.

JASON HAD A BRILLIANT IDEA: THE MORE FORCEFULLY I CHEW MY FOOD, THE MORE CALORIES I'LL BURN, AND THUS THE MORE I CAN EAT WITHOUT GAINING WEIGHT!

WITH THE HOLIDAYS COMING UP, THIS COULD BE A REAL GAME-CHANGER!

FEEL FREE TO BAKE A FEW EXTRA PIES FOR THANKSGIVING.

GRAW GRAW GRAW...

ABOUT THESE STUPID IDEAS OF YOURS...

IT'S NOT MY FAULT DAD LISTENS TO ME!

Cartman

HOLIDAY DISH TOWELS...

A NEW CHEESE GRATER...

A DOZEN BALLPOINT PENS...

PROCEED TO CHECKOUT... AND...

YOUR TOTAL IS $542.57.

WILL YOU QUIT LEAVING VIDEO GAME CONSOLES IN OUR AMAZON CART?!

THERE'S AN EASY WAY TO GET ME TO STOP...

AMEND

NoPro

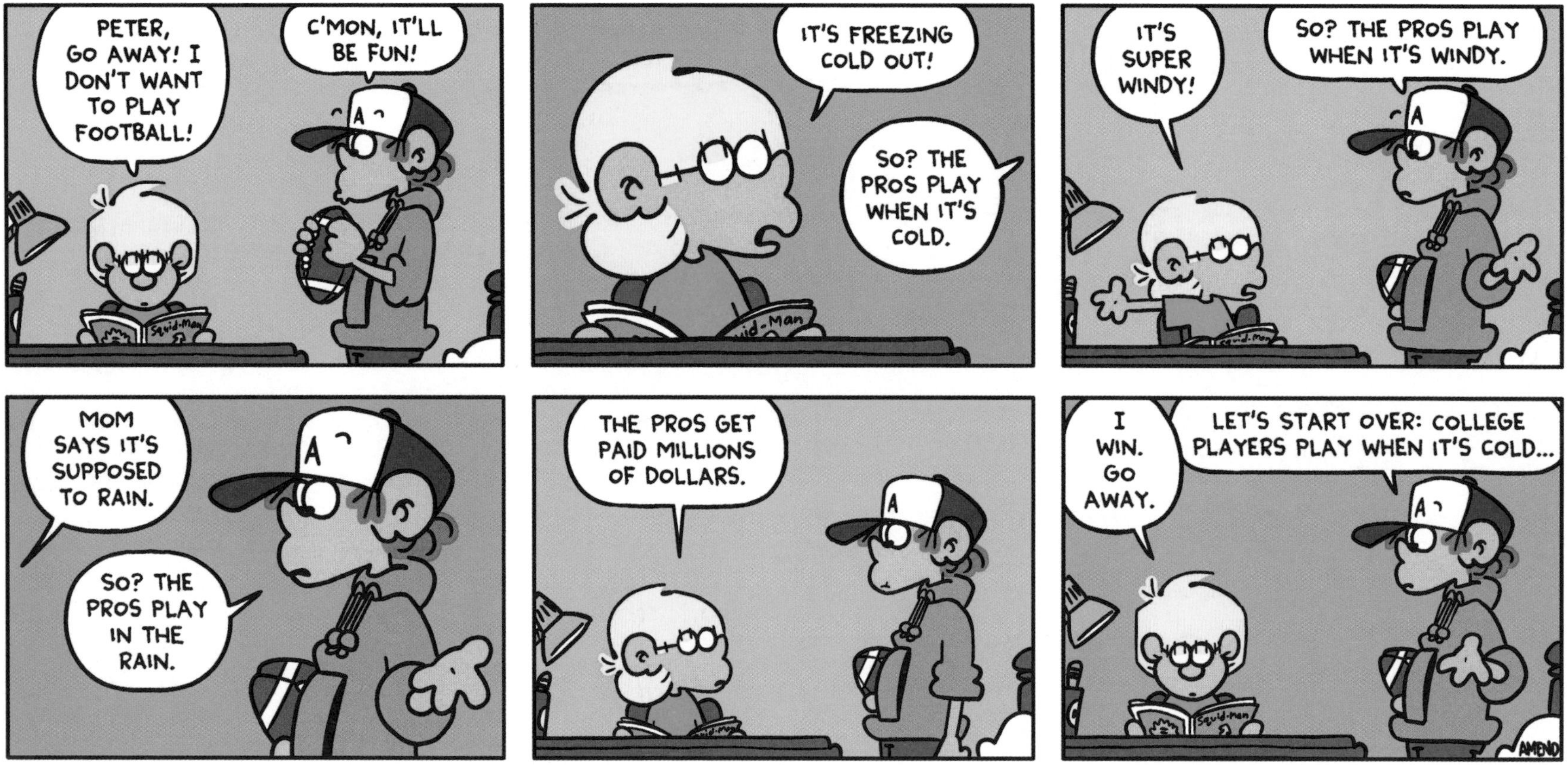
PETER, GO AWAY! I DON'T WANT TO PLAY FOOTBALL!
C'MON, IT'LL BE FUN!
Squid-Man
IT'S FREEZING COLD OUT!
SO? THE PROS PLAY WHEN IT'S COLD.
IT'S SUPER WINDY!
SO? THE PROS PLAY WHEN IT'S WINDY.
MOM SAYS IT'S SUPPOSED TO RAIN.
SO? THE PROS PLAY IN THE RAIN.
THE PROS GET PAID MILLIONS OF DOLLARS.
I WIN. GO AWAY.
LET'S START OVER: COLLEGE PLAYERS PLAY WHEN IT'S COLD...
AMEND

The Spice Must Flow

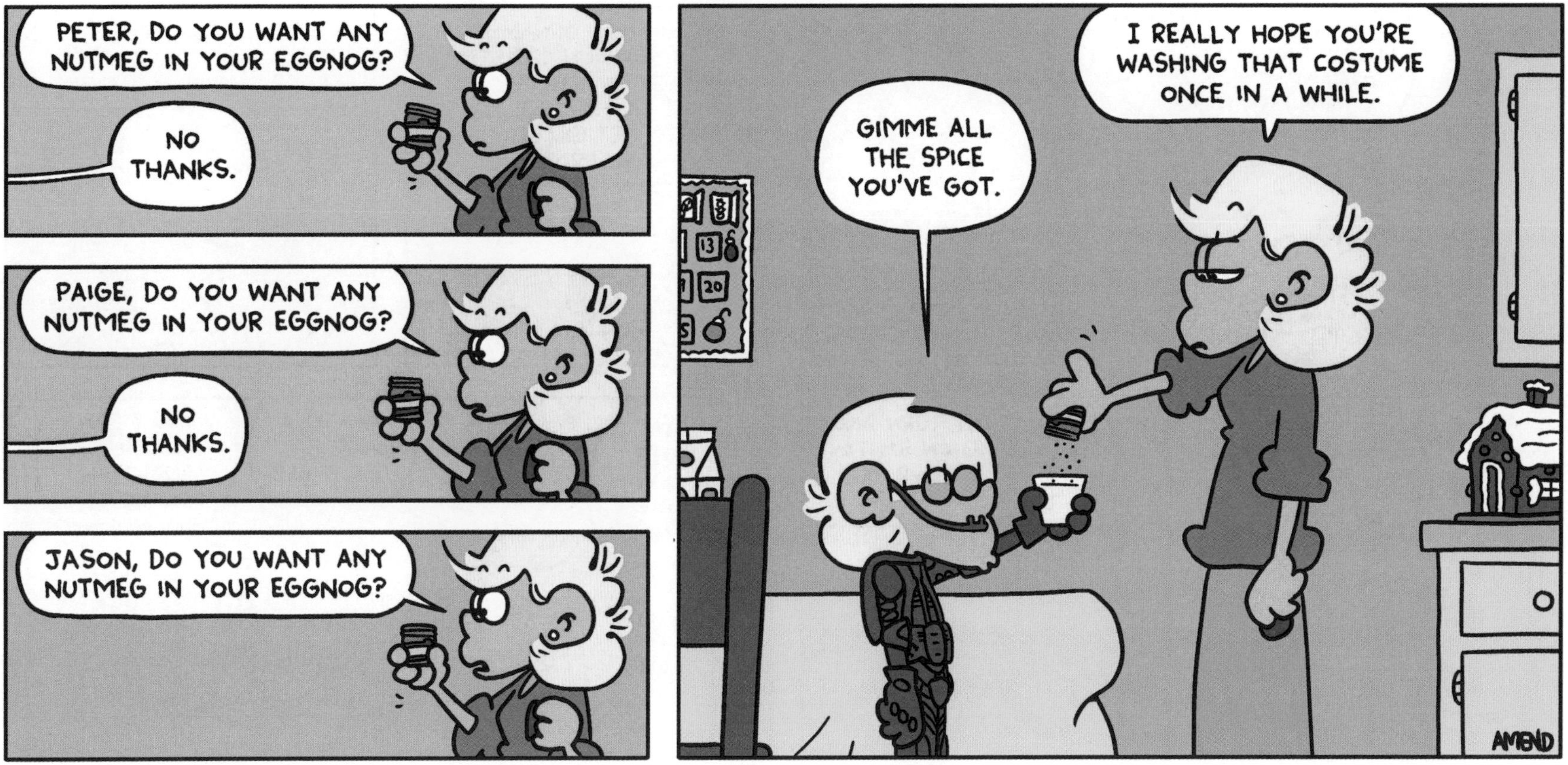
PETER, DO YOU WANT ANY NUTMEG IN YOUR EGGNOG?
NO THANKS.
PAIGE, DO YOU WANT ANY NUTMEG IN YOUR EGGNOG?
NO THANKS.
JASON, DO YOU WANT ANY NUTMEG IN YOUR EGGNOG?
GIMME ALL THE SPICE YOU'VE GOT.
I REALLY HOPE YOU'RE WASHING THAT COSTUME ONCE IN A WHILE.
AMEND

Ornamental

AAAA! THE LUCKY SNOWMAN ORNAMENT IS MISSING!

THE WHAT?

THAT SNOWMAN ORNAMENT WE GOT AT FUN-FUN CHRISTMAS VILLAGE! WHICHEVER KID HANGS IT ON THE TREE ALWAYS SEEMS TO GET EXACTLY WHAT THEY WANT FROM SANTA!

TWO YEARS AGO, PETER HUNG IT AND GOT THAT ELECTRIC BASS GUITAR AND AMP...

LAST YEAR, PAIGE HUNG IT AND GOT THAT DANCE-DANCE K-POP GAME...

THIS YEAR IS **MY** TURN AND I WAS BANKING ON SANTA BRINGING ME A 750-ROUND GATLING NERF GUN!

AAAA! I CAN'T BELIEVE THIS IS HAPPENING!

ANY IDEA WHERE IT MIGHT BE?

YOU MEAN THIS **UN**LUCKY SNOWMAN ORNAMENT?...

AMEND

Boxing Day

SO I WAS THINKING WE'D START WITH THE O.G. "ROCKY"...

THEN SKIM THROUGH ROCKYS "II" THROUGH "V" IN ORDER...

THEN CHECK OUT SOME OLD MUHAMMAD ALI AND MIKE TYSON CLIPS ON YOUTUBE...

THEN FINISH STRONG WITH "ROCKY BALBOA," "CREED" AND "CREED II."

YOU CAN'T LEAVE OUT "RAGING BULL"!

IT'S RATED R, SO WE CAN'T WATCH IT WITH MOM HOME.

PHOOEY.

HEY, PAIGE, WANNA CELEBRATE BOXING DAY WITH US?

I'M PRETENDING I DON'T KNOW EITHER ONE OF YOU.

Winter Games

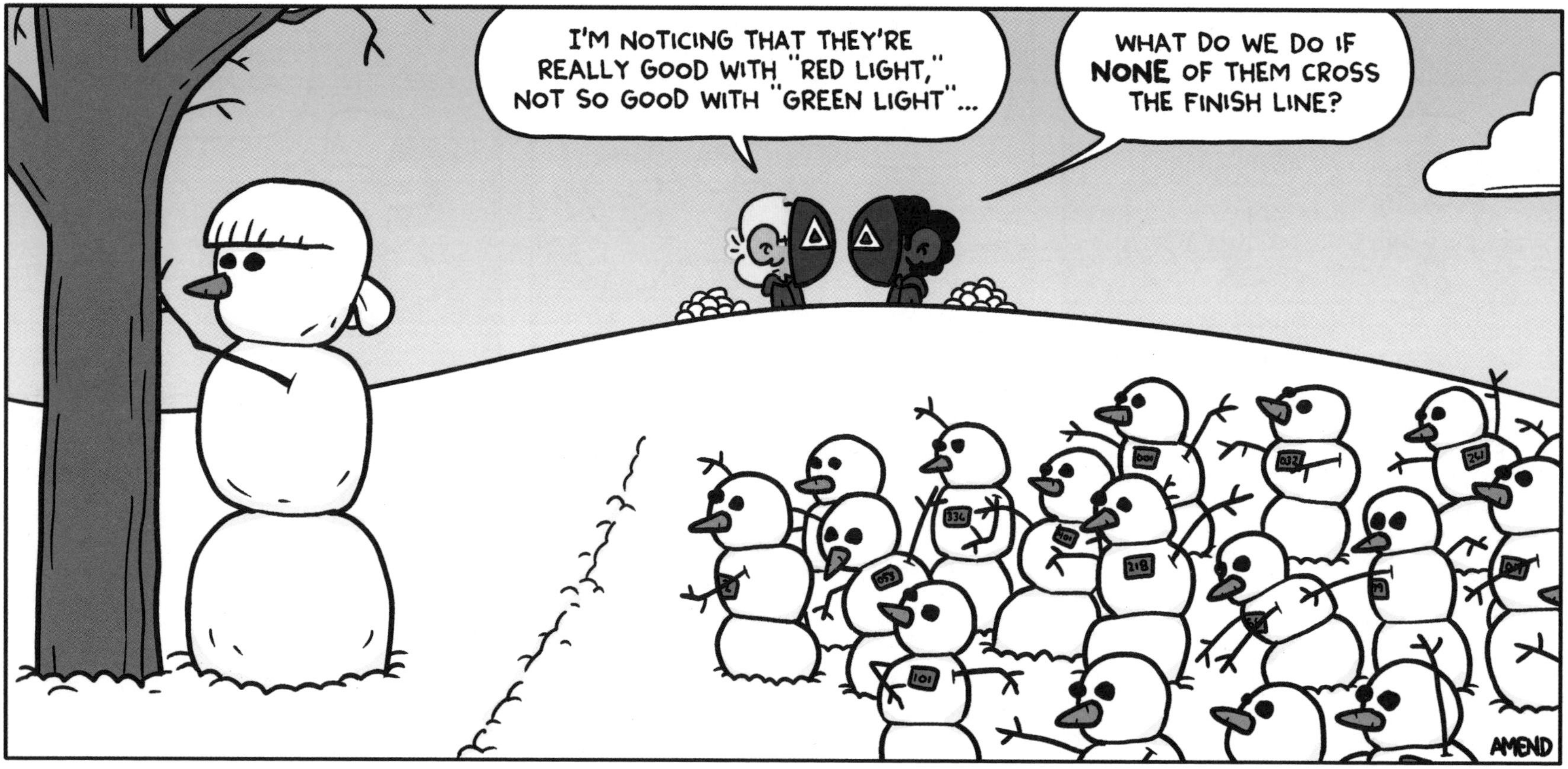
I'M NOTICING THAT THEY'RE REALLY GOOD WITH "RED LIGHT," NOT SO GOOD WITH "GREEN LIGHT"...
WHAT DO WE DO IF NONE OF THEM CROSS THE FINISH LINE?
AMEND

Retrograndes

MY GRADES CAME.

AND?...

WHAT WOULD YOUR REACTION BE IF I TOLD YOU I GOT STRAIGHT A's?

LET'S SEE.... I'D PROBABLY HAVE A HEART ATTACK FROM THE SHOCK.

THEN AT THE HOSPITAL I'D ASK TO HAVE MY HEARING TESTED.

AND IF MY EARS CHECKED OUT, I'D CONSULT A NEUROLOGIST ABOUT THE HALLUCINATIONS I WAS OBVIOUSLY HAVING.

OK, SO THINK OF THIS AS ME SPARING YOU ALL THAT.

ACTUALLY, YOU STILL MIGHT HAVE A HEART ATTACK.

PETER FOX!

AMEND

Supreme Combo

CAN I GET A SLICE WITH PEPPERONI...

A SLICE WITH SAUSAGE...

A SLICE WITH MUSHROOMS...

A SLICE WITH ONIONS...

A SLICE WITH BLACK OLIVES...

AND, LASTLY, A SLICE WITH GREEN PEPPERS.

WEIRDO.

YOU'RE JUST JEALOUS THAT MY SUPREME COMBO IS **MORE** SUPREME.

Early Decisions

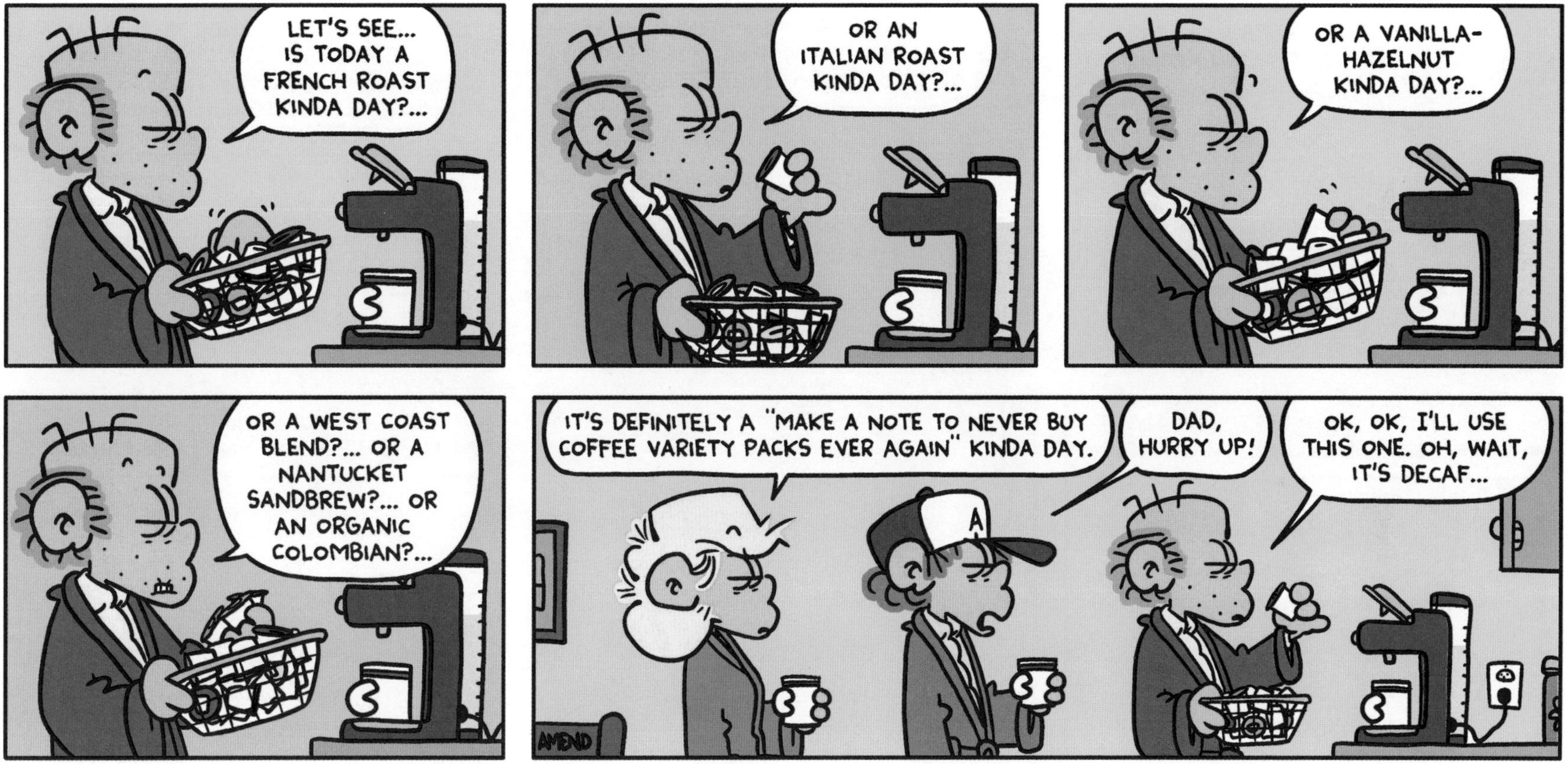

LET'S SEE... IS TODAY A FRENCH ROAST KINDA DAY?...
OR AN ITALIAN ROAST KINDA DAY?...
OR A VANILLA-HAZELNUT KINDA DAY?...
OR A WEST COAST BLEND?... OR A NANTUCKET SANDBREW?... OR AN ORGANIC COLOMBIAN?...
IT'S DEFINITELY A "MAKE A NOTE TO NEVER BUY COFFEE VARIETY PACKS EVER AGAIN" KINDA DAY.
DAD, HURRY UP!
OK, OK, I'LL USE THIS ONE. OH, WAIT, IT'S DECAF...
AMEND

Barbie Girl

G'DAY, MATE!

WHAT'S WITH THE AUSTRALIAN ACCENT?

WITH ALL THE WARM WEATHER WE'VE BEEN HAVING THIS WINTER, I'VE DECIDED ONE OF TWO THINGS MUST BE GOING ON.

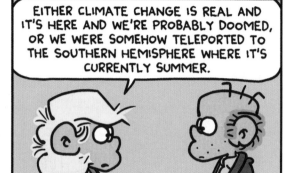

EITHER CLIMATE CHANGE IS REAL AND IT'S HERE AND WE'RE PROBABLY DOOMED, OR WE WERE SOMEHOW TELEPORTED TO THE SOUTHERN HEMISPHERE WHERE IT'S CURRENTLY SUMMER.

I FIND THAT I SLEEP BETTER AT NIGHT IF I EMBRACE THE SECOND EXPLANATION.

SHALL I THROW A SHRIMP ON THE BARBIE FOR YA?

DEAR, THOSE ARE PANCAKES.

Playing Games

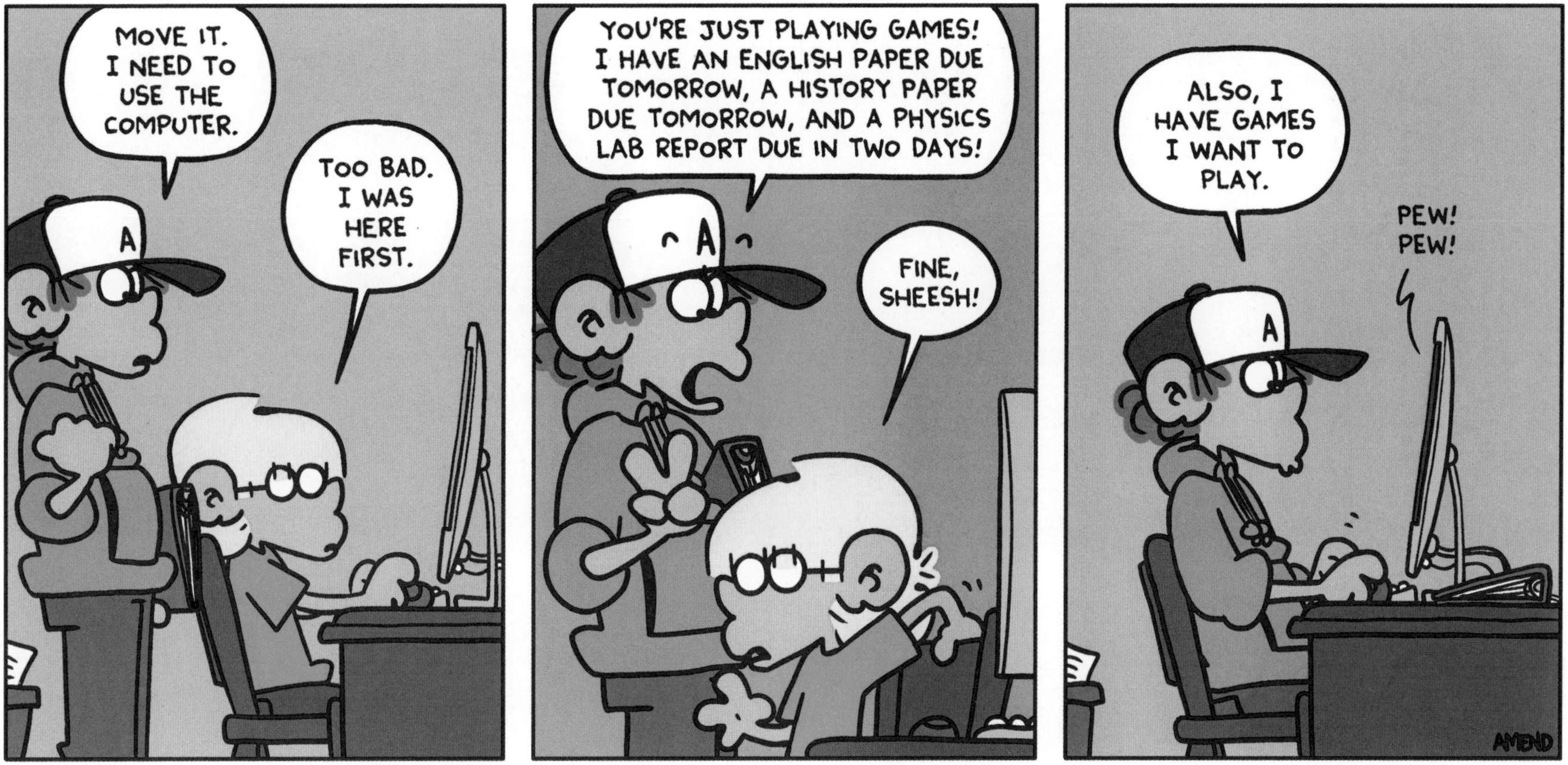
MOVE IT. I NEED TO USE THE COMPUTER.
TOO BAD. I WAS HERE FIRST.
YOU'RE JUST PLAYING GAMES! I HAVE AN ENGLISH PAPER DUE TOMORROW, A HISTORY PAPER DUE TOMORROW, AND A PHYSICS LAB REPORT DUE IN TWO DAYS!
FINE, SHEESH!
ALSO, I HAVE GAMES I WANT TO PLAY.
PEW! PEW!
AMEND

Super Shoppers

OK, LET'S TAKE A COUNT OF WHAT WE'VE GOT.

POTATO CHIPS... TORTILLA CHIPS... CHEEZOS... PRETZELS... SALSA... QUESO... GUAC... ONION DIP... HAMBURGER MEAT... HAMBURGER BUNS... HOT DOGS... HOT DOG BUNS... BEER... SODA... AN ASSORTMENT OF FROZEN PIZZAS...

THINK THAT'LL BE ENOUGH FOR THE SUPER BOWL?

HEH, MAYBE THE FIRST QUARTER.

RIGHT. I'LL GET US THREE MORE CARTS.

SON, I WAS EXAGGERATING! JUST GET ONE!

AMEND

Momio Kart

AAA! THAT GUY JUST PASSED US! GO FASTER!

GET BEHIND HIM! I'LL NAIL HIM WITH A SHELL!

WHY AREN'T YOU DRIFTING?! YOU HAVE TO DRIFT ON THESE TURNS!

TRY TO GET AIRBORNE ON THIS NEXT HILL! I THINK THERE'S A POWER-UP!

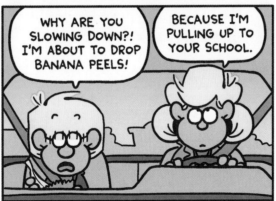

WHY ARE YOU SLOWING DOWN?! I'M ABOUT TO DROP BANANA PEELS!

BECAUSE I'M PULLING UP TO YOUR SCHOOL.

OK, SEE YOU AT 3:00. ALSO, "MOMIO KART" WOULD BE A LOT MORE FUN IF YOU PLAYED ALONG.

I'D LIKE TO STEER CLEAR OF PRISON, THANKS.

AMEND

Difficult Math

Mary Lou has a master's degree and earns x dollars per month teaching high school math.

If her monthly housing costs are $\frac{1}{3}x$, and her heat and utility bills are $\frac{1}{8}x$...

And her food expenses are $\frac{1}{7}x$, and her car-related costs are $\frac{1}{6}x$...

And her monthly health, clothing, furnishings, tax and student loan payments total $\frac{1}{4}x$...

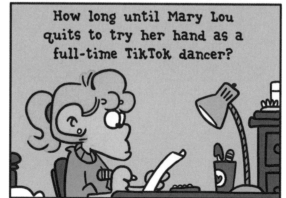

How long until Mary Lou quits to try her hand as a full-time TikTok dancer?

I'D SAY MY TEACHER WAS TRYING TO TELL US SOMETHING, BUT HER NAME'S NOT MARY LOU.

HEY! MINE ASSIGNED THIS PROBLEM ALSO!

Good Ideas

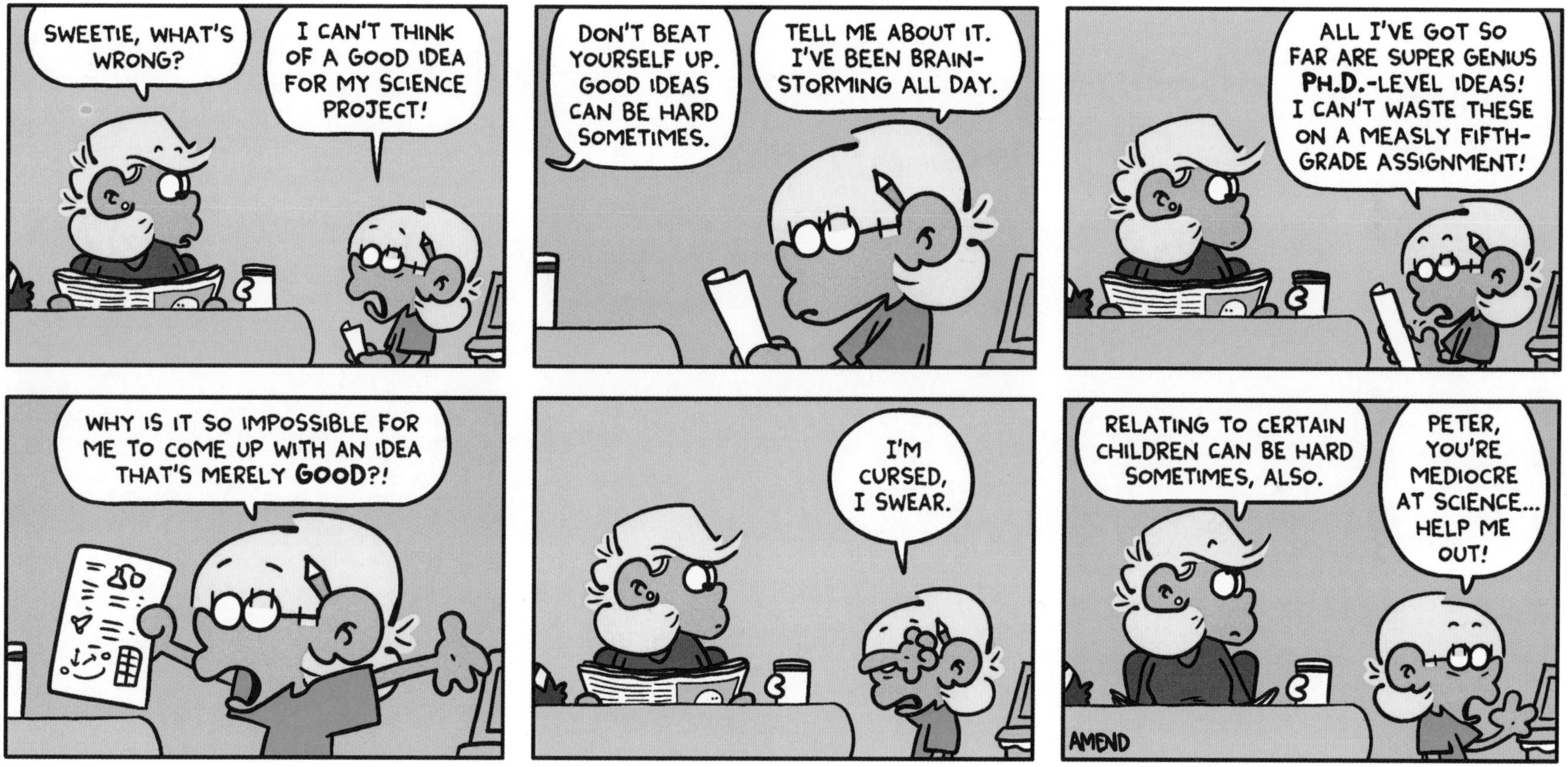
SWEETIE, WHAT'S WRONG?
I CAN'T THINK OF A GOOD IDEA FOR MY SCIENCE PROJECT!
DON'T BEAT YOURSELF UP. GOOD IDEAS CAN BE HARD SOMETIMES.
TELL ME ABOUT IT. I'VE BEEN BRAIN-STORMING ALL DAY.
ALL I'VE GOT SO FAR ARE SUPER GENIUS **PH.D.**-LEVEL IDEAS! I CAN'T WASTE THESE ON A MEASLY FIFTH-GRADE ASSIGNMENT!
WHY IS IT SO IMPOSSIBLE FOR ME TO COME UP WITH AN IDEA THAT'S MERELY **GOOD**?!
I'M CURSED, I SWEAR.
RELATING TO CERTAIN CHILDREN CAN BE HARD SOMETIMES, ALSO.
PETER, YOU'RE MEDIOCRE AT SCIENCE... HELP ME OUT!
AMEND

Pendantic

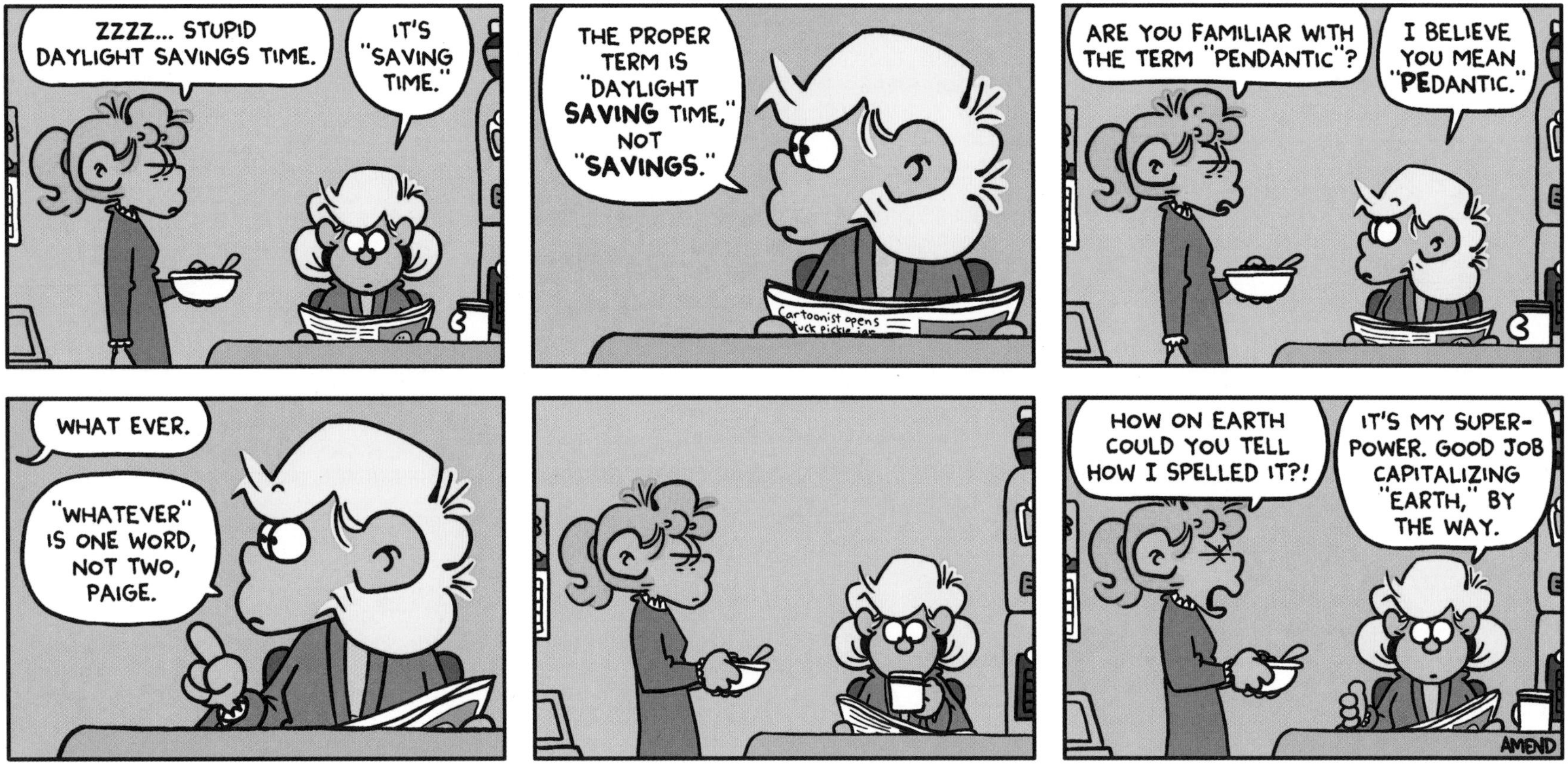
ZZZZ... STUPID DAYLIGHT SAVINGS TIME.
IT'S "SAVING TIME."
THE PROPER TERM IS "DAYLIGHT **SAVING** TIME," NOT "**SAVINGS**."
Cartoonist opens
ARE YOU FAMILIAR WITH THE TERM "PENDANTIC"?
I BELIEVE YOU MEAN "**PE**DANTIC."
WHAT EVER.
"WHATEVER" IS ONE WORD, NOT TWO, PAIGE.
HOW ON EARTH COULD YOU TELL HOW I SPELLED IT?!
IT'S MY SUPER-POWER. GOOD JOB CAPITALIZING "EARTH," BY THE WAY.
AMEND

Hot Meal

SINCE WE'RE NOT GOING ANYWHERE FOR SPRING BREAK, MAYBE YOU COULD TAKE US TO WARM PLACES VIA FOOD.

YOU COULD MAKE TACOS AND WE COULD PRETEND WE'RE IN MEXICO...

YOU COULD MAKE POKE AND WE COULD PRETEND WE'RE IN HAWAII...

YOU COULD MAKE JERK CHICKEN AND WE COULD PRETEND WE'RE IN JAMAICA...

I CAN'T DO THAT TONIGHT. I ALREADY HAVE A JELLIED YAM CASSEROLE IN THE OVEN.

I GUESS WE COULD PRETEND WE'RE IN HELL.

PRETEND?

AMEND

Comical Signs

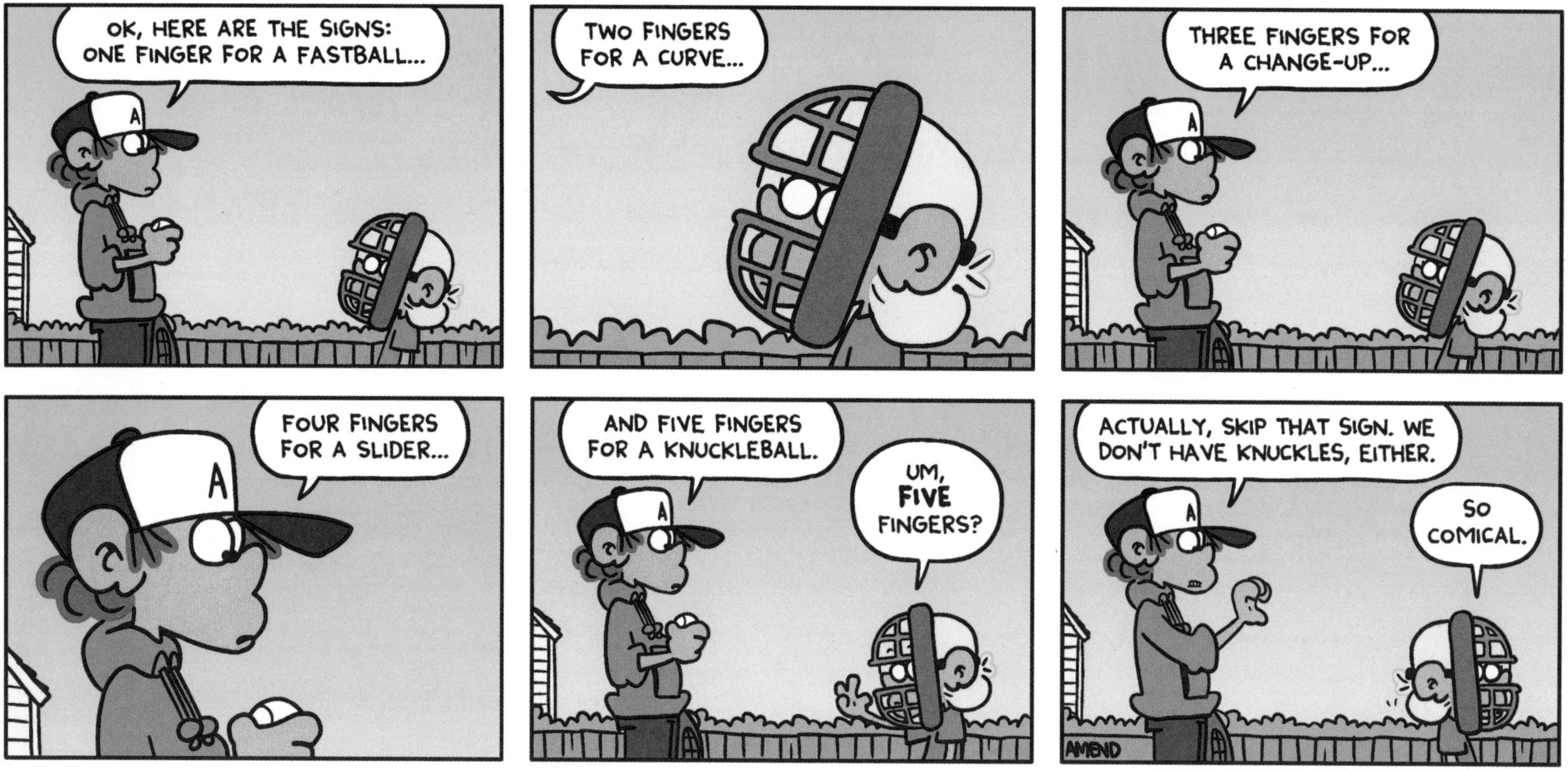
OK, HERE ARE THE SIGNS: ONE FINGER FOR A FASTBALL...
A
TWO FINGERS FOR A CURVE...
THREE FINGERS FOR A CHANGE-UP...
A
FOUR FINGERS FOR A SLIDER...
A
AND FIVE FINGERS FOR A KNUCKLEBALL.
UM, FIVE FINGERS?
A
ACTUALLY, SKIP THAT SIGN. WE DON'T HAVE KNUCKLES, EITHER.
SO COMICAL.
A
AMEND

Shower Season

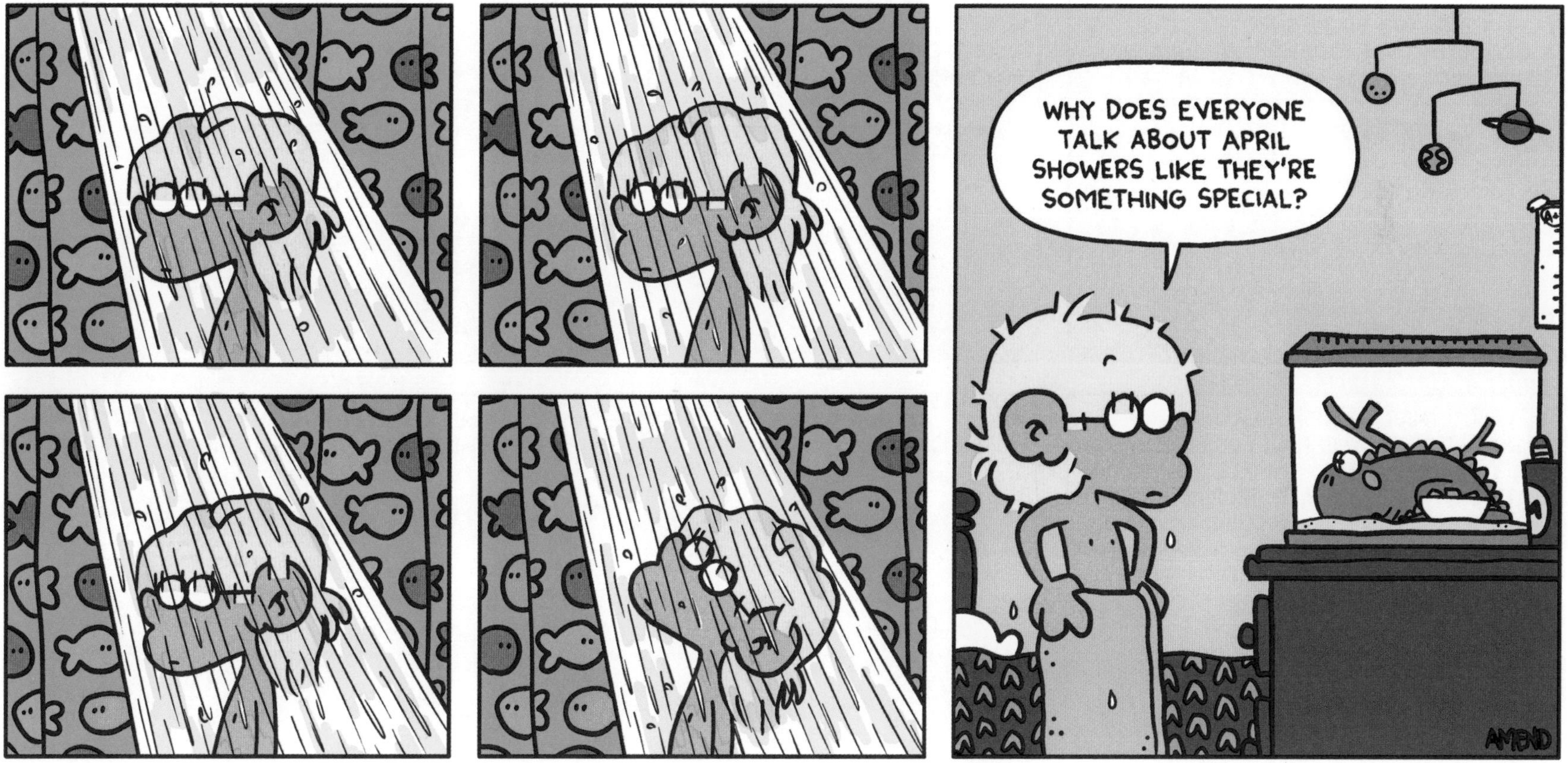

WHY DOES EVERYONE TALK ABOUT APRIL SHOWERS LIKE THEY'RE SOMETHING SPECIAL?
AMEND

Golfing Brilliance

WHY ARE YOU WATCHING BEGINNER GOLF VIDEOS?

I'VE COME UP WITH A BRILLIANT PLAN.

WITH PHIL MICKELSON TAKING "TIME AWAY" FROM THE PGA TOUR, THERE'S NOW AN OPENING FOR A MIDDLE-AGED-AND-NOT-QUITE-SKINNY GUY LIKE ME TO TAKE HIS SPOT.

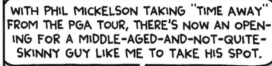

DAD, I'VE GOLFED WITH YOU. NO OFFENSE, BUT YOU'RE AWFUL.

YES, BUT THAT WAS ME PLAYING **RIGHT**-HANDED. TO REPLACE PHIL, I'LL BE PLAYING **LEFT**-HANDED. I'M A COMPLETELY BLANK SLATE ON THAT SIDE. WITH PROPER INSTRUCTION, WHO KNOWS? I COULD BE AMAZING!

WHICH REMINDS ME, I'LL NEED TO BUY A SET OF LEFTY CLUBS.

DOES "BRILLIANT" HAVE A DEFINITION I'M NOT AWARE OF?

I SHOULD PROBABLY PUT THEM ON A CREDIT CARD YOUR MOTHER DOESN'T SEE...

Dye Harder

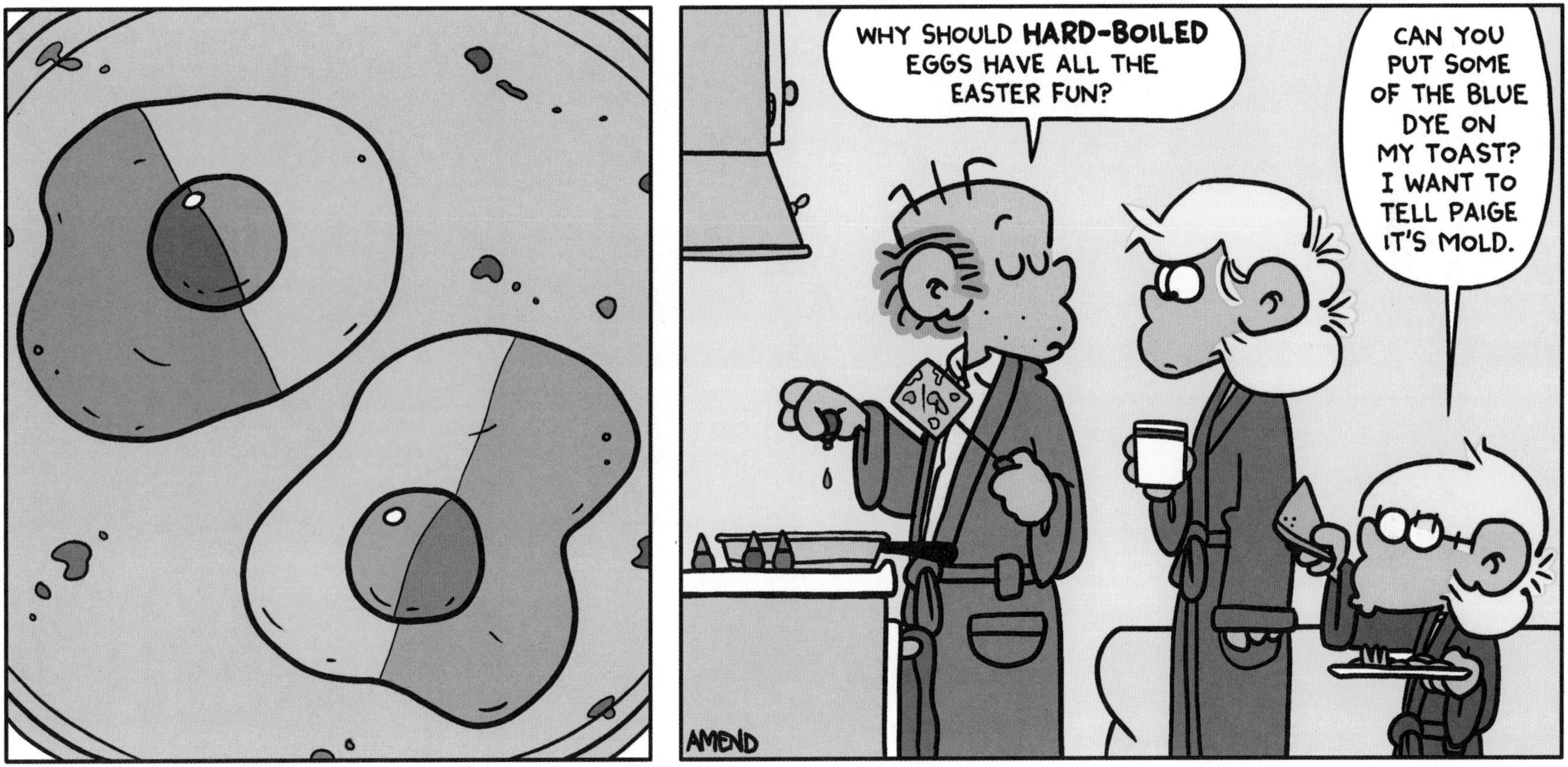
WHY SHOULD **HARD-BOILED** EGGS HAVE ALL THE EASTER FUN?
CAN YOU PUT SOME OF THE BLUE DYE ON MY TOAST? I WANT TO TELL PAIGE IT'S MOLD.
AMEND

Comedy of Errors

I DID ALL THAT ON PURPOSE, BY THE WAY!

THEY STILL COUNT AS ERRORS, FOX.

I NEED TO FIND A SPORT THAT **APPRECIATES** PHYSICAL COMEDY.

May Fools

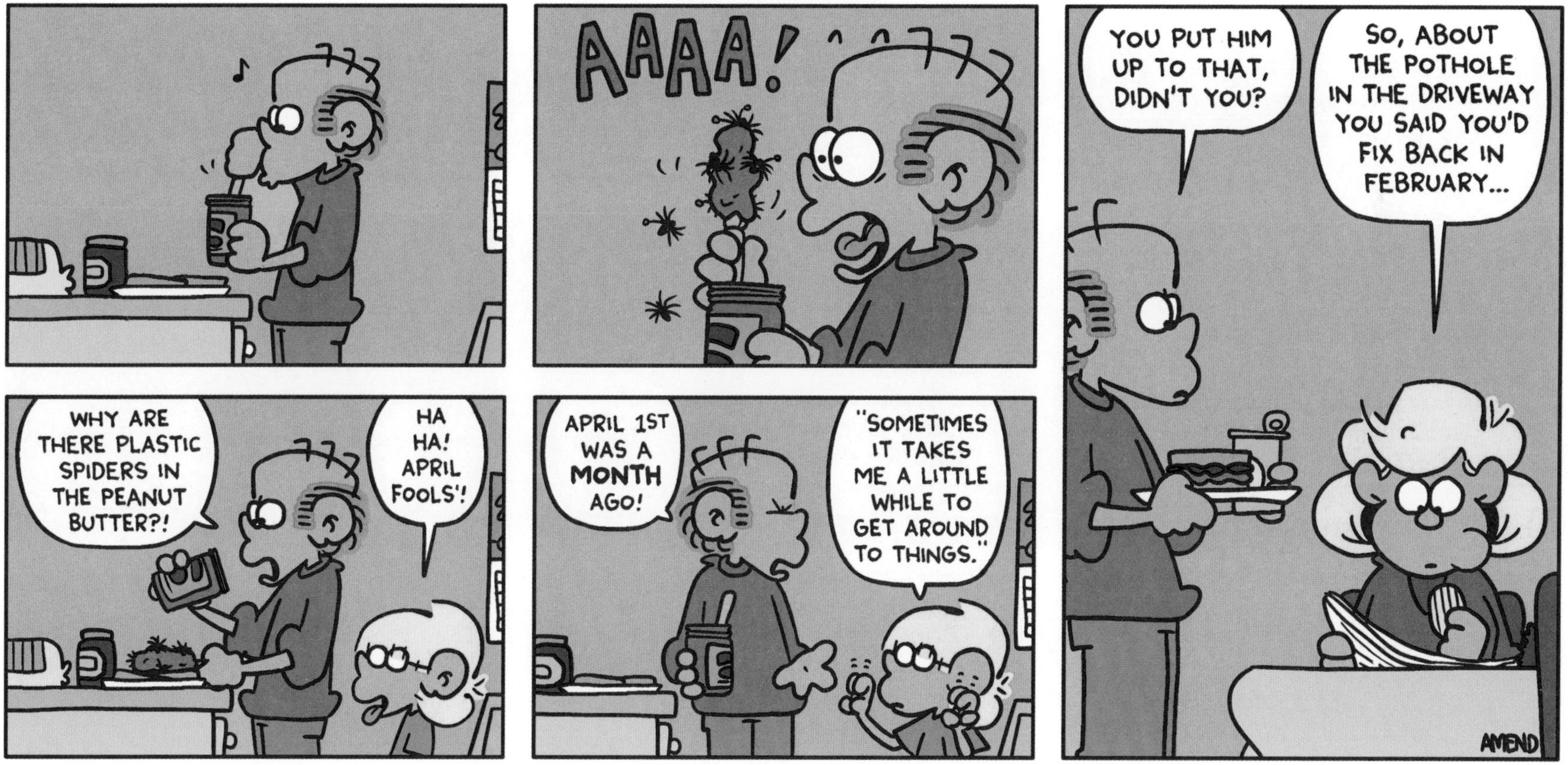
AAAA!
WHY ARE THERE PLASTIC SPIDERS IN THE PEANUT BUTTER?!
HA HA! APRIL FOOLS'!
APRIL 1ST WAS A MONTH AGO!
"SOMETIMES IT TAKES ME A LITTLE WHILE TO GET AROUND TO THINGS."
YOU PUT HIM UP TO THAT, DIDN'T YOU?
SO, ABOUT THE POTHOLE IN THE DRIVEWAY YOU SAID YOU'D FIX BACK IN FEBRUARY...
AMEND

Smaugy Bottom Boy

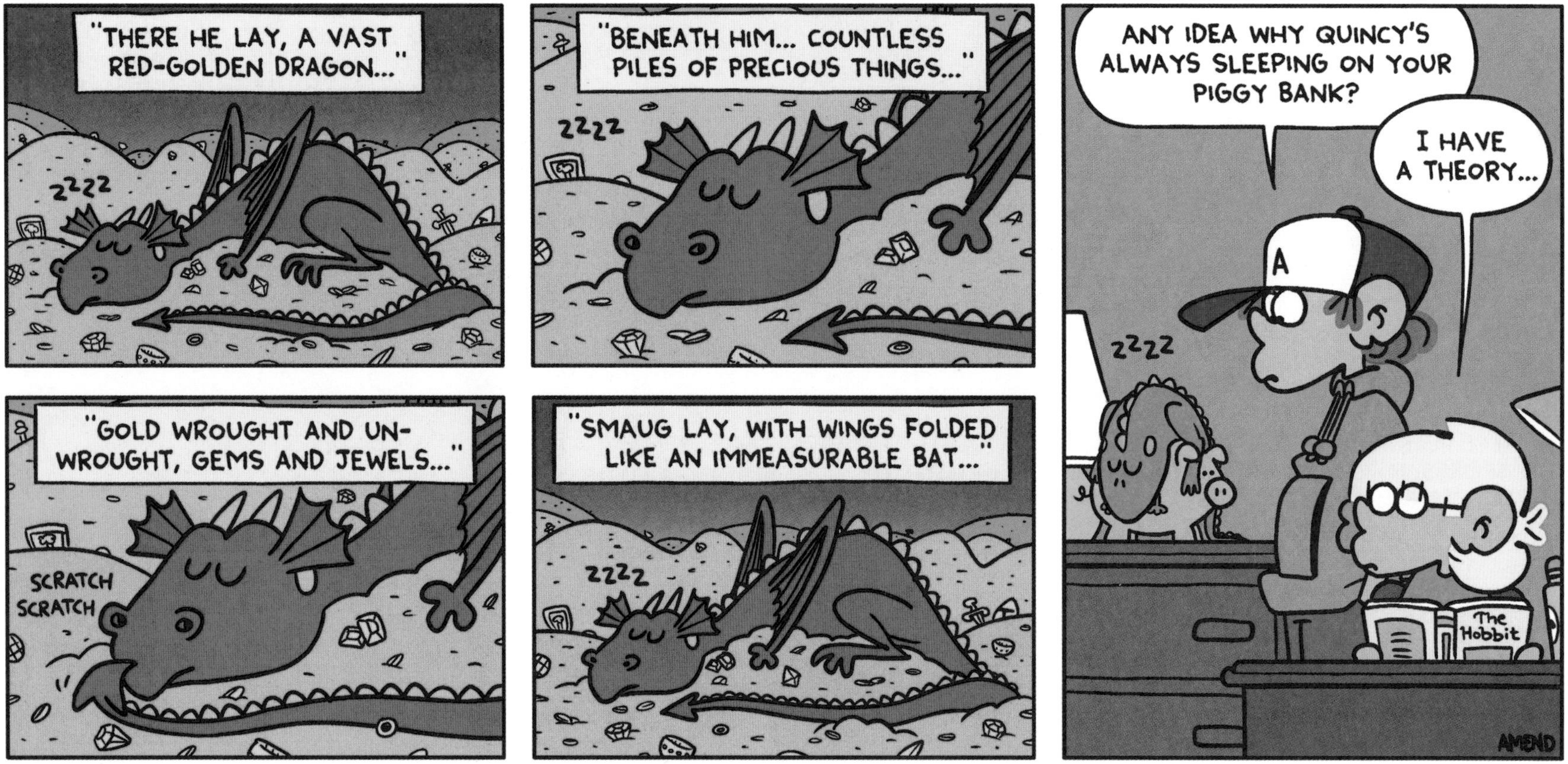

"THERE HE LAY, A VAST RED-GOLDEN DRAGON..."
ZZZZ
"BENEATH HIM... COUNTLESS PILES OF PRECIOUS THINGS..."
ZZZZ
"GOLD WROUGHT AND UN-WROUGHT, GEMS AND JEWELS..."
SCRATCH SCRATCH
"SMAUG LAY, WITH WINGS FOLDED LIKE AN IMMEASURABLE BAT..."
ZZZZ
ANY IDEA WHY QUINCY'S ALWAYS SLEEPING ON YOUR PIGGY BANK?
I HAVE A THEORY...
ZZZZ
A
The Hobbit
AMEND

Tie Game

LET'S SEE... I WAS WEARING THIS HAIR TIE WHEN I DID PRETTY WELL ON THAT ONE MATH TEST... BUT I WAS WEARING **THIS** HAIR TIE WHEN I ACED MY HISTORY PRESENTATION...

BUT I WAS WEARING **THIS** HAIR TIE WHEN I GOT SUPER LUCKY ON THAT BIOLOGY TEST... BUT I THINK I HAD ON **THIS** HAIR TIE WHEN I SCORED A MIRACULOUS 15/15 ON MY VOCABULARY QUIZ...

DOES MY HAIR LOOK WEIRD LIKE THIS?

I THOUGHT YOU WERE PREPPING FOR FINALS.

AMEND

They're Gr-r-rades!

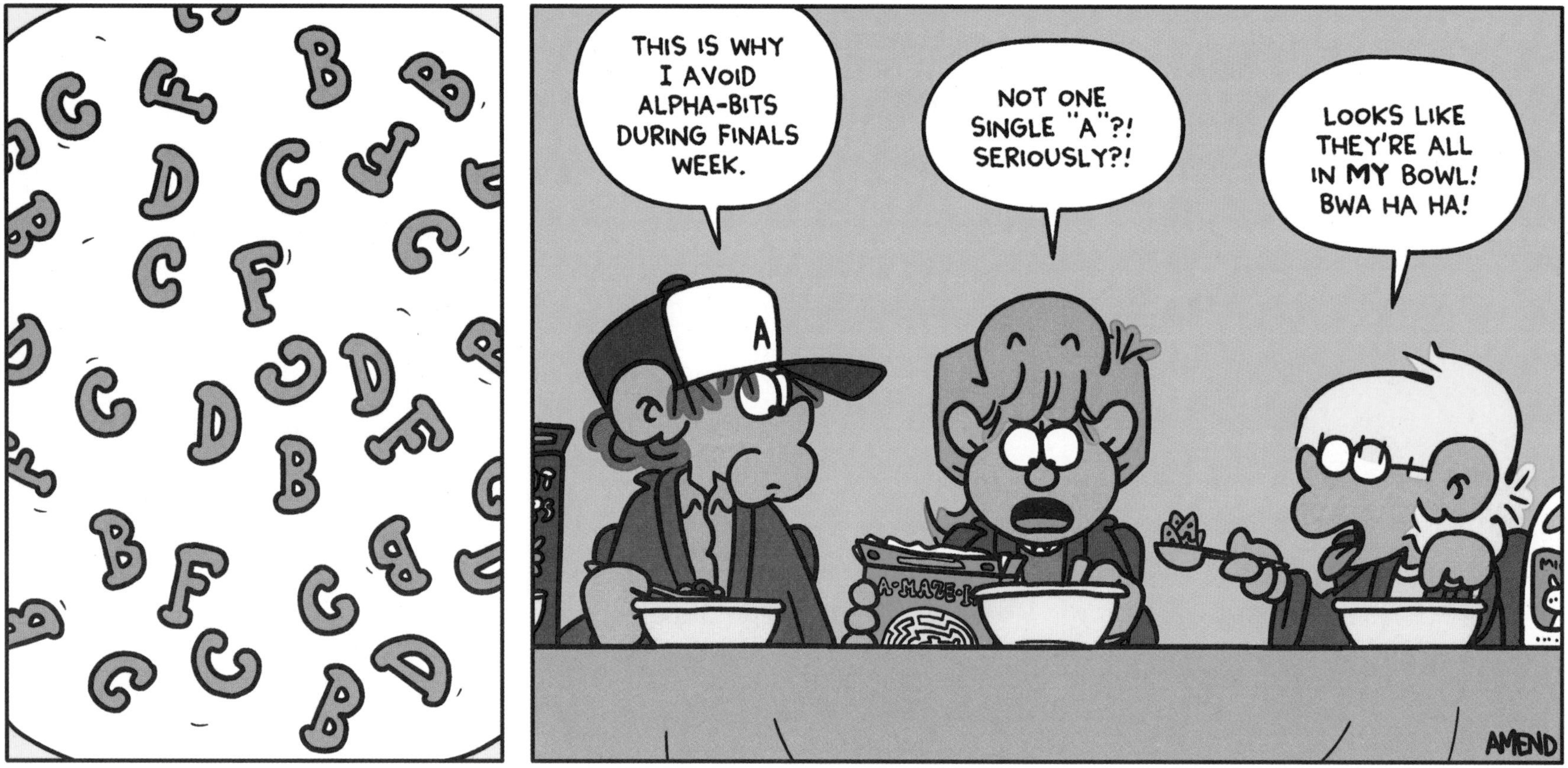
THIS IS WHY I AVOID ALPHA-BITS DURING FINALS WEEK.
NOT ONE SINGLE "A"?! SERIOUSLY?!
LOOKS LIKE THEY'RE ALL IN MY BOWL! BWA HA HA!
AMEND

Hot Grill Summer

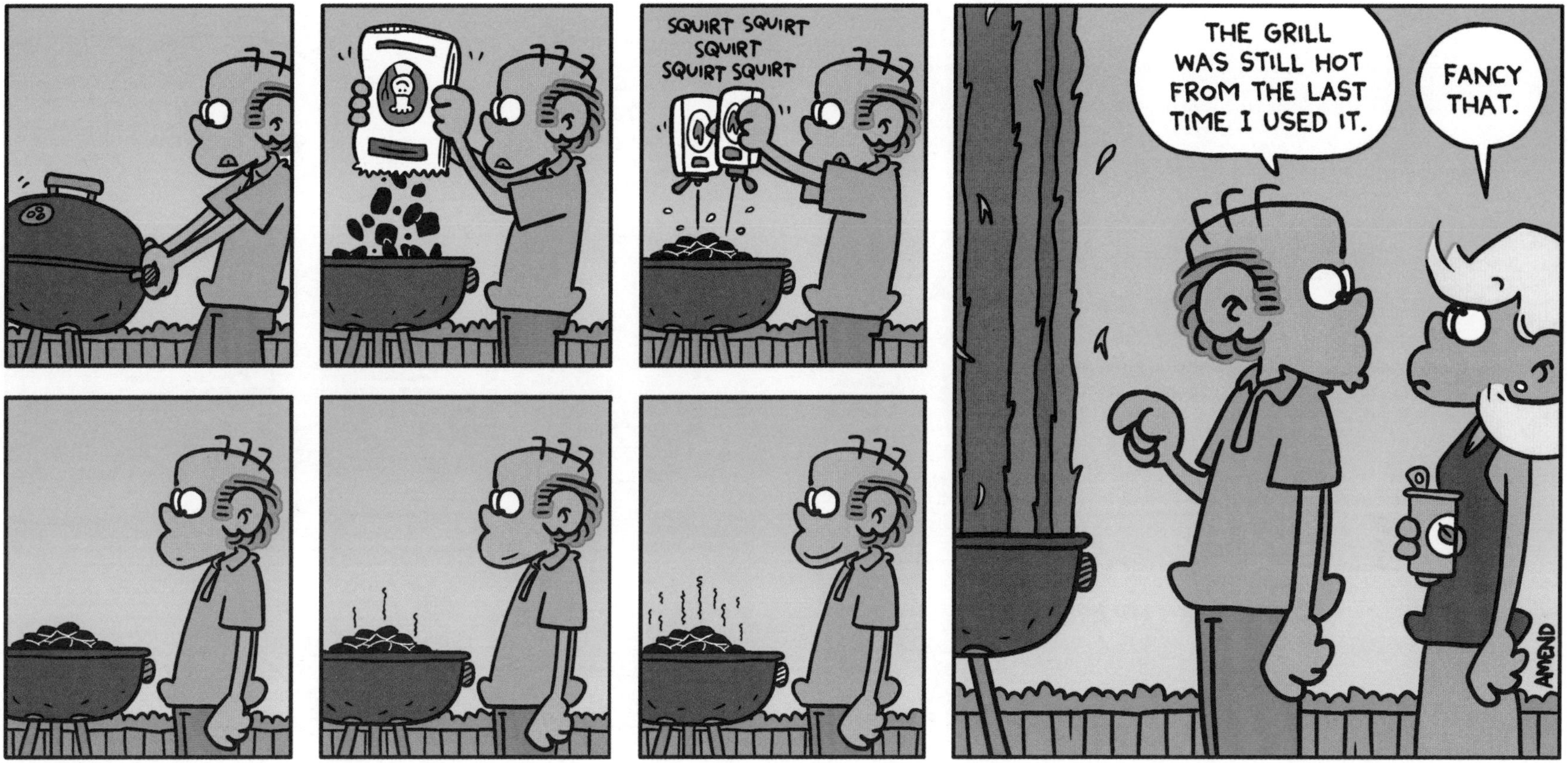
SQUIRT SQUIRT
SQUIRT
SQUIRT SQUIRT
THE GRILL WAS STILL HOT FROM THE LAST TIME I USED IT.
FANCY THAT.
AMEND

When Life Gives You Lemon JPEGs

Think Difference

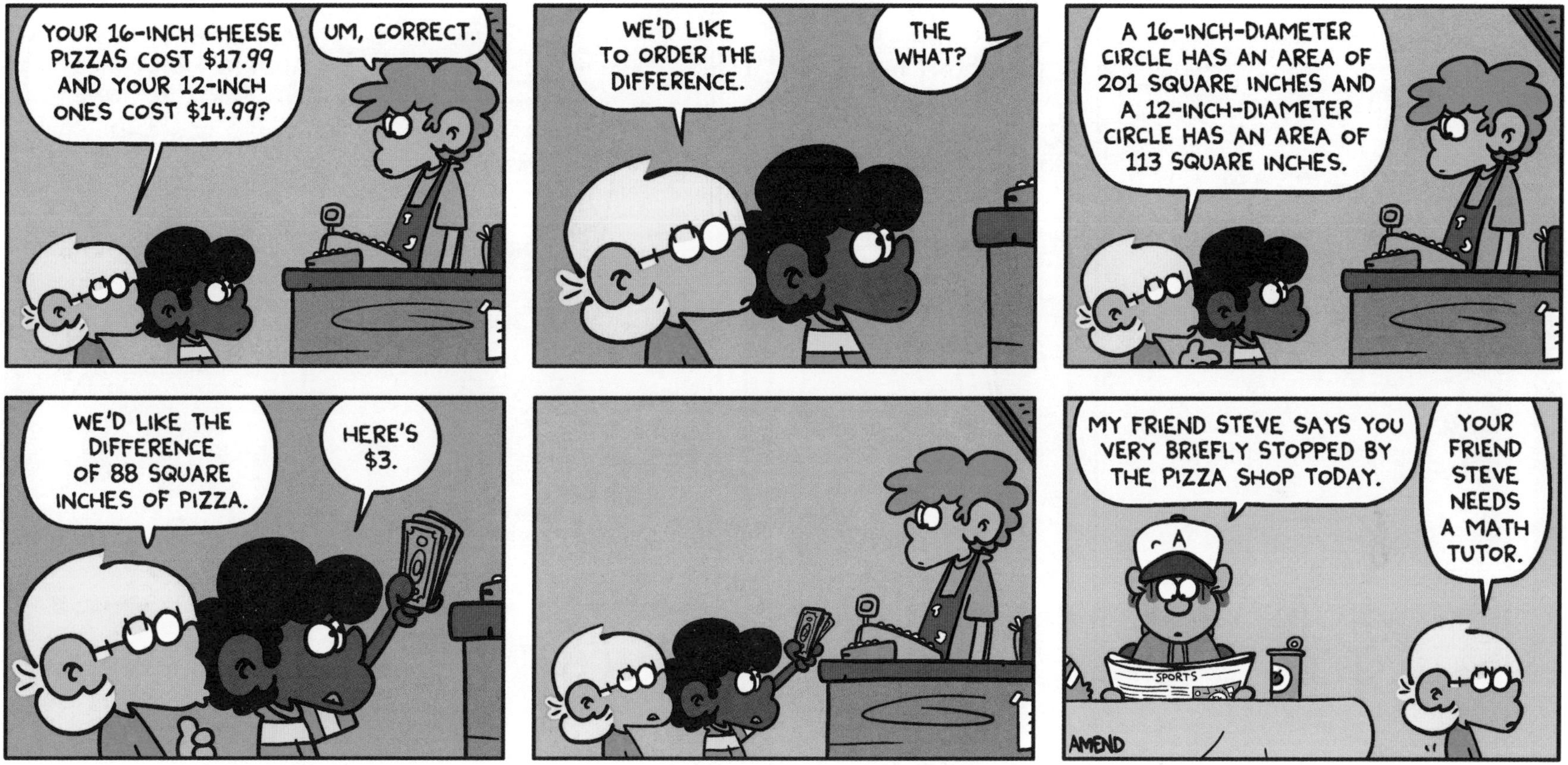

YOUR 16-INCH CHEESE PIZZAS COST $17.99 AND YOUR 12-INCH ONES COST $14.99?
UM, CORRECT.
WE'D LIKE TO ORDER THE DIFFERENCE.
THE WHAT?
A 16-INCH-DIAMETER CIRCLE HAS AN AREA OF 201 SQUARE INCHES AND A 12-INCH-DIAMETER CIRCLE HAS AN AREA OF 113 SQUARE INCHES.
WE'D LIKE THE DIFFERENCE OF 88 SQUARE INCHES OF PIZZA.
HERE'S $3.
MY FRIEND STEVE SAYS YOU VERY BRIEFLY STOPPED BY THE PIZZA SHOP TODAY.
YOUR FRIEND STEVE NEEDS A MATH TUTOR.
SPORTS
AMEND

Partial Credit

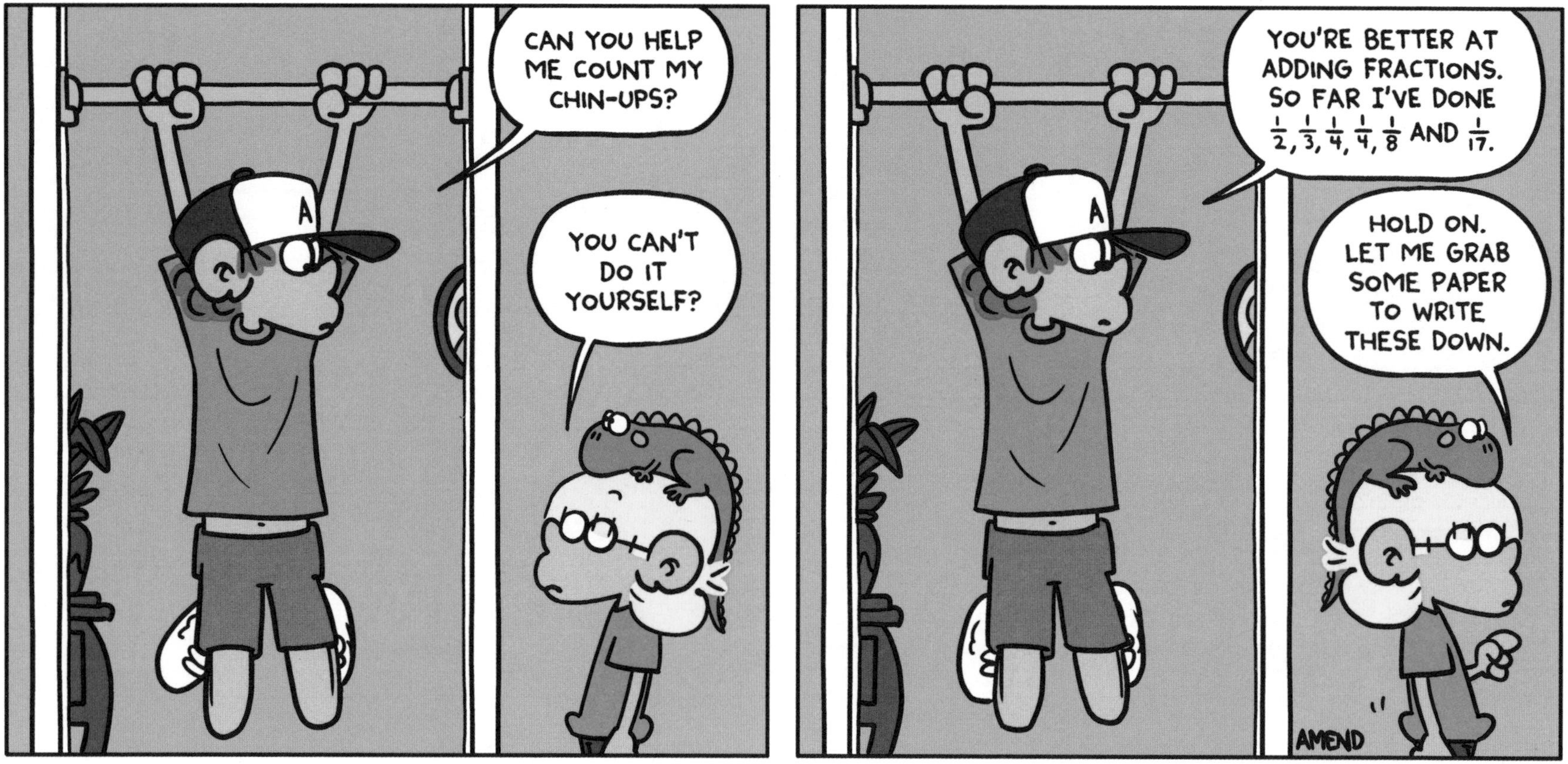
CAN YOU HELP ME COUNT MY CHIN-UPS?
YOU CAN'T DO IT YOURSELF?
YOU'RE BETTER AT ADDING FRACTIONS. SO FAR I'VE DONE $\frac{1}{2}, \frac{1}{3}, \frac{1}{4}, \frac{1}{4}, \frac{1}{8}$ AND $\frac{1}{17}$.
HOLD ON. LET ME GRAB SOME PAPER TO WRITE THESE DOWN.
AMEND

Never Dull

IS IT MY TURN TO MOW THE LAWN?
I THINK SO. WHY?
I WANT TO TEST OUT MY SUPER-BRILLIANT IDEA.
I'VE ATTACHED RAZOR BLADES TO THE PROPELLERS OF MY RADIO-CONTROLLED DRONE!
THIS WAY I CAN FLY IT LOW AROUND THE YARD AND TRIM THE GRASS, ALL FROM THE COMFORT OF OUR AIR-CONDITIONED HOME!
I JUST HOPE THE GLUE HOLDS AND THE BLADES DON'T FLY OFF. THAT COULD BE BAD.
I **TOLD** YOU IT WAS A SUPER-BRILLIANT IDEA.
BUT DAD! IT'S JASON'S TURN TO MOW THE LAWN!
PETER, DON'T ARGUE. JUST DO IT.
AMEND

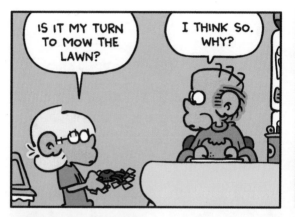

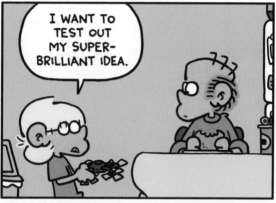

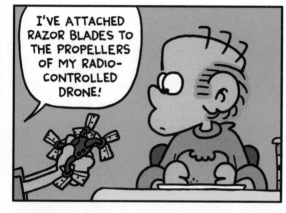

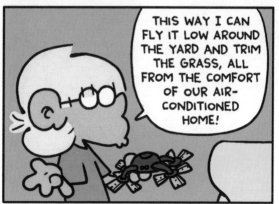

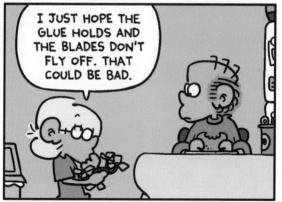

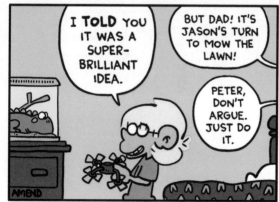

Infinite Appetite

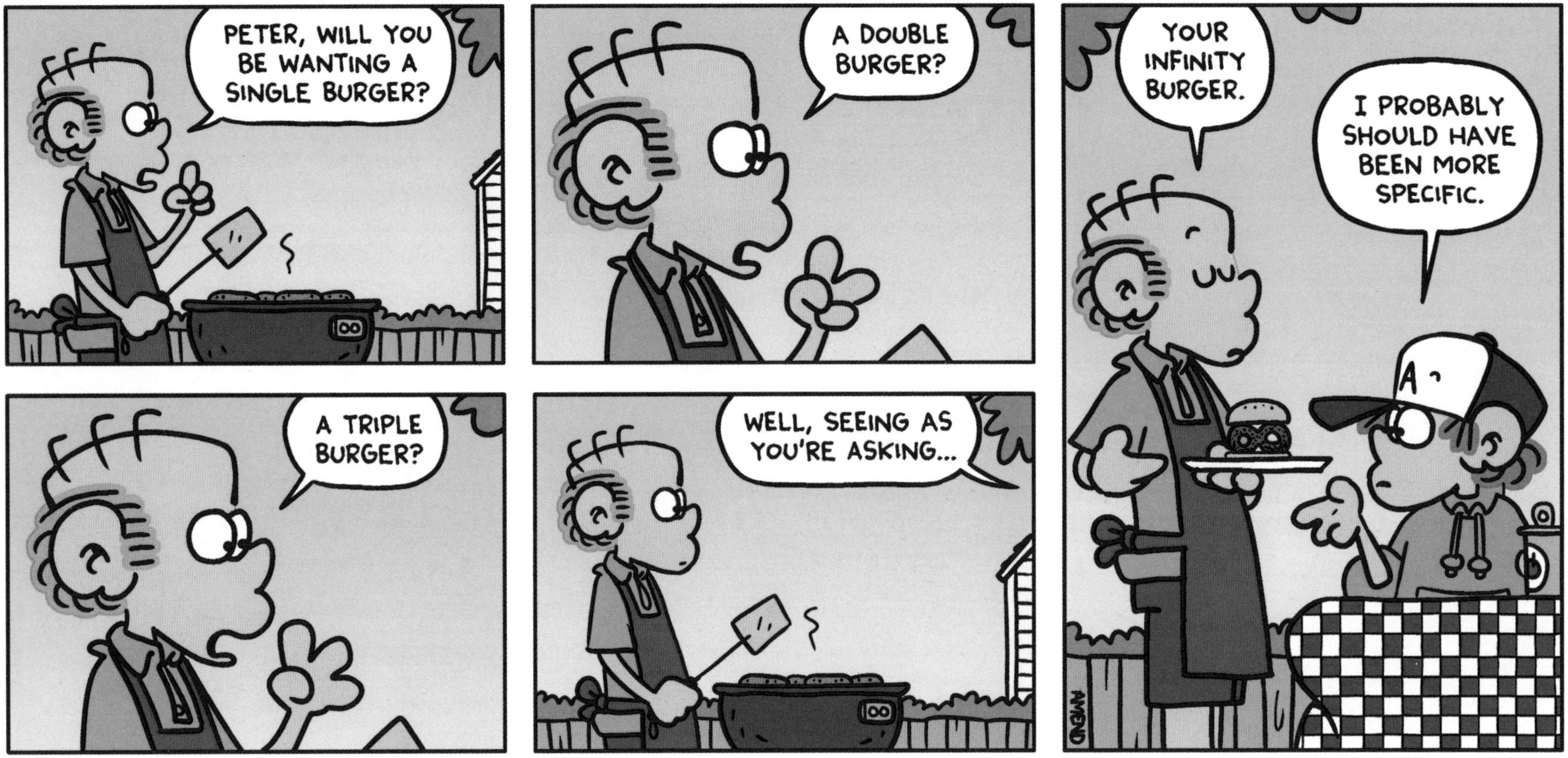
PETER, WILL YOU BE WANTING A SINGLE BURGER?
A DOUBLE BURGER?
A TRIPLE BURGER?
WELL, SEEING AS YOU'RE ASKING...
YOUR INFINITY BURGER.
I PROBABLY SHOULD HAVE BEEN MORE SPECIFIC.
A
AMEND

Froggering

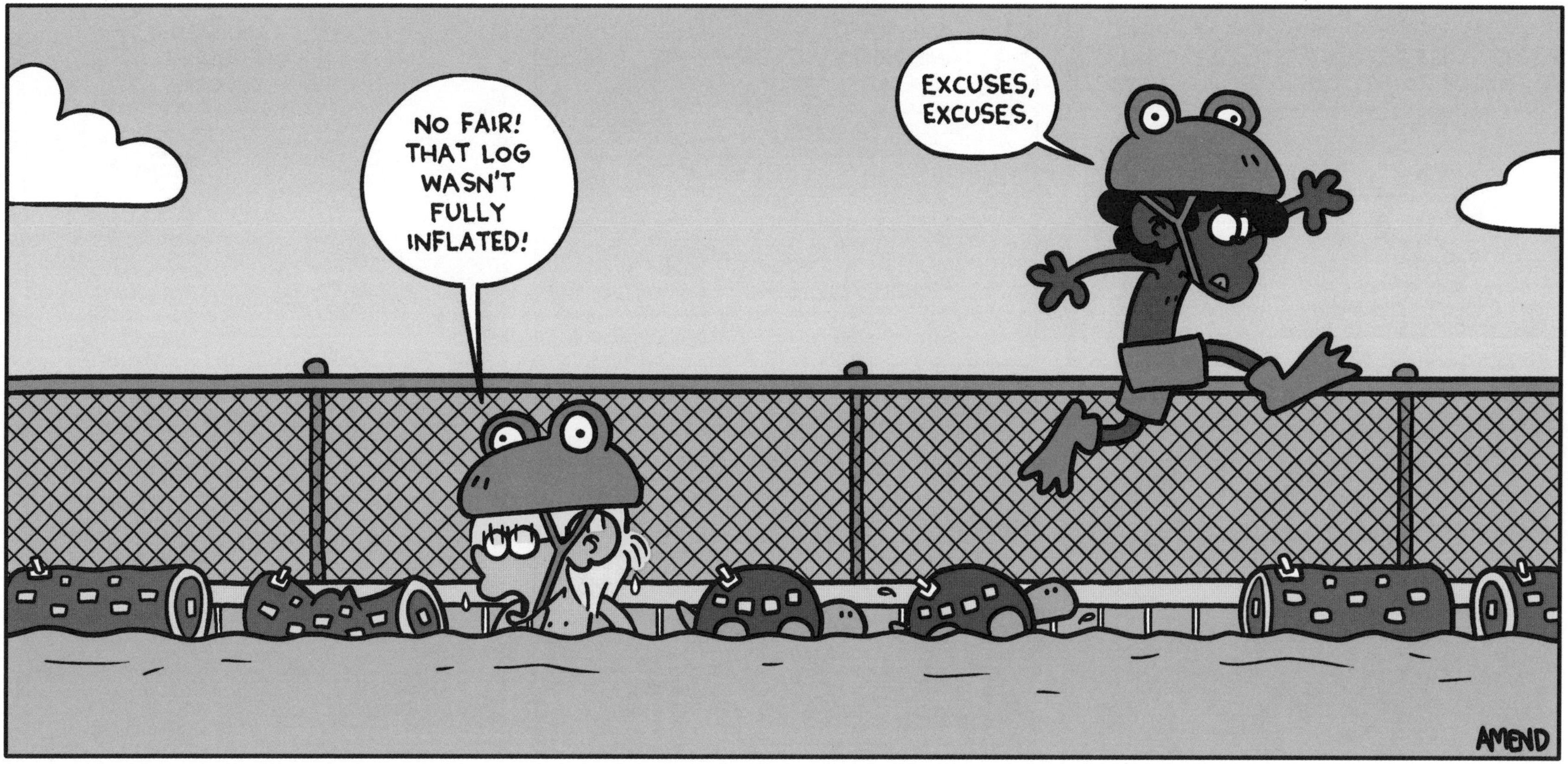
NO FAIR! THAT LOG WASN'T FULLY INFLATED!
EXCUSES, EXCUSES.
AMEND

Need For Speed

PETER, CAN YOU DRIVE TO THE STORE REALLY FAST? I FORGOT TO GET CARROTS.
"FAST," YOU SAY?
A
AVIATOR SUNGLASSES... CHECK!
A
CALL SIGN ON HELMET... CHECK!
"TOP GUN" SOUNDTRACK QUEUED UP ON PHONE... CHECK!
Maverick
CAR KEYS...
Maverick
ACTUALLY, I'LL JUST GO MYSELF.
BUT I DRIVE AT MACH 10! THINK OF THE TIME SAVINGS!
Maverick
AMEND

Icecreamahedron

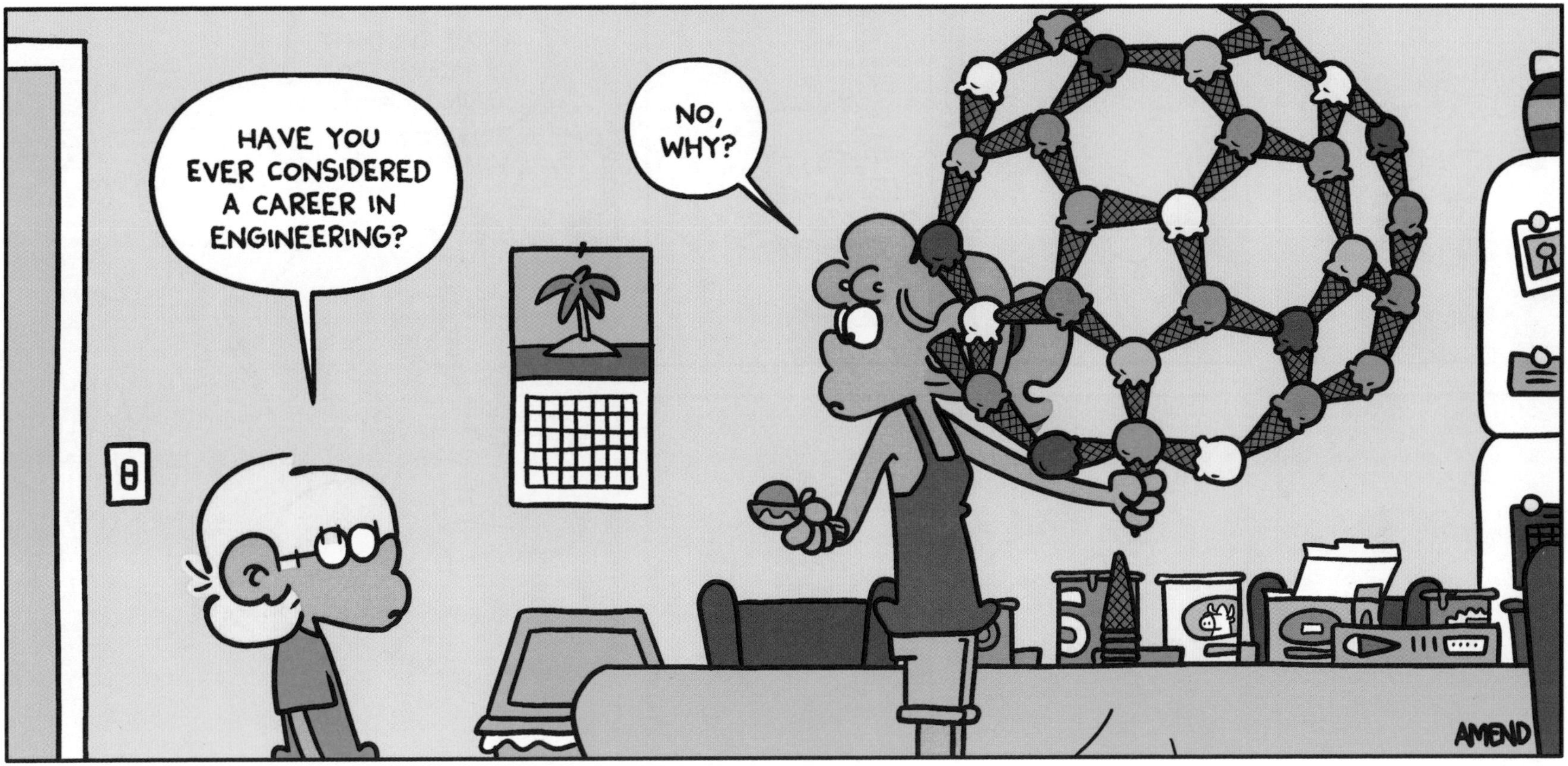
HAVE YOU EVER CONSIDERED A CAREER IN ENGINEERING?
NO, WHY?
AMEND

Light Winds

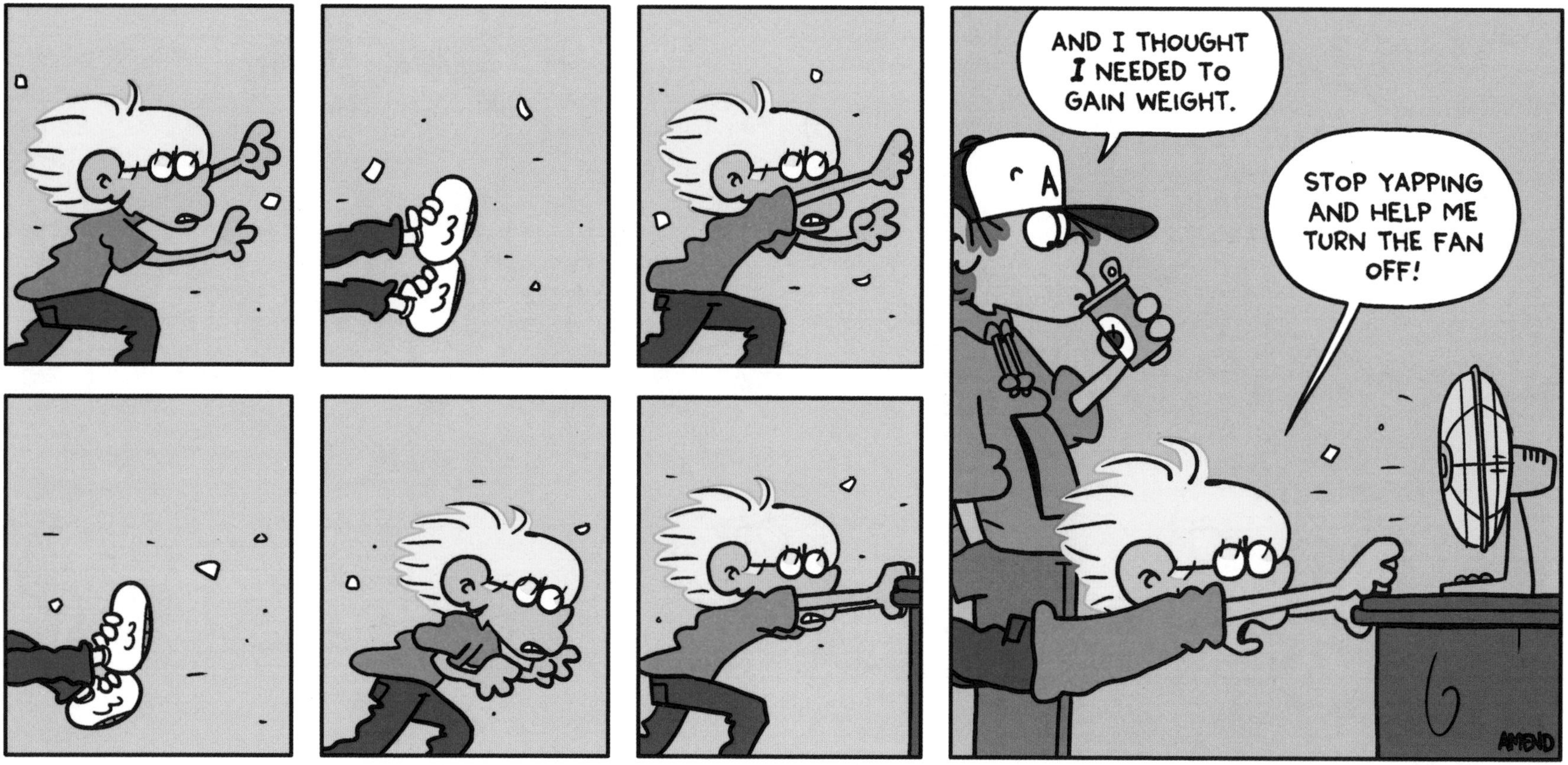
AND I THOUGHT *I* NEEDED TO GAIN WEIGHT.
STOP YAPPING AND HELP ME TURN THE FAN OFF!
AMEND

Skimping

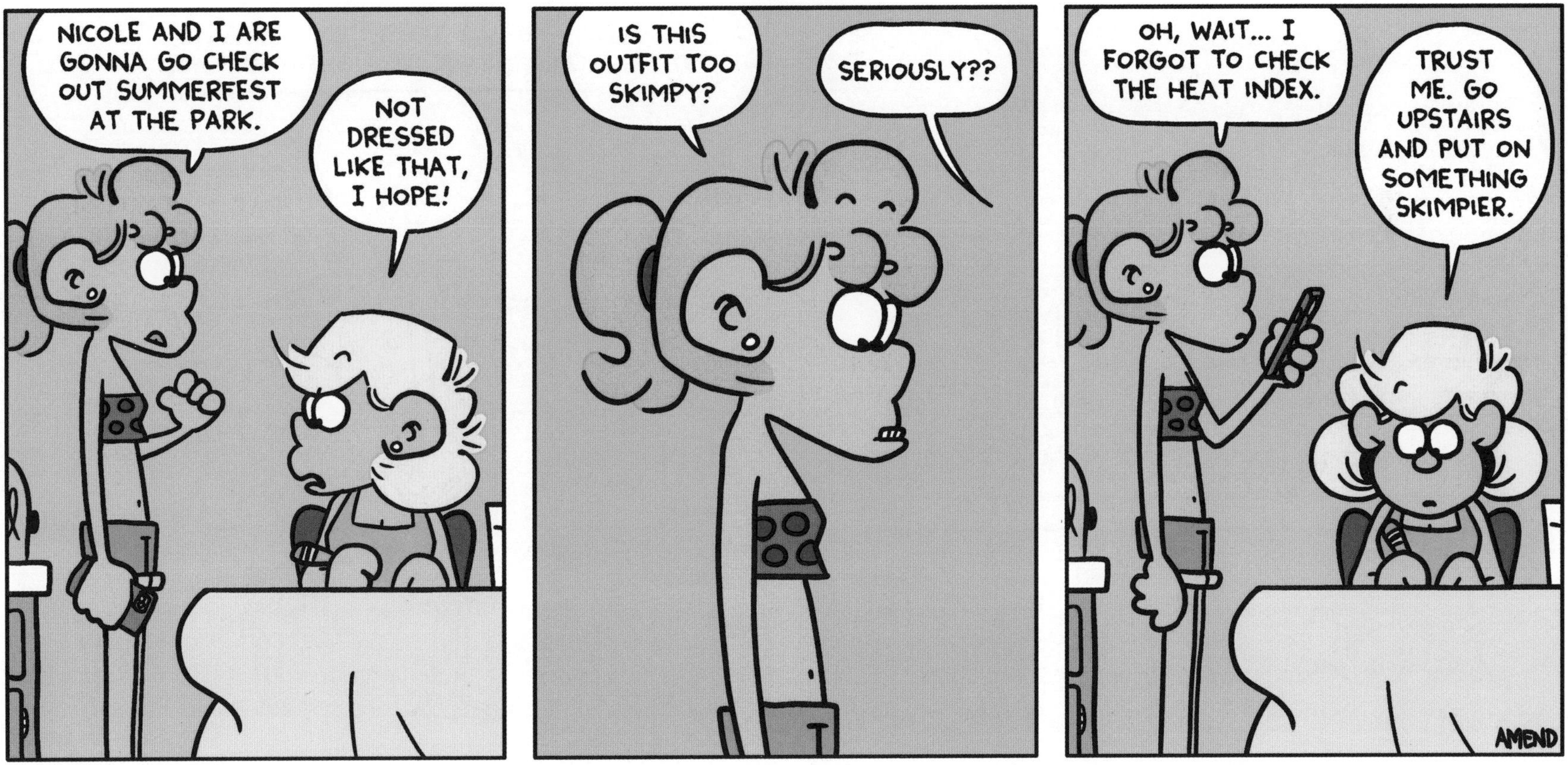
NICOLE AND I ARE GONNA GO CHECK OUT SUMMERFEST AT THE PARK.
NOT DRESSED LIKE THAT, I HOPE!
IS THIS OUTFIT TOO SKIMPY?
SERIOUSLY??
OH, WAIT... I FORGOT TO CHECK THE HEAT INDEX.
TRUST ME. GO UPSTAIRS AND PUT ON SOMETHING SKIMPIER.
AMEND

Sea Cells

Paige F.
Beautiful beach but no cell service.

PETER F.
AWESOME WAVES BUT NO CELL SERVICE.

Jason F.
No wifi _or_ cell service. Why are we here???

Out of Date

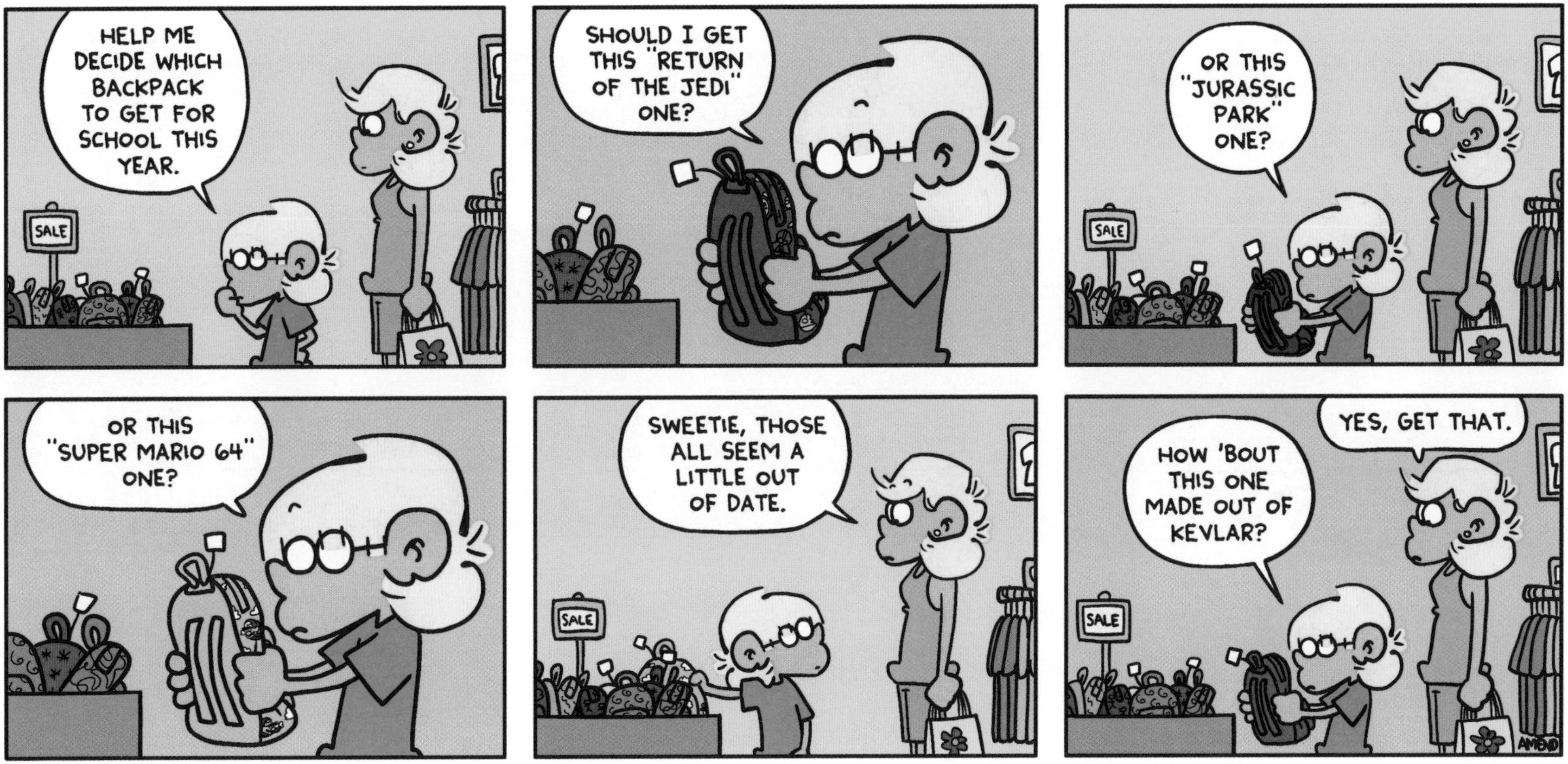
HELP ME DECIDE WHICH BACKPACK TO GET FOR SCHOOL THIS YEAR.
SALE
SHOULD I GET THIS "RETURN OF THE JEDI" ONE?
OR THIS "JURASSIC PARK" ONE?
SALE
OR THIS "SUPER MARIO 64" ONE?
SWEETIE, THOSE ALL SEEM A LITTLE OUT OF DATE.
SALE
HOW 'BOUT THIS ONE MADE OUT OF KEVLAR?
YES, GET THAT.
SALE
AMEND

Easy B-

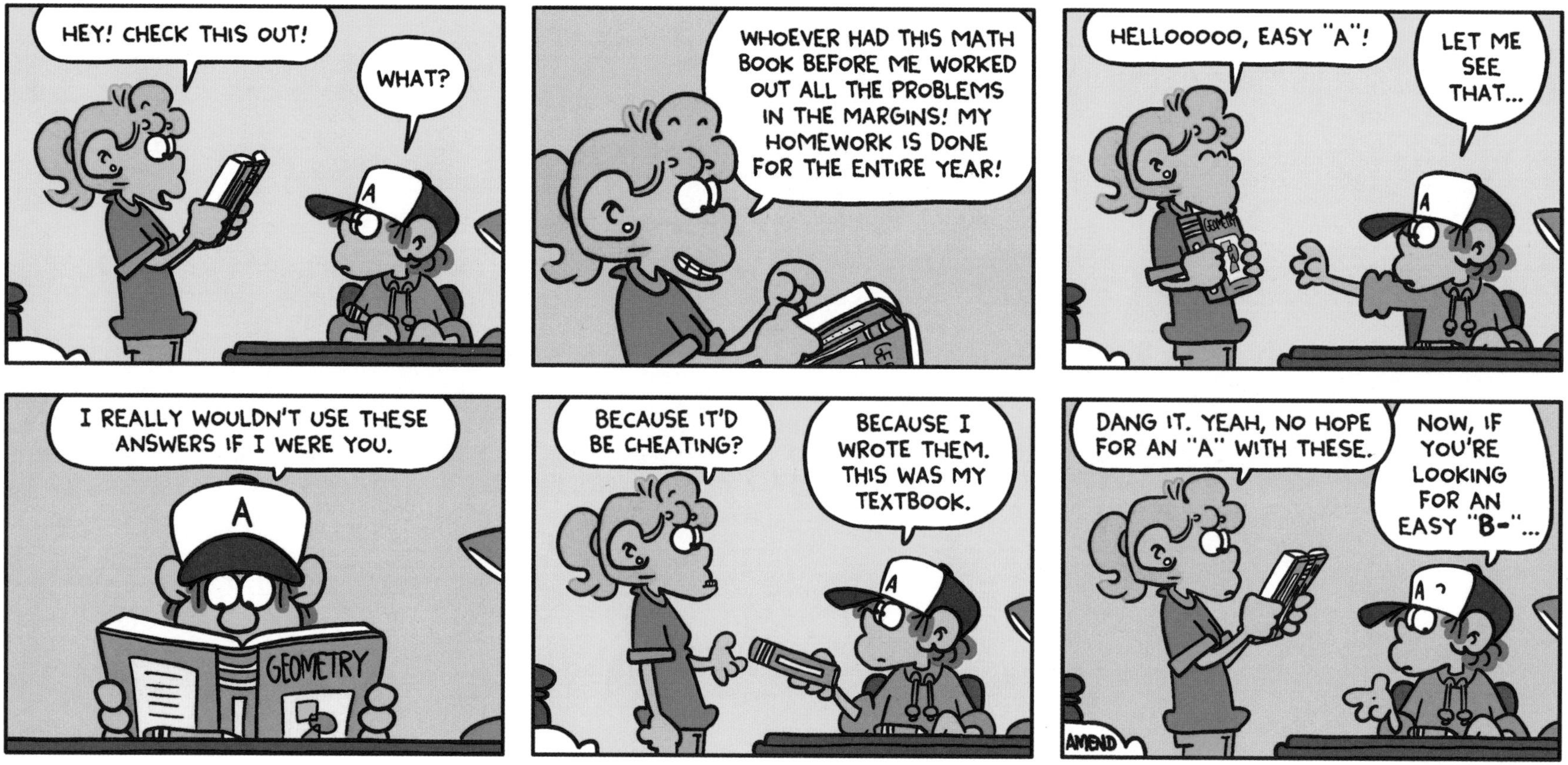
HEY! CHECK THIS OUT!
WHAT?
WHOEVER HAD THIS MATH BOOK BEFORE ME WORKED OUT ALL THE PROBLEMS IN THE MARGINS! MY HOMEWORK IS DONE FOR THE ENTIRE YEAR!
HELLOOOOO, EASY "A"!
LET ME SEE THAT...
I REALLY WOULDN'T USE THESE ANSWERS IF I WERE YOU.
GEOMETRY
BECAUSE IT'D BE CHEATING?
BECAUSE I WROTE THEM. THIS WAS MY TEXTBOOK.
DANG IT. YEAH, NO HOPE FOR AN "A" WITH THESE.
NOW, IF YOU'RE LOOKING FOR AN EASY "B-"...
AMEND

Lab Day

MIND IF I PIPETTE A FEW MILLILITERS OF YOUR ICED TEA?

WHAT FOR?

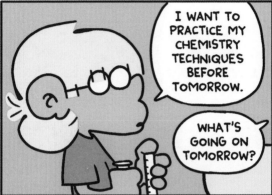

I WANT TO PRACTICE MY CHEMISTRY TECHNIQUES BEFORE TOMORROW.

WHAT'S GOING ON TOMORROW?

IT'S LAB DAY!

IT'S **LABOR** DAY.

OHHH. I JUST ASSUMED THE CALENDAR HAD A TYPO.

GUESS I WON'T BE PIPETTING.

MOM, DO WE HAVE ANY STEEL GIRDERS IN NEED OF WELDING?

SON, COME BACK! THE PIPETTING WAS FINE!

AMEND

Degree of Difficulty

MISS O'MALLEY, ABOUT TOMORROW'S MATH QUIZ...

WILL YOU BE IMPLEMENTING A "DEGREE OF DIFFICULTY" SCALE IN YOUR GRADING?

A WHAT?

LIKE HOW IN OLYMPIC DIVING AND GYMNASTICS, ONE CAN SCORE MORE POINTS BY DOING THINGS IN A MORE DIFFICULT FASHION.

FOR EXAMPLE, IF I WERE TO TAKE THE QUIZ HOLDING A SHARPIE WITH MY TEETH WHILE STANDING ON MY HEAD, COULD I POTENTIALLY EARN A SCORE HIGHER THAN THE 10/10 BASELINE?

NO, 10/10 IS THE MAXIMUM GRADE.

PHOOEY.

CAN I DO THOSE THINGS ANYWAY? I KINDA SPENT ALL SUMMER PRACTICING.

SPEAKING OF SUMMER, NEXT YEAR'S IS **HOW** MANY MONTHS AWAY?

Dangerous Game

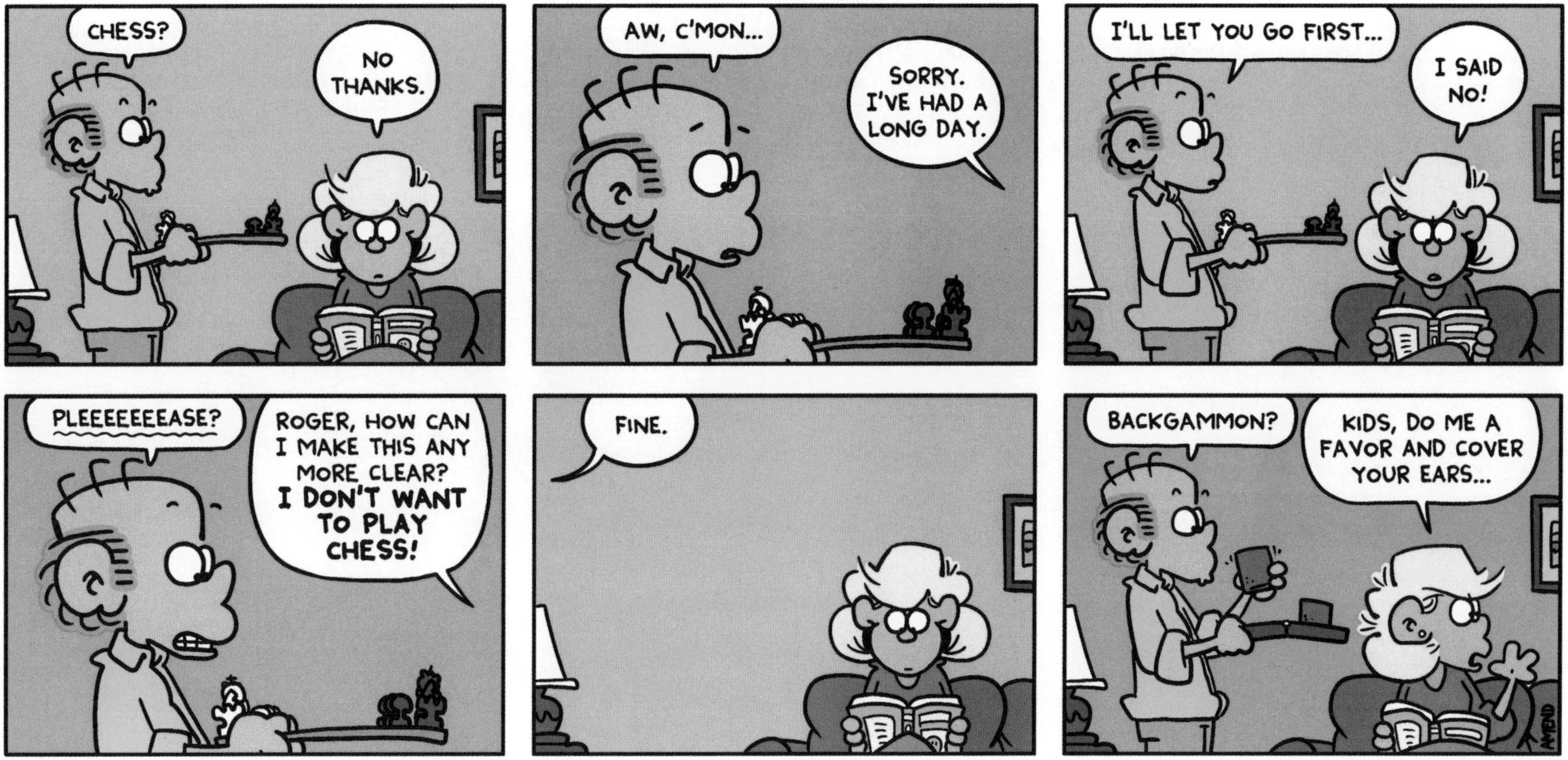

CHESS?
NO THANKS.
AW, C'MON...
SORRY. I'VE HAD A LONG DAY.
I'LL LET YOU GO FIRST...
I SAID NO!
PLEEEEEEEASE?
ROGER, HOW CAN I MAKE THIS ANY MORE CLEAR? I DON'T WANT TO PLAY CHESS!
FINE.
BACKGAMMON?
KIDS, DO ME A FAVOR AND COVER YOUR EARS...

Safety First

I THOUGHT LUNCH WAS LASAGNA TODAY.

THIS **IS** LASAGNA.

IT DOESN'T LOOK LIKE LASAGNA. IT LOOKS LIKE GRAY GLOP.

WE MAKE IT THAT WAY ON PURPOSE. IT'S FOR YOUR SAFETY.

THIS SCHOOL HOUSES 1,200 RAVENOUS TEENAGERS. IMAGINE THE STAMPEDES EVERY LUNCHTIME IF THE CAFETERIA SERVED APPETIZING FOOD.

IF WE DIDN'T DO THINGS LIKE ADD GRAY FOOD COLORING TO FOOL PEOPLE, YOU'D LIKELY BE GETTING TRAMPLED RIGHT NOW.

I SEE.

YOU'RE WELCOME.

IT DOESN'T SMELL LIKE LASAGNA, EITHER.

AGAIN, YOU'RE WELCOME.

Gravity Gravity

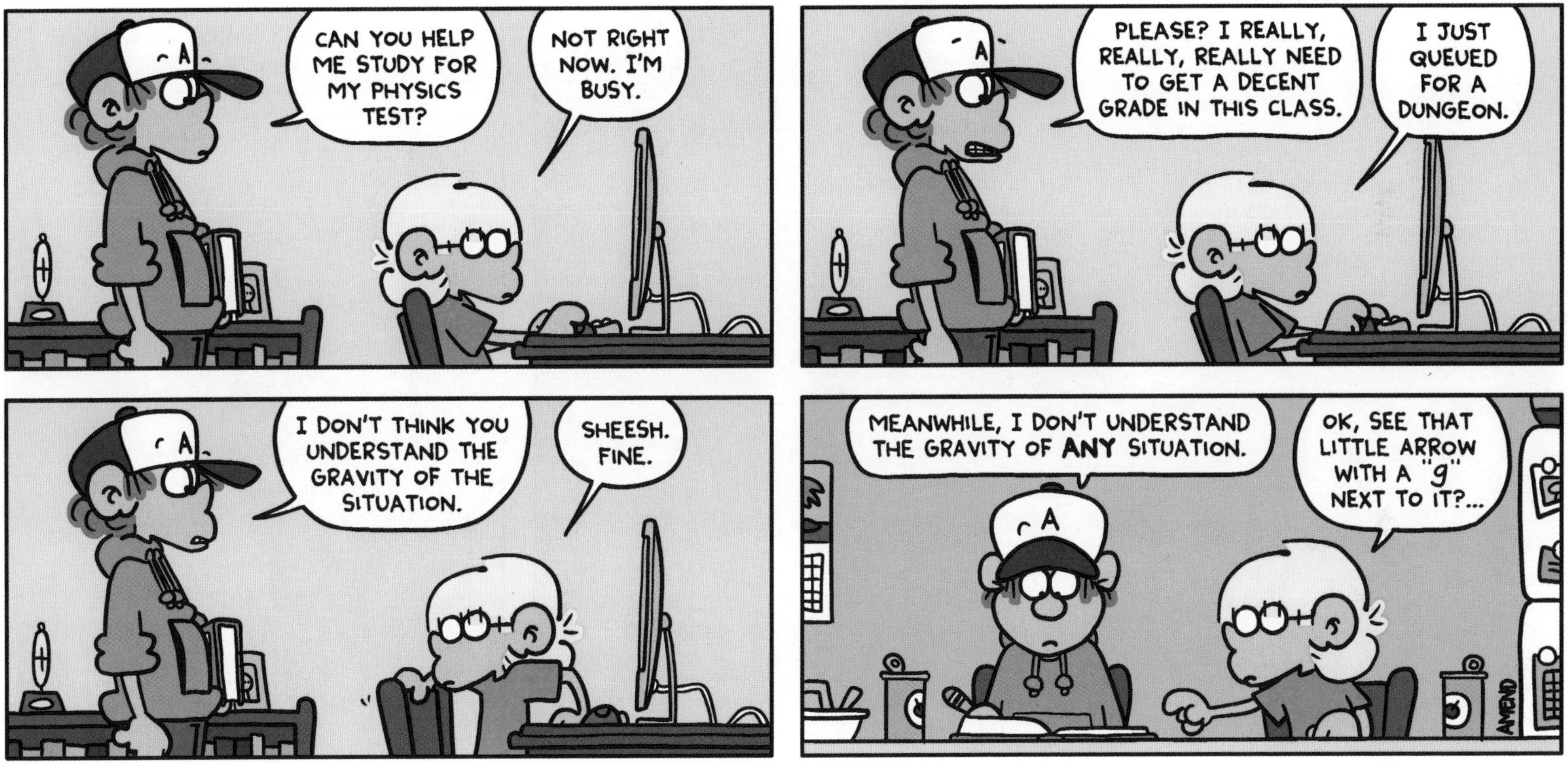
CAN YOU HELP ME STUDY FOR MY PHYSICS TEST?
NOT RIGHT NOW. I'M BUSY.
PLEASE? I REALLY, REALLY, REALLY NEED TO GET A DECENT GRADE IN THIS CLASS.
I JUST QUEUED FOR A DUNGEON.
I DON'T THINK YOU UNDERSTAND THE GRAVITY OF THE SITUATION.
SHEESH. FINE.
MEANWHILE, I DON'T UNDERSTAND THE GRAVITY OF ANY SITUATION.
OK, SEE THAT LITTLE ARROW WITH A "g" NEXT TO IT?...
AMEND

Rerouted

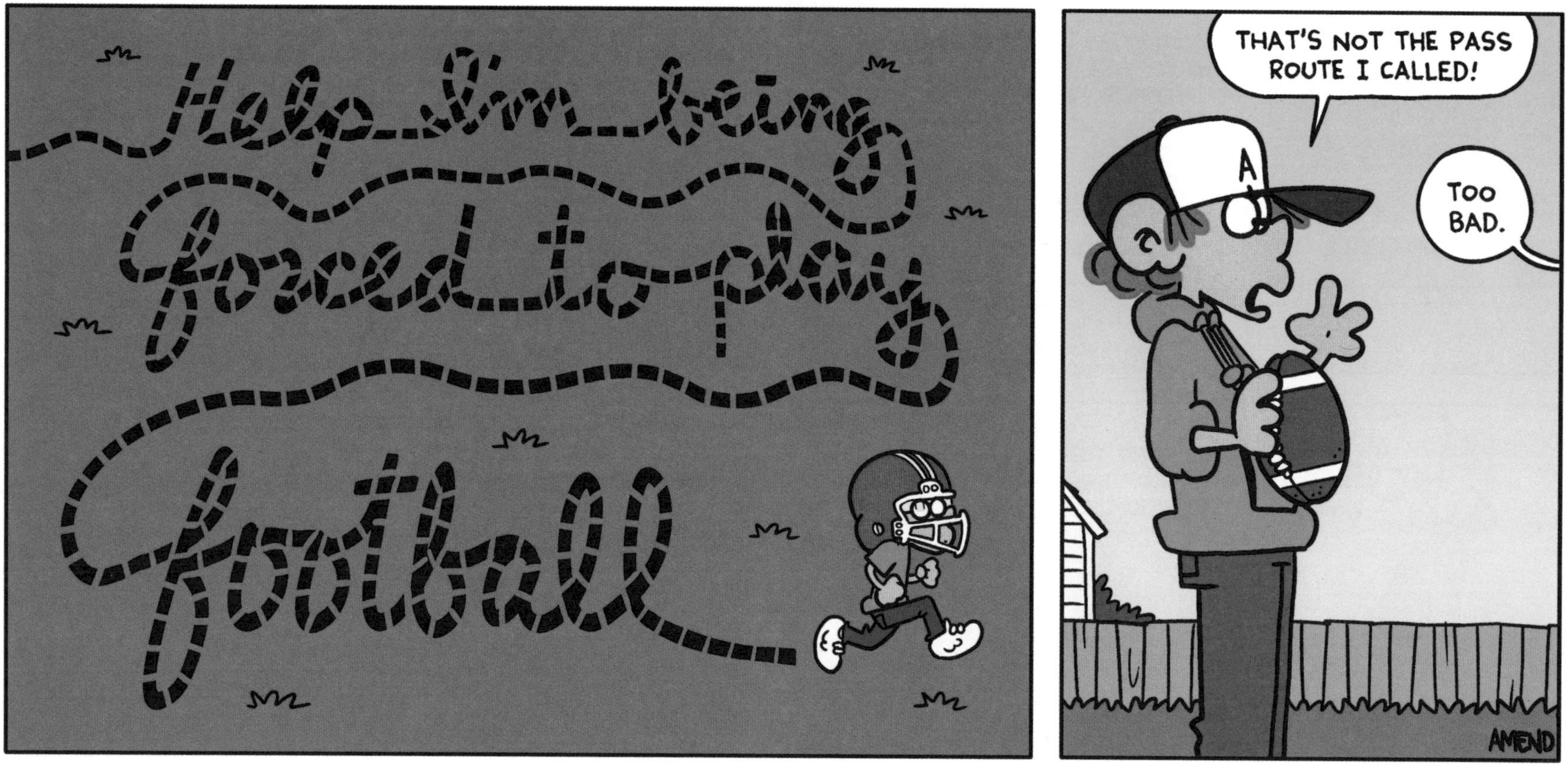
Help I'm being forced to play football
THAT'S NOT THE PASS ROUTE I CALLED!
TOO BAD.
AMEND

QuincyTok

I'M STARTING TO THINK QUINCY WASN'T MEANT FOR TIKTOK.

IS THIS A VIDEO OR A PHOTO?

Murder, She Watched

ANY THOUGHTS ON DINNER?

I MEANT TO MAKE SQUASH BALLS, BUT I FORGOT.

NO PROB. I CAN ORDER US PIZZA.

SORRY... I'VE BEEN OBSESSIVELY BINGEING THIS NEW SHOW.

IT'S A TRUE-CRIME JUNKIE'S DREAM: A DOCUSERIES INVESTIGATING EVERY MURDER IN HUMAN HISTORY.

IT'S CRAZY HOW MANY THERE'VE BEEN! I'M ON EPISODE 27, AND THEY'RE BARELY INTO THE BRONZE AGE!

MAYBE YOU AND THE KIDS SHOULD JUST PLAN ON ORDERING PIZZA FOR THE NEXT FEW MONTHS.

LOOKS LIKE NETFLIX GOT YOUR SUGGESTION LETTER.

WOOHOO! I'LL HAVE PEPPERONI AND SAUSAGE.

Spicing Things Up

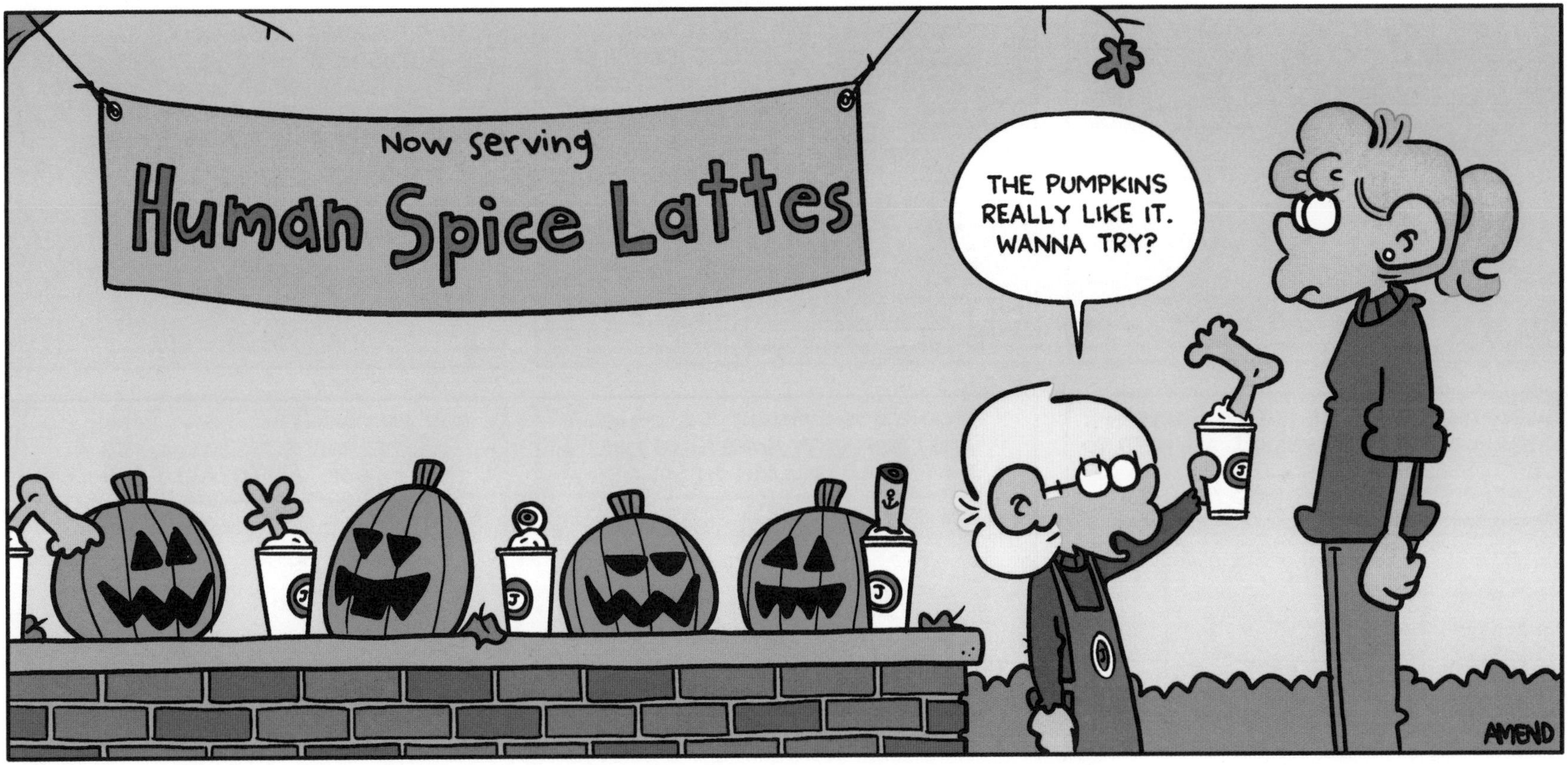
Now serving
Human Spice Lattes
THE PUMPKINS REALLY LIKE IT. WANNA TRY?
AMEND

Extra Hours

I LOVE HOW IN THE FALL WE GET TO SET OUR CLOCKS BACK AND GET AN EXTRA HOUR OF SLEEP.

I JUST WISH WE COULD DO IT EVERY NIGHT.

THAT WOULD MAKE EVERY "DAY" 25 HOURS LONG.

ON SOME DAYS NOON WOULD BE SUNNY LIKE IT IS NOW, ON OTHER DAYS IT'D BE PITCH BLACK. GOOD LUCK TRYING TO PLAN OUTDOOR ACTIVITIES.

ALSO, THERE'D BE LIKE 15 FEWER DAYS IN A YEAR. OUR CALENDARS WOULD ALL NEED TO BE TOSSED FOR NEW ONES. MILLIONS OF PEOPLE'S BIRTHDAYS WOULD VANISH.

I CAN'T EVEN IMAGINE THE CHAOS AND COMPLEXITY SOMETHING LIKE THAT WOULD UNLEASH ON SOCIETY.

BUT WE'D GET TO SLEEP AN EXTRA HOUR.

LOOK, I'M NOT SAYING IT'S A **TOTALLY** BAD IDEA...

Literally Everything

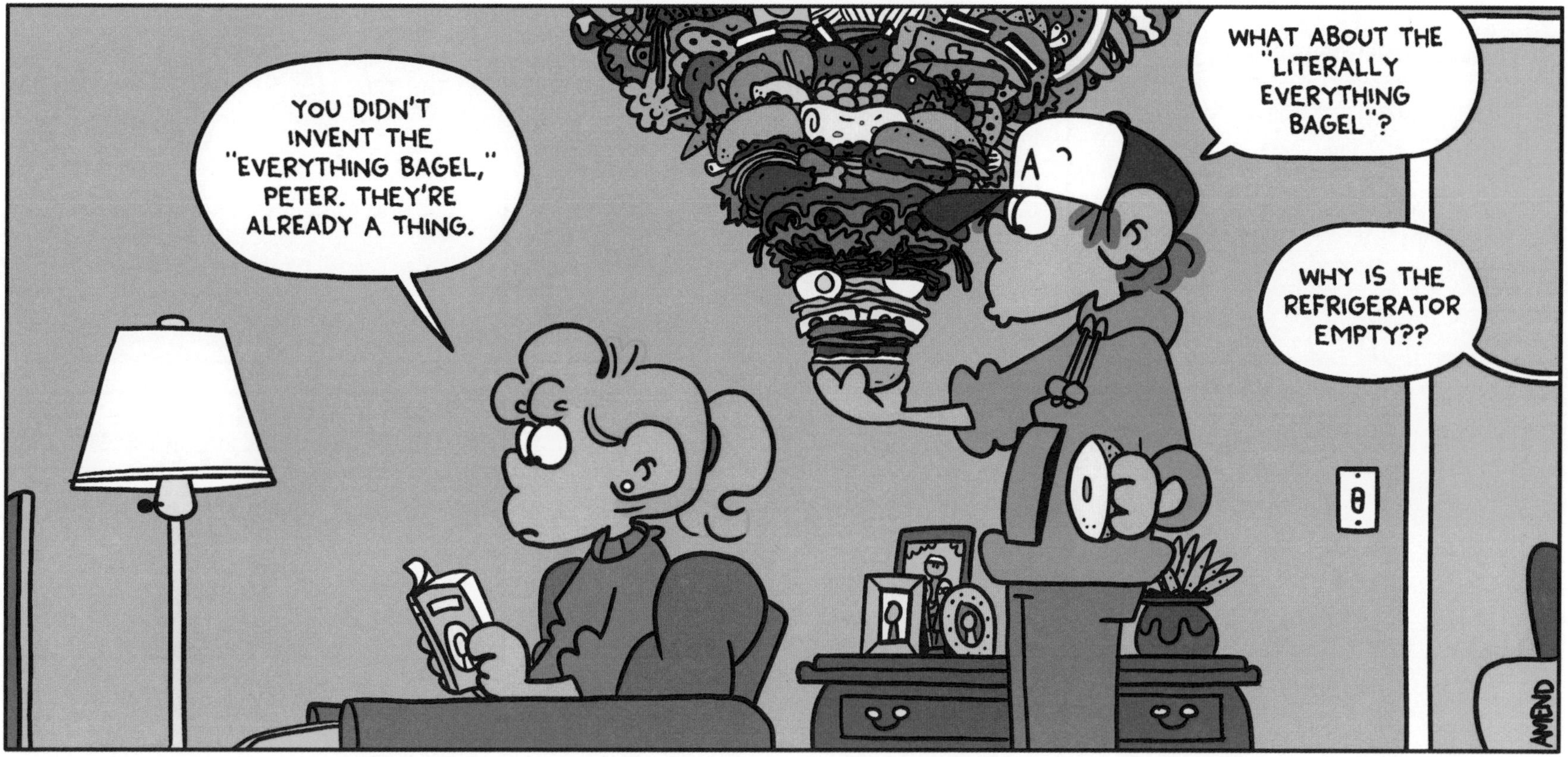
YOU DIDN'T INVENT THE "EVERYTHING BAGEL," PETER. THEY'RE ALREADY A THING.
WHAT ABOUT THE "LITERALLY EVERYTHING BAGEL"?
WHY IS THE REFRIGERATOR EMPTY??
AMEND

Holiday Preparations

HAVE YOU SEEN A PHILLIPS SCREWDRIVER ANYWHERE?

NO, WHY?

I'M TRYING TO GET THINGS READY FOR THE HOLIDAYS, AND I NEED ONE.

TO PUT TOGETHER THE TREE STAND?

TO ATTACH LIGHTS TO THE HOUSE?

TO ASSEMBLE THAT ANNOYING BANJO SANTA YOU BOUGHT AT COSTCLUB?

TO TAKE THE BATTERIES OUT OF OUR BATHROOM SCALE.

I'LL CHECK THE GARAGE.

Wizarding

YOU ARE IN A LARGE CIRCULAR ROOM WITH A RADIUS OF (ROLL ROLL) 24 FEET. CALCULATE ITS CIRCUMFERENCE!
48π FEET.
THE CEILING IS (ROLL ROLL) 51 FEET HIGH. CALCULATE THE VOLUME OF THE ROOM IN CUBIC METERS!
LESSEE... 831.8π?
SUDDENLY, A BALROG APPEARS! CALCULATE THE ODDS OF YOUR SURVIVING!
HOW THE HECK DO I DO THAT??
HEY, YOU'RE THE ONE WHO WANTED TO PLAY AS A MATH WIZARD.
I ASK THE BALROG IF HE NEEDS HELP WITH HIS HOMEWORK...
AMEND

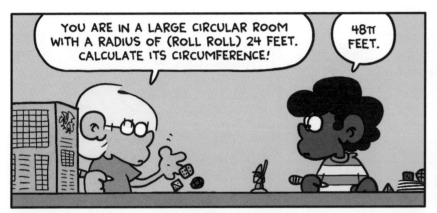

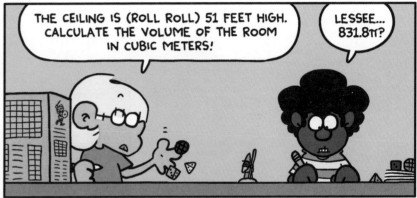

Decimate

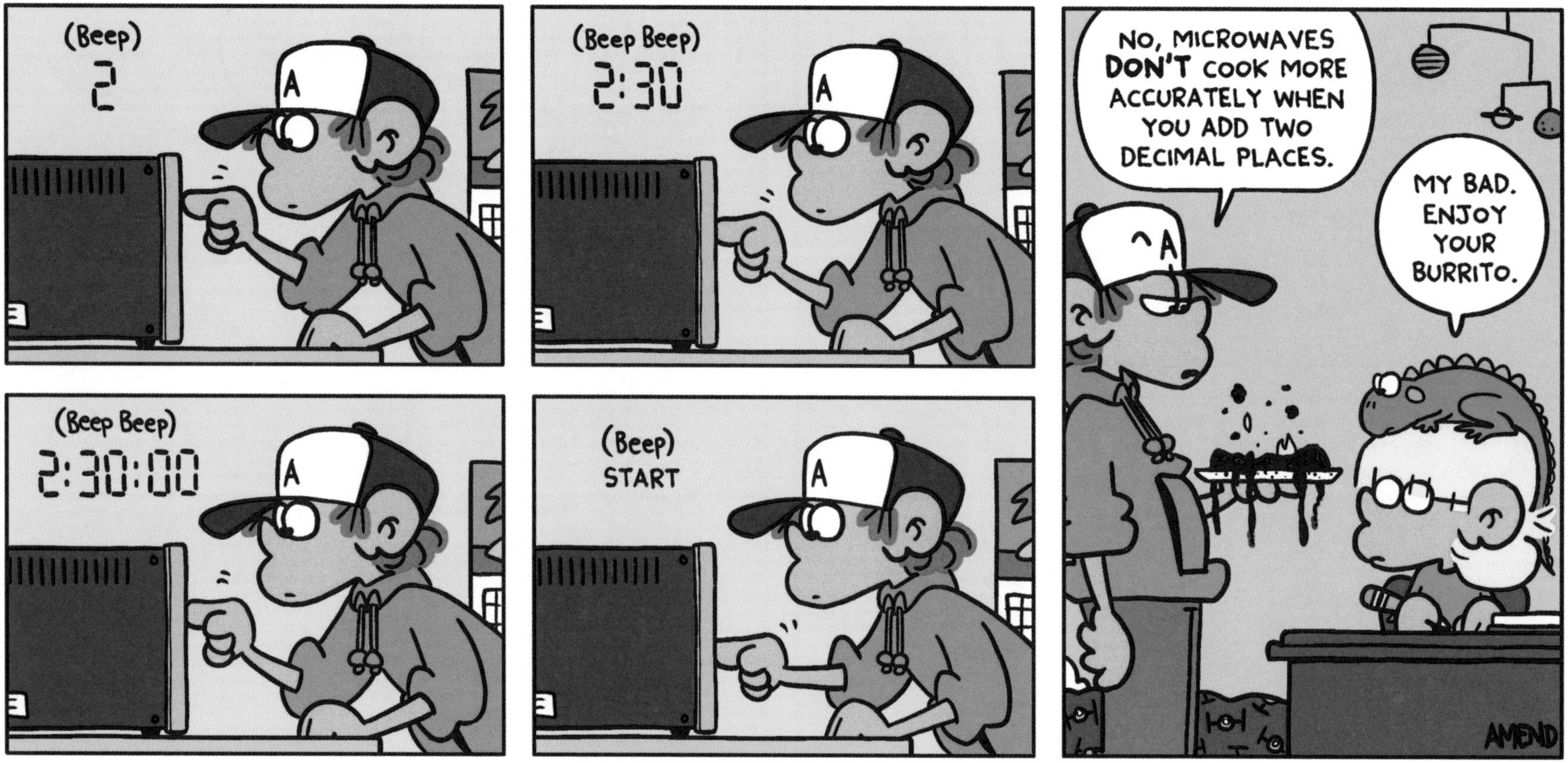
(Beep)
2
(Beep Beep)
2:30
(Beep Beep)
2:30:00
(Beep)
START
NO, MICROWAVES **DON'T** COOK MORE ACCURATELY WHEN YOU ADD TWO DECIMAL PLACES.
MY BAD. ENJOY YOUR BURRITO.
AMEND

#Loophole

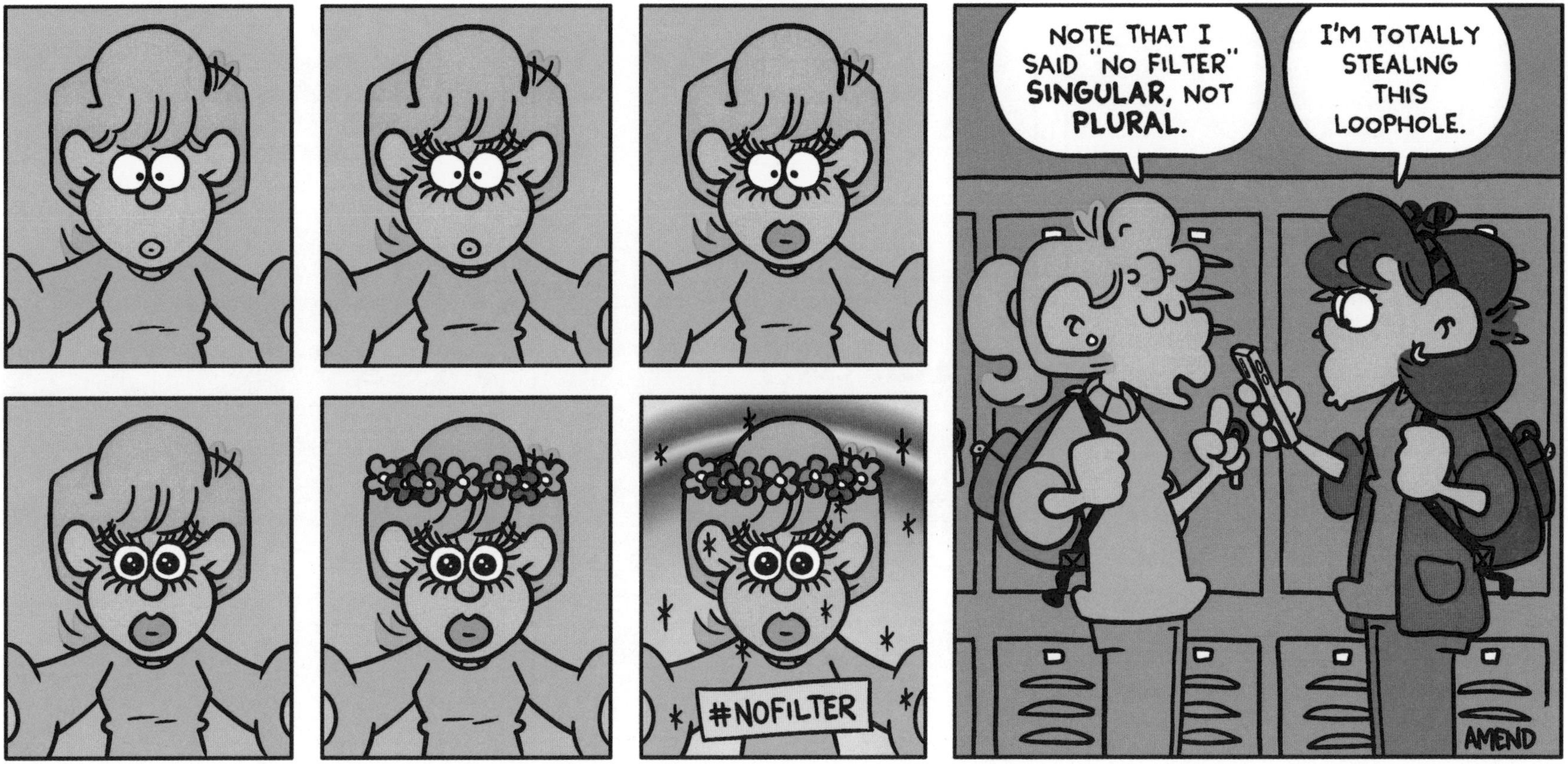
#NOFILTER
NOTE THAT I SAID "NO FILTER" SINGULAR, NOT PLURAL.
I'M TOTALLY STEALING THIS LOOPHOLE.
AMEND

A Three Hour Recipe

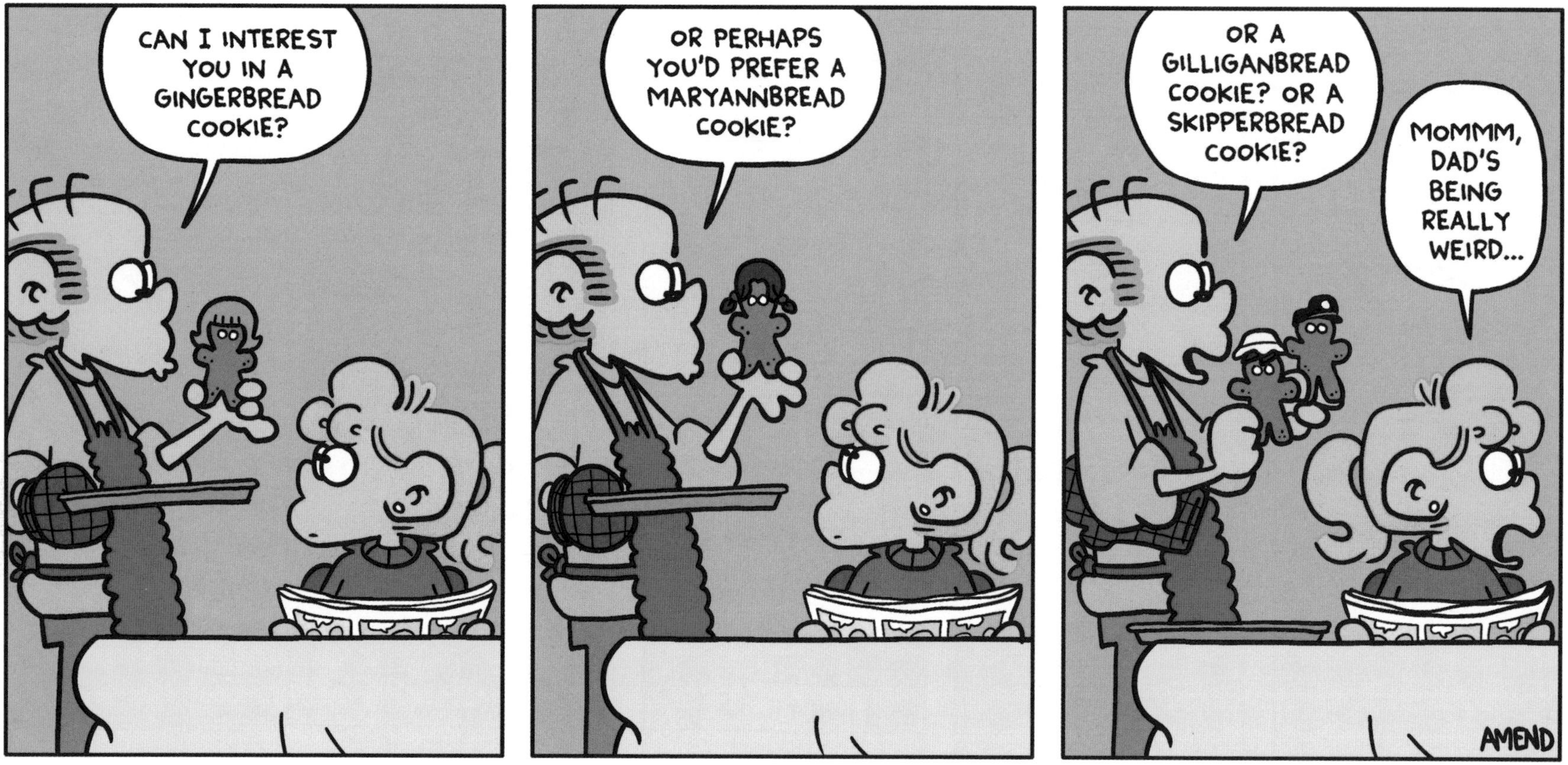
CAN I INTEREST YOU IN A GINGERBREAD COOKIE?
OR PERHAPS YOU'D PREFER A MARYANNBREAD COOKIE?
OR A GILLIGANBREAD COOKIE? OR A SKIPPERBREAD COOKIE?
MOMMM, DAD'S BEING REALLY WEIRD...
AMEND

Dream On

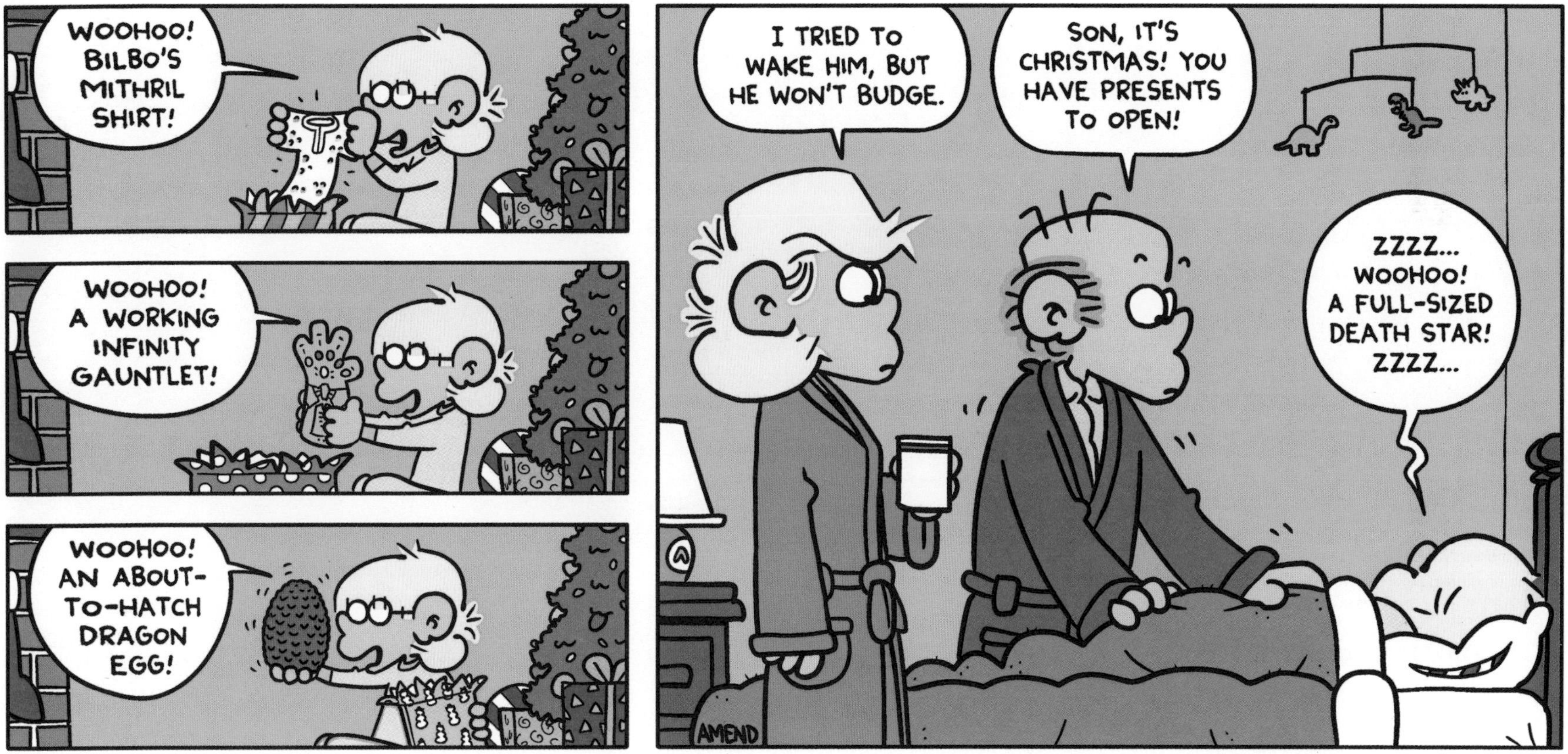

WOOHOO! BILBO'S MITHRIL SHIRT!
WOOHOO! A WORKING INFINITY GAUNTLET!
WOOHOO! AN ABOUT-TO-HATCH DRAGON EGG!
I TRIED TO WAKE HIM, BUT HE WON'T BUDGE.
SON, IT'S CHRISTMAS! YOU HAVE PRESENTS TO OPEN!
ZZZZ... WOOHOO! A FULL-SIZED DEATH STAR! ZZZZ...
AMEND

FoxTrot is distributed internationally by Andrews McMeel Syndication.

FoxTrot Big Dweeb Energy © 2024 by Bill Amend. All rights reserved. Printed in China. No part of this book may be used or reproduced in any manner whatsoever without written permission except in the case of reprints in the context of reviews.

Andrews McMeel Publishing
a division of Andrews McMeel Universal
1130 Walnut Street, Kansas City, Missouri 64106

24 25 26 27 28 IGO 10 9 8 7 6 5 4 3 2 1

ISBN: 978-1-5248-8748-3

Library of Congress Control Number: 2023943123

www.andrewsmcmeel.com

www.foxtrot.com

ATTENTION: SCHOOLS AND BUSINESSES

Andrews McMeel books are available at quantity discounts with bulk purchase for educational, business, or sales promotional use. For information, please e-mail the Andrews McMeel Publishing Special Sales Department: sales@amuniversal.com.